D0296921

WILDFLOWER SAFARI
The Life of Mary Richards

WILDFLOWER
SAFARI

The Life of Mary Richards

William Condry

First impression—1998

ISBN 1 85902 558 7

Photographs by the author unless otherwise stated

Printed in Wales at
Gomer Press, Llandysul, Ceredigion

AUTHOR'S PREFACE

This life of Mary Richards has sprung as naturally as a river from its sources. It comes from the many papers she left behind, the letters she wrote and the memories people still have of her. Above all, it springs out of what has survived of the diaries she kept over the years. She long intended to write an account of her life and made several efforts to get down to it. But though she obviously enjoyed writing her diary every evening, she was never the sort to sit at a desk day after day and write a whole book. She was one of nature's extroverts. Even into extreme old age she wanted an active life, out of doors whenever possible; and so she never got very far with her autobiography.

When, after she died, much material about her life was entrusted to me, I felt an obligation, as an old friend, to complete her task. Years have passed since then and not until now have I been able to find the time to write this chronicle of a remarkable life. To her many friends and relations I am indebted for a great deal of information. Her son and daughter-in-law, Lt Commander and Pamela Richards, have supplied much essential data. It was her elder daughter, Jonnet Oldfield, who passed to me her mother's diaries and other papers. Jonnet's sister, Kate Heywood, wrote down many precious reminiscences of their mother. Among past and present members of staff at Kew Herbarium I am indebted to Dr Phillip Cribb, Peter Taylor, the late Edgar Milne-Redhead and especially to Dr R.K. Brummit whose help has been crucial. The National Library of Wales at Aberystwyth has been an unfailing source of information. So has the Department of Botany at the National Museum in Cardiff, where Dr George Hutchinson went to much trouble to assist my research. The Birmingham Central Library and the Birmingham City Museum and Art Gallery provided valuable information. Others who have helped in various ways include Andrew and Shirley Agnew, David Allen, John Beesley, Peter Benoit, B.L. Burtt, Arthur Cadman, Valerie Charlton, Arthur Chater, Ann Connolly, the County Archivist at Dolgellau, Christine Demmar, David Elias, Ernest

5

and Christine Evans, the late Evan Price Evans, Ray Evans, John Harrison, Wilf and Dora Holmes, Peter Hope Jones, John Leedal, the late Father G.P. Leedal, Roger and Mary Long, Cedric Maby, A.P.G. Michelmore, Tony and Judith Newbery, Dorothy Paish, Ruth Pearce, Harlow Phibbs, the late Tim Ruck, the late Kathleen Stevens, Robert Stjernstedt, Maldwyn and Betty Thomas, Janet Trant, the late Ion Trant, the late Hon Mary Vaughan and Gwyn Walters. I am grateful to Tim and Ruth Jones for enormous help with word-processing and to Dyfed Elis-Gruffydd of Gwasg Gomer for great editorial support.

CHAPTER ONE

It is the middle of June, 1953. A group of us, botanists or would-be botanists belonging to the West Wales Field Society, are floundering across the peatbogs that lie below the vast north-facing cliffs of Cader Idris, that best-loved of the mountains of southern Snowdonia. All morning the wind and the rain have been driving in off the Irish Sea and I don't doubt that by now most of us are feeling we'd like to get out of the weather. But how can you admit to abject defeat when your leader is apparently oblivious of the squalls as she stoops to point out an orchid, demonstrate a sedge or hold forth about the ecology of a club-moss with the excitement given only to real enthusiasts?

This sparsely built woman in her late sixties, with only a lightweight raincoat and a thin headscarf to protect her from the elements, does she really not notice that her shoes go under water with nearly every step she takes? We who gather round her, well protected by rainproofs and gumboots, are probably as much impressed by her indifference to physical discomfort as by her gift for putting across her botanical knowledge with such ardour. In a commanding yet attractive voice she holds our attention for a whole afternoon without us realising how time has passed. Then quite suddenly, as if coming out of a trance, she looks round at us and shouts: 'Come on, it's time for tea. I'm sick of botany. I can't look at another plant!'

*   *   *

Mary Richards used to describe herself, with a twinkle in her eye, as a Victorian lady, though in fact she was only sixteen when Queen Victoria died. It was on 3 August 1885 that she was born Mary Alice Eleanor Stokes at the home of her mother's parents, Charles and Mary Edwards of Dolserau, an historic house a mile east of Dolgellau in Merioneth. Born in Wales of a Welsh mother she quite legitimately described herself as Welsh though her father, Frederick Stokes, was English, the proprietor of a leather-making business at Walsall, Staffordshire. So it was that though

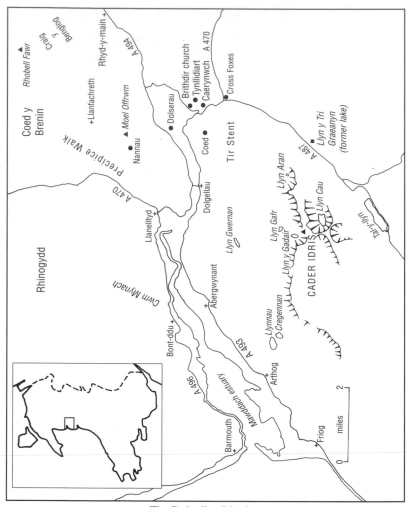

The Dolgellau District.

she had many a holiday at Dolserau, Mary spent most of her first twenty-two years far from Wales at her parents' house, Knowle Hurst, in Lichfield which is ten miles north-east of Walsall.

She liked to recall the influences on her childhood, especially those which turned her towards natural history. As was then still the fashion for daughters of middle-class parents, she was not sent to school until well into her teens. Instead she was educated at home, first by a French nurse who taught her to speak French from a tender age, then by an English governess until she was twelve.

From then on there was a German governess whose influence, Mary always acknowledged, was crucial. Along with other accomplishments, Fraulein Wahl taught her to speak German; but, of more significance, the *fraulein* happened to have a bent for natural history and was eager to guide her pupil along the same lines. The result was that many a fine afternoon was spent in the Lichfield countryside, learning to recognise the birds, insects and wildflowers they encountered in the woods, fields and lanesides. It was Fraulein Wahl who taught her how to pick a wildflower, dry it, mount it on a sheet of botanical paper and label it with name, date and locality. In after years Mary often mentioned Fraulein Wahl's training with gratitude. The inspiring *fraulein* also taught her much about English literature and, in the fashion of those days, Mary learnt by heart long passages of poetry which she remembered all her life. That she was never taught any Welsh is not surprising since she lived so far from Wales. And her mother, though Welsh, belonged to a time when the Welsh language was quite out of fashion among the Welsh middle class. Music was very important and was especially encouraged by Mary's musical father who one year took her to the Bayreuth festival. At some stage in her upbringing Mary's imagination was fired by the legends of ancient Greece which left her with a longing to visit the sites of classical antiquity. She might well have grown up to be an archaeologist but there was never any influence in her life strong enough to turn her in that direction.

Seven childhood letters (one in very good French) from Mary to her mother still exist. Three were sent to Lichfield from Dolserau where Mary spent quite a lot of time, looked after by Fraulein Wahl. In one letter we find them on a nature walk:

> We went to church yesterday and in the afternoon Fraulein and I went up the Torrent Walk and got two burnet moths, a hairstreak and a wood tiger and a lot of brown butterflies and beetles.

Grandmama Mary Edwards enjoyed having her young grand-daughter at Dolserau: 'Mary is in her element when she is down here', was her comment.

Throughout Mary's early years the impact of her frequent visits to Wales was immense. After the long-tamed countryside of the Midlands, the wildness of the mountains that surround Dolgellau had a strong appeal. Dolserau, long her mother's parents' home, though not a large estate by the standards of that time, was beautifully placed in its riverside setting. William Bingley in 1804 speaks of Dolserau's 'luxuriant woods, meadows and cornfields intersected by the River Wnion which serpentises along the vale'. In his *County Families of Wales* (1872), Thomas Nicholas wrote:

> The mansion of Dolserau was rebuilt by the present owner in 1864 and the old house was pulled down in 1865. The situation is sheltered and pleasant, in the vale of the Wnion, above Dolgelley, over which river a picturesque bridge leads from the high-road to the entrance gates. To the north are the heights of Nannau and to the south those of Caerynwch.

It is often difficult to say what helps to form young minds, but a major force in Mary's youth was undoubtedly her mother's brother, Munro Edwards. Uncle Munro was a vigorous, out-door type, very willing to pass on to Mary his interest in wildlife. A pioneer of camping, he had a passion for walking the mountains with a tent and a fishing rod. He angled for trout in streams and lakes for miles around and was delighted, as Mary grew up, to find in her a kindred spirit. Often, when she was staying at Dolserau, they went off on camping, walking and fishing expeditions. Where better for an out-door girl to have holidays than here in the heart of Merioneth, 'this county beyond question the wildest and most picturesque in Wales', to quote Thomas Nicholas again.

12 September 1898 was a memorable date: it saw the consecration of Brithdir church which for three years had been under construction in a roadside field on Tŷ Glyn farm, part of the Caerynwch estate. Brithdir's first church (in its early years often referred to as Caerynwch church), it was built and endowed by Mrs Louisa Tooth of Caerynwch. For twenty-one years she had been the widow of Richard Meredyth Richards (1821-73) and had then married the Rev Charles Tooth. The creation of the church was a dream they shared; but after only four months of marriage Charles Tooth died and the church became his memorial. It was dedicated to St Mark because he had been chaplain of St Mark's English church in Florence. Today Brithdir church is well known among the smaller churches of Wales, especially for its magnificent copper altar front. Among those at the opening ceremony were the Edwardses of Dolserau, long closely linked with the Richards family. Mary Stokes, aged 13, was also at the opening of this church which was destined to play a central role in her life.

10

Prominent among her childhood heroes were the explorers of darkest Africa who, not very long before, had ventured intrepidly into the unknown interior to find and map the great lakes and rivers. It was only fourteen years before Mary was born that Stanley had found Livingstone at the north end of Lake Tanganyika. Livingstone died only two years before she was born. She was nineteen when Stanley died. In after years she liked to relate how her childhood imagination had been fired by reading the books of Speke, Grant, Stanley and Livingstone.

At fifteen Mary was sent to her only school. It was Les Peupliers at Valvide outside Brussels and it was much more than a place for training girls in the social graces. It was a school with advanced ideas, its headmistress fervently believing that science should be part of a girl's education. One of the first things she told Mary was to take off her laced corsets, for the school regarded them as unhealthy, a somewhat revolutionary opinion in those days. At Les Peupliers Mary made good progress, especially in botany, so much so that when she left after two years, the school wrote to her parents recommending that she should go on to a university to read botany. But at the beginning of the twentieth century the idea was still widely held that young ladies when they left school had finished their education and that universities were not for them. The conventional role for young ladies, before they married, was to be at home learning how to run a household. They might also pick and arrange the flowers, perhaps do a little light gardening or become proficient in art, music or needlework. They were also expected to take part in a whirl of social activities which might include a season in London, if their parents could afford it.

The study of plant life had been a recommended part of the education of young ladies since as far back as Jean-Jacques Rousseau, himself a keen botanist. His ideas were taken up by others such as Thomas Martyn, Professor of Botany at Cambridge. In 1785 he had published his popular translation of Rousseau's *Letters on the elements of Botany addressed to a lady* and had added letters of his own, in one of which he wrote: 'The study of nature abates the taste for frivolous amusements, prevents the tumult of the passions and provides the mind with a nourishment which is salutary.' Well before the end of the nineteenth century it was becoming increasingly accepted that girls should take up science, botany for example, as a career.

It was a frustrated Mary Stokes who came home from her

Brussels school. By now she had set her heart on going to a university with a view to becoming a professional botanist and all she got from her parents was opposition. But, as she wrote in later years: 'I was always a rebel and always different'; and she soon began to work out a ploy of her own. She had discovered that in Birmingham, only sixteen miles from home, there was a Department of Botany at Mason College which was just then being metamorphosed into becoming Birmingham's first university. So to Birmingham she duly went and told her story to the man in charge of botany, Professor William Hillhouse. Perhaps the good professor was persuaded by her seventeen-year-old charm and enthusiasm. At all events, although her parents refused to pay any tuition fees, he agreed to let her attend lectures unofficially and use the facilities of his laboratory whenever she could get into Birmingham. This may seem an unorthodox arrangement to us today but, as Asa Briggs wrote in his *History of Birmingham*: 'Mason College was designed to be as liberal as possible in the character and extent of its teaching, the system of management and the mode and terms of admission.' So for a year, defying her parents who even declined to pay her rail-fare, Mary went two or three times a week with a packet of sandwiches in her pocket, in earnest pursuit of botany at the college in Edmund Street, a tall, rabbit-warren of a building on a site now occupied by the city's Central Library. Her rail-fare she found by saving up her pocket-money and any gift money from Christmas and her birthday. She even kept chickens and sold eggs to help her along.

Mary could hardly have had a better mentor than William Hillhouse. Born in Bedford in 1850, he graduated at Cambridge and became Mason College's first and only Professor of Botany in 1882 and then first Professor of Botany at the new Birmingham University. As well as being an academic he was deeply involved in local natural history. Before moving to the Midlands he had long been interested in the flora of Bedfordshire. In his Birmingham days he became a popular lecturer to natural history societies, was a co-editor of the *Midland Naturalist*, honorary secretary of the Birmingham Botanical and Horticultural Society and honorary director of the Botanical Gardens in Edgbaston not far from where he lived in Calthorpe Road. A pioneer of women's education, Hillhouse was just the sort to be sympathetic to the aspirations of a keen, intelligent youngster like Mary Stokes. As he tells us himself, girls were only just beginning to break through the ancient barriers that kept so many of them out of higher education:

> Perhaps the most striking feature of Mason College is that within its walls male and female students mingle on terms of perfect equality. All the classes and laboratories are open to both sexes alike, the first institution of importance in which the experiment of mixed education was given a fair trial.

Hillhouse also claimed that in 1890 Mason College had the largest school of botany in England, outside London and Cambridge.

Did Mary nurse the hope that when they saw how conscientiously she was attending college lectures, her parents would come round to agreeing to her becoming a registered student? If so, she was disappointed. At the end of the academic year Professor Hillhouse advised her that since she could find no means of becoming a full-time student, she had better abandon thoughts of a scientific career. He suggested that now she had grasped the elements of plant study, she might get lasting satisfaction from remaining an amateur botanist. The Lichfield countryside, he pointed out, had many attractive woodlands and other good habitats; and not far away were the semi-wild heathlands of Cannock Chase and Sutton Park. So it came about that, with much regret, Mary left college with nothing more ambitious to look forward to than perhaps becoming a lady botanist in what had been the Victorian, and was now the Edwardian tradition. No doubt her parents were much relieved by the change. Now she could settle down to a conventional existence in Lichfield which was a garrison town with plenty going on by way of dances, garden parties and other social events. At about this time Mary was presented at court by her mother.

No details of Mary's progress in botany have survived from her earliest teens. The first record we have is of a plant preserved when she was fifteen. It came from neither Lichfield nor Wales but from south-east England. It is an orchid, the white helleborine, which she found at Eastwell in Kent while staying with her aunt, Mrs Marguerite Ashley-Dodd, at Godinton, a fine Jacobean house in an extensive private park near Ashford. The specimen is preserved in Mary's considerable collection of pressed plants now in the National Museum of Wales. As no diaries have come down from those early years, this finding of the white helleborine is all we know about the year 1900. The next year is bleaker still: there is no botanical record or specimen made by Mary in any month. But there is a plant of some interest collected by another hand. It was given, or more probably sent, to her by her kinsman, Alexander Somerville of Glasgow, a distinguished Scottish naturalist. For several years he did much, by correspondence, to encourage Mary in her plant studies; and there are a few others of his specimens in her collection, as well as the lesser water plantain which he had plucked that August of 1901 from the lake at Killarney.

Alexander Somerville (1842-1907), a specialist in botany and marine biology, was well known for encouraging the young. In the *Transactions of the Natural History Society of Glasgow* for November, 1907, the society's president wrote:

> What I shall remember him best by, was his encouragement of young collectors of plants. He saw the young collectors needed encouragement and never passed one over. He was of a cheery disposition and maintained an extensive correspondence with field botanists in all parts of the country.

He also kept in touch with his relations including Nellie Stokes, Mary's mother, and must have been delighted, in the last years of his life, to be told that young Mary Stokes in Lichfield was showing promise in botany. The family link goes back to a John Munro who was in the East India Company in Madras. His daughter, Mary, married William Tate and their daughter, also Mary, married Charles Edwards of Dolserau, Mary Stokes' grandfather. Another daughter of John Munro married into the Somerville family. So both Mary Stokes and Alexander Somerville had Munro blood in their veins. We can speculate that the gene of Mary's vast interest in plants came from her great-grandfather, William Tate: we know he was elected Fellow of the Horticultural Society of London in 1821.

Another influence on Mary's early years was an even more prestigious figure. This was Claridge Druce who, like Alexander Somerville, was well known for helping and inspiring young botanists. Druce was a remarkable character who, though he had a chemist's shop in Oxford for over fifty years, somehow managed to become the leading field botanist of his day, travelling all over Britain and getting to know an amazing number of people. The circumstances are now forgotten but at some stage Druce probably got to know Mary's Dolserau grandparents, Charles and Mary Edwards, who did a great deal of entertaining both at Dolserau, their summer retreat, and in London where they had a house near Hyde Park. Druce was widely known and could well have met the Edwardses in London. However it happened, what is certain is that Druce knew Mary as a youngster and, as she recalled in later years, did his best to encourage her interest in plants.

We can fairly assume that Mary kept an eager eye on the wildflowers during her holidays in 1902 and 1903 at Dolserau and elsewhere. She named common orache at Penmaenpool on 19 July 1902; and in 1903 she saw burnet saxifrage on the heights of both Cader Idris and Rhobell Fawr. Then at Christmas, 1903, her Dolserau grandmama Edwards gave her a copy of *Illustrations of the British Flora* by Fitch and Smith (1901 edition). From then on she got into the habit of pencilling the date and place of her finds in the margins of these drawings. So from 1904 onwards we can, to some extent, follow her progress as she gradually became acquainted with more and more species around Dolgellau and Barmouth.

Outside Wales she had a holiday in Herefordshire that year with her godmother, Mrs 'Clipsie' King-King (so nicknamed because she was born during an eclipse!). Née Robertson (of the Palé estate near Bala), Mrs King-King, who lived at the Spout House, Orleton, did much to encourage Mary's botanical leanings. It was in nearby Stoke Edith Wood that Mary first came upon lime-lovers like spurge-laurel, stinking hellebore and hairy violet. Down in Kent, while staying at Godinton Park, she collected a specimen of that strange little annual of arable fields, Venus' looking-glass. Also from 1904 comes one of her very few pressed wildflowers from Lichfield: it is common Solomon's seal, but its green leaves and white flowers have now all faded to grey.

Two Welsh botanical records from 1905 are of particular interest. Both relate to Rhobell Fawr, a mountain then, as now, largely neglected by botanists because its mainly limeless rocks are poor in plants. Yet Mary managed to find mountain everlasting which may have gone now from Rhobell, for this is a notoriously decreasing plant, perhaps a victim of acid rain. Mary's other find up there (was she with Uncle Munro Edwards on one of their camping trips?) was the mini-shrub, hairy greenweed, whose yellow, pea-like flowers usually open in mid-June and are soon over. This rarity, long known on Cader Idris, had never before been reported from Rhobell and still awaits rediscovery. Also in 1905, in Stoke Edith Wood, Herefordshire, she made the acquaintance of that rather uncommon plant, wood vetch, so elegant with its white blooms, heavily purple-veined.

1906 brought a fateful event. On Sunday afternoon, 14 October, Grandmama Mary Edwards of Dolserau was being driven in a hired brougham to a service in Brithdir church, intending to go to tea afterwards with her young kinsman, Major Harry Richards of Caerynwch. But on the way something frightened the horse which suddenly bolted. The carriage crashed, the coachman was killed and Mrs Edwards received severe head injuries. The tenant of nearby Maes-yr-helmau farm took her back to Dolserau in his pony and trap; and Major Richards was sent for. He wired Mary's mother at Lichfield and next morning Mary and her mother came on the first train. Mrs Edwards died ten days later.

This tragedy was to be a turning point in Mary's life. Grandmama Edwards was succeeded by her eldest son, Mary's Uncle Munro, who had the task of sorting things out at Dolserau. For several months Mary stayed at Dolserau to help him and while there she saw a great deal of Harry Richards of Caerynwch. They went fishing and walking the hills together, found they had much in common, grew ever closer to each other and quite soon their engagement was announced.

We have a few of Mary's botanical records from that year of 1906, including mossy saxifrage on Cader Idris in June. By July she was in Kent, no doubt staying again at Godinton Park. From there she got to Dymchurch where she noted black medick (quite a local plant in Merioneth); and to Hythe where she collected rough clover. She is back at Lichfield in September and in the park at Sutton Coldfield finds plants of acid ground: alder buckthorn, crowberry and cranberry. These are the last plants noted before her marriage.

*   *   *

The sun shone brightly as Mary Stokes and Major Harry Richards were married in Lichfield Cathedral on 22 August 1907. They were distant cousins, both having the Edwardses of Dolserau in their blood. He was 37, she was 22. He had long been in the Royal Welch Fusiliers and had seen service abroad in Crete where an international force established order in 1897; in South Africa (the Boer War) in 1900; and in China (the Boxer rising), also in

The Cader Idris range in southern Snowdonia from Foel Caerynwch. Cader was always Mary Richards' favourite mountain.

Dolserau in the Wnion valley above Dolgellau, where Mary Richards was born on 3 August 1885.

Caerynwch, the house among the trees at the centre of the photograph, is where Mary Richards lived during her married life.

Mary Richards in her nurse's uniform in World War I. She won a Royal Red Cross Medal for running a military hospital at her home, Caerynwch.

(Anon)

Mary Richards in travelling clothes, *c*. 1930.

(Anon)

Major Harry Richards, *c*. 1930.

(Anon)

Major and Mrs Richards, *c*. 1939.

(Anon)

Caerynwch garden showing terraces extended by Mary Richards.
(Photo by Mary Richards)

The mouth of the Mawddach estuary, Barmouth, a favourite haunt of Mary Richards and family for fishing, birdwatching and yachting.

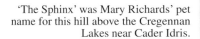

'The Sphinx' was Mary Richards' pet name for this hill above the Cregennan Lakes near Cader Idris.

Greater butterfly orchids were abundant in Dolgellau meadows until modern farming reduced them to scarcity.

Long-leaved sundew, an insect-eating plant of the boggy margins of the Cregennan Lakes.

Globe flowers, like butterfly orchids, were common in meadows around Dolgellau before the 1950s.

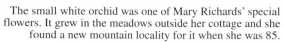

The small white orchid was one of Mary Richards' special flowers. It grew in the meadows outside her cottage and she found a new mountain locality for it when she was 85.

Tynllidiart, a cottage on the Caerynwch estate which Mary Richards occupied from 1950 when she was not in Africa.

Mary Richards and the ecologist, Evan Price Evans, in the garden at Tynllidiart in 1953. Cader Idris in the background.

The Rhinog uplands. Mary Richards (left) and Shirley Beesley on the Roman Steps near Llanbedr, 1957. *(Photo by J. Beesley)*

Mary Richards (right) and Shirley Beesley above Llyn Aran, Cader Idris, 1957. *(Photo by J. Beesley)*

A group of the West Wales Field Society (Merioneth Section) on Ynys Gwylan Fawr, Aberdaron, 31 May 1958. Mary Richards, founder of the section, is standing extreme right.

The dunes of Morfa Harlech, one of Mary Richards' favourite botanical localities. They are now a National Nature Reserve.

Tir Stent, a plant-rich common near Dolgellau, looking north-east towards Caerynwch (distant in the centre of the photograph).

Hairy greenweed (*Genista pilosa*), a rare plant of Cader Idris, was one of Mary Richards' specialities.

Abercorn (now Mbala) as Mary Richards knew it.

Marion (left) and Hope Gamwell at their home, Chilongolwelo, near Abercorn, Northern Rhodesia. It was their invitation that first got Mary Richards to Africa in 1951.
(*Photo by 'Horizon' magazine, Salisbury, Rhodesia, 1964*)

Martial eagle, one of Africa's largest
birds of prey. A pair nested in a tree
close to Chilongolwelo when Mary
Richards first got there.

The International Red-Locust
Control headquarters at
Abercorn (Mbala), Zambia.
The herbarium where Mary
Richards worked on the flora
of Abercorn was in the
building on the right.
(*Photo by Mary Richards*)

Kalambo Falls on the border between
Zambia and Tanzania, a rewarding
locality for botanists and birdwatchers.

1900. The fashionable wedding was fully reported in the *Lichfield Mercury*; and among the guests we find Mary's former governess, Fraulein Wahl. The couple honeymooned on the Continent and, Major Richards being High Sheriff of Merioneth, they had a civic reception when they got back to Dolgellau. The town was abundantly decorated, six-hundred schoolchildren were given tea, a silver band played and hundreds of people waited for the train. Mary and Harry were met at the station by the family carriage but the horses were then taken out and the citizens of Dolgellau hauled the carriage and the newly-weds through the town. This sort of reception may seem bizarre in our more egalitarian age but was not at all unusual in pre-1914 days.

It was literally by accident that Harry Richards had come into possession of Caerynwch, for as a second son he had had little expectation of so doing. His father had died back in 1873 and had been succeeded by the elder son, Richard, aged eight, who took over the estate in due course but was killed in a shooting accident on 13 January 1905, at the age of 40. Harry Richards had succeeded and had forthwith resigned from the army in order to manage the estate.

Caerynwch is a name that takes us all the way back to those shadowy years of the Dark Ages where fact and legend are hopelessly entangled. Assuming that the name has not been grossly mutilated by the centuries, it can be interpreted as meaning the *caer* (stronghold) of Ynwch, or Unwch. Possibly a local chieftain of the sixth century, Ynwch is mentioned in ancient stories as a friend of the slightly historical, mostly legendary, Maelgwn Gwynedd, King of North Wales. Perhaps Ynwch's stronghold was not on the site of the house but up on Foel Caerynwch which rises steeply behind the house. But there are no signs up there of any hill-fort walls or embankments. Another possibility is that the name Caerynwch was brought from some site elsewhere now forgotten.

In modern times, Caerynwch has had a prominent place in local history. It was owned in the eighteenth century by several generations of a family called Humphreys who lived in the early seventeenth-century house now called Plas Hen. Then in 1785 Richard Richards, of the neighbouring Coed estate, married the Caerynwch heiress, Catherine Humphreys, so combining two large estates. This Richards was a man of distinction. Born at Coed in 1752, he went into the law and spent most of his life in London where he was extremely successful, gaining a knighthood and becoming Lord Chief Baron of the Exchequer in 1817. He built the present house at Caerynwch and laid out the grounds, including the now popular Torrent Walk which goes down alongside the Clywedog stream to Dolserau. Sir Richard died in London in 1823 aged 71 and was buried in the Temple. His bust is in Westminster Abbey and there is a memorial to him in Dolgellau church.

*   *   *

Little is recorded about the first few years of life at Caerynwch from 1907 onwards. We know that right from the start Major Harry gave Mary every encouragement to keep up her botanical interests and that in 1908 they got to Sicily, as twenty-seven sheets of pressed wildflowers still bear witness. In 1910 Mary (and Harry?) got far enough up Snowdon to see the purple saxifrage, presumably about Easter when it is at its best. Then in 1911 she climbed the heights of Yorkshire's botanically celebrated Ingleborough in mid-May and made the acquaintance of bird's-eye primrose and cloudberry. A few days later we find her on Place Fell which towers above the south end of Ullswater in the Lake District. Up there she adds yellow mountain saxifrage and alpine lady's-mantle to her life list. Down by the lake she chances on herb Paris, always a good find anywhere. Then she skips up to the top of Helvellyn and finds *Salix herbacea*, that is well-named the least willow since it often has a job to reach two inches in height. In July she got to one of her favourite Welsh places outside Merioneth—that Mecca of botanists, the Great Orme at Llandudno. By that date the Orme's fine show of spring flowers was long over but she was impressed by the beautiful mats of prostrate juniper. Her only Merioneth records for 1911 were the creeping willow and the fragrant orchids she saw on Tir Stent in June.

In those years just before the 1914 war Mary and Harry Richards seem to have indulged their love of travel to the full, holidaying in many parts of Europe, but no account of any of these trips has survived. At home Mary steadily gained confidence in the running of household affairs while Harry settled more and more into the role of a gentleman farmer. They were enjoying the estate immensely and they entertained and visited their many friends. Some of these were far afield; but others were local, for in those days the larger houses around Dolgellau, which

18

are now hotels, boarding houses or divided into flats, were occupied by their owners, at least in summer, and their life was much more social. Field sports were a major preoccupation; and there were trips to London, Henley and Ascot for 'the season'. Most long journeys Mary and Harry made were by train but sometimes in their own carriage. Their first motor-car was still some years into the future.

The fairly large Caerynwch household was virtually self-supporting. The home farm produced beef, lamb and bacon; milk, cream, butter and cheese; and chickens and eggs. There was game in season and they caught trout in the nearby rivers and lakes. The walled garden grew apples, plums, pears, strawberries, raspberries, red and black currants and gooseberries as well as hot-house fruits like peaches, nectarines, melons, grapes, cucumbers and tomatoes. All vegetables for the house were also grown. This picture of life at Caerynwch comes from Kate Heywood, younger daughter of Harry and Mary Richards. She continues:

All cakes and bread were baked in the large kitchen which was surrounded by shelves of gleaming copper pans, polished by the kitchen maid. As a small child I can just remember the laundry with its large coppers for boiling the linen, and flat-irons heated on a fire. The electricity—light only—was made by damming up the river and storing the power in batteries. The electricity frequently failed in winter and we went to bed with silver chamber candlesticks. I am pretty sure there was no housekeeper, so you can see that my mother, still very young, had a lot to oversee.

CHAPTER TWO

1912 was an *Annus Mirabilis* for Harry and Mary Richards, the year they went on a leisurely world tour. They sailed, probably from Tilbury, via Suez to the Indian Ocean. The sea-crossing was no doubt much enjoyed by Harry who was a good sailor but maybe less so by Mary who was not. Sadly, our knowledge of their world tour is very incomplete because although Mary kept a day by day account of it, most of what she wrote has not come to light. We know that they went first to Ceylon (now Sri Lanka) where they visited the famous botanical garden at Peradeniya; and that from Ceylon they sailed to the southern tip of India at Tuticorin which, as a rail-head, gave them access to the rest of India.

It is a special loss that the India part of Mary's chronicle is largely missing because it is known that she and Major Harry had an almost triumphal procession through the country. In those still balmy days of the British Raj, they made contact wherever they went either with government officials or army personnel, often enjoying their hospitality or getting introductions to people in high places, including an Indian prince or two. They travelled in style, taking with them any amount of luggage, including a pile of hat-boxes, for no lady went hatless in those days. We know nothing of the journey from south to north India, of the towns, villages and people they saw and of the wild places they may have got to. And what an epic of travelling on those splendid old Indian railways Mary's lost diary probably told! What we do know, because the story is still remembered, is that they got as far north as the Khyber Pass, as is described by their daughter, Kate:

> They were put up by the colonel commanding at Peshawar in present-day Pakistan, and one day, being rather bored, they took a horse and carriage and went up the Khyber Pass. This was an extremely dangerous and foolish thing to do as it was on the border of Afghanistan (never conquered by the British) and the pass was infested with bandits. Had they been attacked or captured, it would have caused an immense amount of trouble. On

their return (they had enjoyed the excursion very much) they were given a tremendous ticking off by the colonel.

From Peshawar they headed south-east and where the one surviving diary of the tour begins we find our happy travellers on the banks of the sacred Ganges in the very holy city of Benares on 30 January 1912. Next morning, Harry's birthday, they went off from their hotel in a carriage to the oldest part of the city, then got out and walked along streets so narrow there was only room for two people to walk abreast. Mary's diary reports:

> They were extremely picturesque: different coloured muslins just out of the die-pot hung across the street; silver and brass makers working at their trays and bowls; and nearly every other building a temple. We were not allowed inside the temples but looked in from the doorways. The principal Hindu temple, the Golden Temple, dedicated to Shiva, was destroyed by Aurangzeb who built a mosque in its place. Shiva fled in terror to a well close by and this well is held in great reverence. Flowers and offerings are thrown down it and if you drink its waters you learn wisdom; but I would rather not! Another Golden Temple has been built and this is the most sacred spot in Benares. Its roof is coated in gold leaf. We went to see some embroideries and some cloth of gold at a shop which supplies all the brocades and materials for the Rajahs' clothes all over India. I never saw such lovely things—brocades and scarves woven with threads of pure gold and silver, but very expensive. We went back to lunch and the carriage then took us to the station.

So off on the afternoon train down the Ganges valley to Calcutta where they found the Great Eastern Hotel was crowded and they got 'a very bad room'. February began with two days of sightseeing in Calcutta and lunching and dining with old army friends. They went to see the botanical gardens on the other side of the Hooghly River where Mary mentions the colourful bougainvilleas and bignonias, the many different palms and the hugest banyan tree they had ever seen and which is still there. Mary says little about Calcutta itself. She notes its obvious prosperity, its fine buildings and its vast open square, the Maidan; but is disappointed by the Bengali people because their clothes were so drab.

Rangoon was next; and early on 4 February they boarded a British India boat and spent the day going down the 120 miles of the Hooghly River through the delta to the sea. 'It is the most difficult navigation in the world,' Mary wrote, 'and the Hooghly pilots are very highly paid. It is a bad place for cyclones and the currents are very dangerous. We had a smooth sea all the way. Only the boat was too crowded.' From the delta the voyage continued across the Bay of Bengal, heading for Burma.

They should have reached Rangoon at eight that evening but missed the tide and were delayed for over six hours, not reaching Rangoon till 2.30 a.m. But having only one day for seeing the place, they were out before breakfast to visit the city's most famous building, the Golden Pagoda or Shwe Dagon, which dominates Rangoon from high on the north side and is one of the most venerated Buddhist monuments in the world. 'The pagoda is higher than St Pauls,' Mary wrote, 'and is covered in gold leaf. It is built on a high raised platform on which are hundreds of images of Buddha in small shrines. On each side sit vendors of flowers, candles and paper flags which are bought as offerings.' Mary liked the Burmese people partly because, unlike the sombrely dressed Bengalis, 'both sexes wear the brightest colours they can find', and partly because 'the people are charming, especially the women, who all smoke big cigars!'

Next they were off to explore the rest of Burma, heading north by train for Mandalay. At Pegu, two hours from Rangoon, they broke their journey and hired a guide and a conveyance which Mary described as:

> like a wooden box on wheels, drawn by a small Burmese pony and has very poor springs. The roads were awful and we jolted all over the place. Pegu is chiefly famous for its colossal figure of Buddha. It is 186 feet long and 48 feet high. It is not known who made it. Up to a few years ago it was covered with dense jungle and was only discovered by chance when the railway was being built. The figure is lying on its side and is partly gilded. We bumped over a worse road to the Kyaikpur Pagoda which has four big figures of Buddha each 90 feet high, sitting back to back. We dined at the refreshment room and caught our train to Mandalay at 7 p.m., sleeping on the train.

They were out early in the morning to see the sights—many pagodas, a palace, a monastery and the markets. Then they made their way to the riverside to board the cargo boat on which they were to go up the Irrawaddy next day. They slept on board that night because their hotel was 'so bad and so dirty we couldn't stand it any longer. We found there was only one passenger besides ourselves and we have a nice large cabin. The mosquitos were in clouds and drove us to bed early.' Up at seven next morning, they saw the boat start upriver. It was, in fact, three boats in one: 'There is the steamer in the middle on which we live and which has the engines. Then on each side is fastened a cargo boat.'

So off they went on a slow boat up the great Irrawaddy. 'A cargo steamer,' Mary wrote, 'is much more amusing to travel by than a mail boat, as we stop at all the largest villages, and the mail boat goes straight on without stopping except to tie up at night.' All day on 11 February they steamed gently upstream, passing small villages, calling at larger ones. At Mingoon they saw one of the world's greatest bells (weight 87 tons) and the ruins of what Mary describes as 'the largest pagoda in the world'. Cultivations were thick along the river wherever the jungle had been cleared to make way for fields of rice, tobacco, maize, plantains and mangoes. There were many cranes, cormorants, herons, geese and ducks. The night air was deliciously scented. 'All Burma smells of flowers' was how Mary ended her diary that day.

Next day a change: cultivations gave place to thick jungle on both banks; and high mountains which had been distant were now close. The river broadened and was hazardous in its shallows; then it narrowed and deepened between wooded hills. When the boat called at a village they went on a long walk on winding jungle paths, marvelling at the number of different tree species. They saw monkeys eating fruits and leaping from branch to branch with their babies clinging to them. Then failing light sent them hurrying back to the boat.

They reached Katha which they found was a centre for the teak industry, the trees being hauled from the forest by elephants. It was the chief town of the district and home for many Europeans. But Harry and Mary were not enamoured of the place. True, it was rich in pagodas but by now they had seen all the pagodas they ever wished to see. So, having posted letters home, they continued their journey upriver. Next day began amid scenic splendour. They were on deck at sunrise to see the boat pass through the second, and most spectacular, of the navigable Irrawaddy's three defiles where the river narrows to a hundred yards as it squeezes between limestone cliffs 300 feet high. 'There are hills on each side,' Mary observed, 'covered with the most luxurious vegetation—palms, feathery bamboos, huge ferns and great trees covered with creepers. Mist hung in wreaths over the hills and the light was beautiful.'

They came upriver to Bhamo, 900 miles from the sea, the head of all-year-round navigation and almost the highest town on the Irrawaddy. Mary noted

> there are heaps of Chinese in Bhamo which is only 39 miles from the Chinese frontier. There is a big Chinese bazaar and a joss-house very much carved and painted. A hideous idol sat in the middle with a row of Chinese on each side, joss-sticks in brass pots burning before them.

The British military had a base at Bhamo: 'On our way back we saw officers of the East Surrey Regiment playing polo. They asked us to come in and watch, which we did.' They had intended to continue upriver to Myitkyina, the highest town reachable by steamer, but when they collected their mail at Bhamo they found a letter from friends inviting them to stay at Muiktila, south of Mandalay. So they abandoned their Irrawaddy adventure, though not without regret. They had become very friendly with their skipper, Captain Taylor, who had entertained them with wonderful stories about the Irrawaddy's great tributary, the Chindwin, along which he had previously served. He had thrilled Mary by his account of tree orchids in the Chindwin forests, orchids which he claimed grew nowhere else in the world.

Up at 5.30 a.m., they caught a boat downriver to Katha where they got on the 5.00 p.m. train to take them on southwards. They found their friends living in the hills by a lake near Muiktilo. Two days with them and they were off by rail again, sleeping on the train and getting into Rangoon for breakfast. That afternoon they embarked for Singapore. 'The boat is the "Elephanta",' writes Mary. 'She is not very full, mostly Americans and some Germans. Our cabin is very hot and it is almost impossible to sleep.' And did she have memories of Wales when she added: 'There are several hundred sheep on board which smell horrible'?

Next morning, 23 February, was 'a hot day. I didn't feel very fit and sat still all day and read. We slept on deck last night.' The ship passed through the Mergui Archipelago—'small islands with rich vegetation, some had yellow sandy beaches and some had rocky coasts. It is cooler today. I wrote a lot of letters and postcards.' Then they passed down the coast of the Malay

Peninsula to Penang where they got ashore in a sampan 'rowed by a man standing up in the same way as in a Venetian gondola'. At Penang, despite great heat, Harry and Mary went off in rickshaws to visit the botanical gardens where they saw an immense variety of palms and flowering trees.

They had meant to be carried on sedan chairs up to a hill-top hotel for lunch but when they failed to find anyone to take them they decided to walk up and soon wished they hadn't:

> It is almost four miles and very very steep. The heat was terrific and by the time we got to the top we were just as if we had been put, clothes and all, into a bucket of water. The moisture was dripping off my ear-rings. We undressed and dried our clothes as best we could and ate an enormous lunch. Then it rained hard, so we sat and looked at the view.

From 2,260 feet they had a wonderful prospect of Penang and its harbour and far along the Malay coast.

That night it was still very hot and again they slept on the ship's deck as they passed through the Straits of Malacca on the way to Singapore which they reached at 9.00 o'clock in the morning. As nearly everywhere, they had friends to stay with at Singapore. The Days (Mrs Trixie Day was the daughter of the Rev Owen, Vicar of Brithdir) lived on the nearby island of Karimon and to get there they had to transfer themselves and their luggage to a launch.

> She was a funny little boat full of Chinese and natives and we had to step over the cooking stove and cooking pots to get on to the top deck. We reached Karimon at 5.40 p.m. and Mr Day met us on a very rickety landing stage.

Karimon, they found, was an island 15 miles long, mainly jungle-covered and edged all round by mangrove swamps. The main product was rubber from the British-run factory (supervised by Mr Day) occupying a clearing in the forest. After two days of tropical island life Harry and Mary were again on the move, this time on a mail-boat bound for the Dutch East Indies. The sea was rough and Mary was sick. It was the same next day and all she could manage to report was that they had crossed the Equator and that 'we passed many islands and in the afternoon went through the straits between Banka and Sumatra'.

Their arrival in Java was not propitious. They had meant to stay in Batavia (now Jakarta) but, finding the hotels full, they had to get themselves and all their luggage to the station in heavy rain to catch a train for Buitenzorg (now Bogor), 2½ hours away. There things improved:

> We went to the Hotel Belle Vue, very comfortable and we have a lovely view across to Mount Salak. We had lunch and made our acquaintance with the national dish. A soup plate is first piled high with rice, then a procession of waiters offer you from ten to fourteen different dishes—eggs, ducks, chickens, vegetables, two or three sorts of curries and the usual chutney, chillies, coconut, etc. All these you mix up together and eat. No wonder the Dutch ladies are enormously stout!

After lunch they went to the botanical gardens which were reputed to be the finest in the world. Mary certainly thought them better than those at Peradeniya in Ceylon:

> We went along an avenue of trees up each of which was grown a specimen of the big-leaved tropical creepers and huge tree-ferns and orchids. Further on was a lake in which the *Victoria regia* lily was flowering luxuriantly, and behind was a huge mass of white lotus. In another pond were water lilies—rose, pale-pink and blue. There was a fine collection of tree and other ferns and every variety of palm, some of them huge. There were many hundreds of orchids, all growing on frangipani trees.

On 5 March, they made for the mountains. It meant an early start and they were on the road by 5.45 a.m.:

> We sent on our bigger luggage by train and took our small things with us. We had the funniest little two-wheeled cart drawn by three ponies. We were very cramped when we and all our baggage got inside and the driver looked most uncomfortable perched on top. Each side of the road were palms, plantains, fields of paddy and hedges of pineapples, the fruit hanging into the road. We walked up the worst hills. About 11 o'clock we changed ponies and cart and got into a thing like a governess cart with a hood and two cream ponies. We passed huge bushes of daturas making large white patches on the hillsides. We went up and up and presently came into virgin forest—huge ferns, palms and creepers and every tree covered with orchids. We went right up into the clouds and the

26

whole place was like a huge greenhouse, every leaf dripping with moisture, the beauty of the vegetation beyond description. It was very hot and steamy walking up and we must have climbed about 5,000 feet. At the top we got into the cart and plunged down an equally steep descent. The views were splendid, a broad valley below us green with cultivations and paddy fields; and range after range of blue mountains.

So they came down into the lowlands, had an excellent hotel lunch, then took a train to continue their journey eastwards.

On 8 March, in the town of Garut, they rose really early:

We were called at 4 a.m. and were very loath to get up. It was still quite dark when we started at 4.45 after cocoa, tea and bread and butter. We had the usual odd little cart and three ponies.

They climbed steeply to the hills, eventually changing their vehicle for riding ponies, Mary going side-saddle. So up again into the rain forest:

Everything was dripping with moisture as at this height there are generally mists. There were huge ferns, a tangle of palms, creepers and foliage plants. Suddenly the vegetation changed and the soil became stony and sulphurous. We came to a huge cliff and saw a mass of yellow, burning sulphur and huge clouds of smoke and steam. We went right into the crater, the mist had come down and it was raining hard. All round the ground was steaming and sulphur water bubbling up; and volcanic dust nearly suffocated us when the wind blew it our way. At the top end of the crater issued a river of boiling water. After our guide had broken us off some pieces of sulphur we went down. The rain had made the path slippery and our ponies slipped and slithered.

Java's many volcanoes clearly fascinated Harry and Mary. Next day, just as early, they were off again up to the wilds of the rain forest and this time Mary felt it safer to ride astride her pony rather than side-saddle. There were huge trees smothered in ferns and orchids, each tree-trunk surrounded by hartstongues six feet tall. They passed through a small mountain village into dense forest:

So thick were the trees that the light was dim, long mosses and filmy ferns hung from the trees. The whole place was silent, dank and weird. As we got up it grew less dense and the ferns, palms

27

and creepers more and more beautiful. Huge rattan cane palms climbed in a wild tangle, a crimson-flowered creeper clung like ivy to the trees. Suddenly at a turn in the path we came upon a pool of boiling sulphur and mud sending up clouds of steam. All round, the dense vegetation and the tree ferns hanging over, looked as if they enjoyed it. Further on we came to a hut where we left our ponies. This hut was built in the very middle of scorched and smoking ground and holes in which huge cauldrons of boiling mud bubbled and seethed with noises which shook the hollow ground. We threaded our way with great care as the ground was hot and little more than a crust in places. Ahead of us rose a huge column of steam which came with a roar out of a cavern. Below ran a stream of boiling sulphur and water, and hanging over the stream, its stems coated with sulphur, grew a glorious orange-red rhododendron, its flowers three inches across. I found several beautiful white terrestrial orchids. We came to three big mud volcanoes which were boiling with great violence. We went back to our ponies and started down, collecting plants on the way.

Next day, Sunday, was a rest day. In the morning they went to church and in the afternoon Mary went shopping and bought hats to add to their mountain of luggage. Then on Tuesday they left high-placed Garut by an early morning train on 'a lovely journey down through the mountains'. There followed two days of sightseeing at Yogyakarta where they saw Buddhist temples and a sultan's palace. On 16 March they took a train back to Batavia and their Java visit was over. A boat the same day took them to Singapore where they stayed at the Raffles Hotel which Mary did not think much of, confiding to her diary: 'This hotel is not good and the servants very impertinent.' We are left guessing what had happened to upset her.

At noon on 23 March they left Singapore for Hong Kong on the *Delta* (10,000 tons) and were given 'a nice three-berth cabin on the breezy side'. The voyage took five days and on the last morning, Mary tells us:

> We got into a fog and the hooter was going all night. At 5 a.m. Harry woke me and we went on deck as we were getting into Hong Kong. There was a thick mist over the harbour and the Peak. We got alongside about 7 o'clock at Kowloon.

They went over to Hong Kong in a ferry-boat, then a funicular train took them up to their hotel on the Peak. Mary thought Hong

Kong 'a very fine town with broad European streets, good buildings and tramways. It has grown so much in the last ten years Harry did not know his way about.'

Next day, a military friend of Harry's took them round the harbour on his yacht. Mary was enchanted:

> This place is one of the prettiest I have ever seen, the harbour with all its shipping, dotted with islands, and the mainland with its high, bare hills and rose-coloured rocks and Hong Kong itself with its buildings along the sea front, the Peak behind with houses climbing up it. The sea a beautiful deep blue. After lunch we started to walk to the reservoir above the Happy Valley and had glorious views of the rest of the island and of the sea dotted with islands large and small.

Two days later they left Hong Kong on a boat for Canton:

> We went across the harbour past many islands and past the limit of British territory. We went through open sea but it was as smooth as a mill-pond and land was in sight all the time. The water got a thick, yellow colour which showed we were in the estuary of the Canton River. We got into more and more shipping, till at last we arrived at the pier. The river was thick with junks of all shapes and sizes and it was wonderful how the bigger boats and steamers got through. A large part of the population live on these junks.

They had two days of sightseeing and gift-buying in Canton. They saw a water-clock claimed to be six centuries old:

> Water trickles into a jar with a floating indicator inside which shows the time as the water rises. The jar takes twelve hours to fill and is then emptied. We went next to the place where the Chinese dead are kept till the astrologers have fixed a time and place for burial. One coffin we saw had been there thirty years.

Having had their fill of the sights, sounds and, most memorably, the smells of Canton (the sewers were decidedly noxious), they sailed away downriver at four in the afternoon. That evening there was 'a lovely full moon and we sat on deck and watched the junks. We got into Macoa at 12.30 but I was fast asleep.' Macoa, on the west side of the Canton estuary, had been a Portuguese colony for centuries and had long been infamous for gambling and opium-making. Mary, on her first morning, thought it 'quite the prettiest place we have been to. It is like a bit of the Italian Riviera. It is on a rocky promontory with the sea on one side dotted with islands, and the river on the other.' After lunch they took a boat back to Hong Kong, 'a delightful journey all through islands'.

On Tuesday, 9 April, they sailed for Shanghai:

> Twelve miles from Hong Kong we got into a dense fog and had to anchor after very nearly having a collision with a ship of the Douglas line. We were so close we could have stepped on to her. It was bitterly cold.

Wednesday was no warmer: 'Such a cold day and very rough. I am very proud of myself as I didn't miss a meal all day. But I was not happy and could not keep warm.' Next day was smoother but even colder and Mary stayed in bed. 'A strong wind and no sun and everybody grumbling,' she reports. Things began to improve on the third day: 'A lovely day, cold, but brilliant sun and the sea like glass. We are going along the coast past hundreds of sailing junks.' At this point the chronicle comes to an abrupt end. No doubt it was continued in another notebook now lost, for it is unthinkable that Mary made no record of the rest of the tour which took them up through China to Japan and then right across Canada.

Although the diary covering China is missing, one snippet of their visit has come down by word of mouth. As Kate recalls:

> My father, when serving with the Royal Welch Fusiliers, had been stationed in China and took part in the relief of Peking during the Boxer Rising of 1900. When he and my mother arrived in Shanghai twelve years later they were surprised when Bonzo, who had been my father's servant on his previous visit, was waiting for them on the quayside and accompanied them to Peking. There was a remarkable grape-vine in Shanghai in those days and a close watch was kept by the Chinese on the passenger lists of arriving ships. Peking at that time was dominated by the Forbidden City near which was a maze of winding streets. One day my parents hired two coolie-drawn rickshaws, my mother travelling in front. Suddenly she heard blood-curdling screams. Her coolie began to run in great excitement, saying: 'Execution, Missee, we go see.' Round the corner came a procession headed by a man carrying a huge sword. Behind him a screaming prisoner was being dragged by guards. My mother said those screams haunted her for weeks.

She had difficulty in preventing her coolie from following the procession, to his great disappointment.

Though China was then torn by civil war, tourism was evidently unimpeded, for we have a note among Mary's papers saying: 'Fighting among the Chinese was going on but Europe was not involved.' So they had no problem in getting to see the Ming tombs near Peking and also in visiting the Great Wall.

In Japan we can again quote Kate:

> From China my parents travelled on to Japan which must have been little visited by tourists in those days. They covered about 400 miles, my mother often walking and my father riding because he had injured a knee. They put up at very primitive rest-houses, at one of which my mother was somewhat disconcerted when the male Japanese proprietor came into the room where she was bathing naked and offered to scrub her back. This, he assured her, was a Japanese custom and an honour paid to visitors of both sexes.

A reminiscence written by Mary in after years mentions that while in Japan they had an exciting close view of a volcano in eruption and also experienced a minor earthquake in Tokyo.

A precious souvenir of the Japanese part of the tour is a collection of 137 wild plants made by Mary as they travelled through the countryside. The plants are unnamed and if she intended to get them identified when she got home there is no sign that she ever did. Many of the specimens are small, delicate and beautiful, some still so fresh-looking they might have been gathered yesterday. Very possibly beech fern was the only plant among them which Mary recognised, so often had she seen it on Cader Idris. There is one other much-valued survivor from that visit to Japan: at Caerynwch there is a bonsai tree (*Chamaecyparis obtusa*), still in its original dish, which Mary brought back in 1912. It is in good health and was exhibited at the Chelsea Show some years ago. One final memory of that world tour: when they got to Canada, Mary recalled many years later, they went by train from Vancouver to Montreal and 'here we got a boat for England; but a day's journey out, in the Strait of Belle Isle, we got into thick fog and ran into a cargo boat. We had a large hole in our side so went back to Quebec and caught a train to New York.' There they boarded a ship for England.

CHAPTER THREE

Although in much of Britain the years just before 1914 were a time of strikes and industrial unrest, life for the comfortably off was still going on as smoothly as it had for many decades. Home from their world tour, Harry and Mary Richards could look to the future with a fair degree of satisfaction. There was only one cloud in the sky: they had been married several years without any sign of children on the way. Yet even that cloud dispersed in the spring of 1914. There came a happily expectant few months until life exploded for everyone on 4 August 1914, and Britain was at war. As a reserve officer, Major Harry Richards was called up immediately to Wrexham to be second in command of the sixteenth battalion of the Royal Welch Fusiliers; and Mary was left at Caerynwch to get through the last months of pregnancy. In December she moved to her parents at Lichfield and there a baby girl, Jonnet, was born on 30 December.

It was not an easy birth and Mary, in poor health afterwards, remained at Lichfield for the next three months. By then Major Harry had been moved with the battalion to Llandudno and there Mary joined him with the baby and a young nanny, Edna Horton, who was to remain with the family for many years. So Mary passed a summer at Llandudno where, despite the exigencies of wartime and motherhood, her botanist's eyes can hardly have missed the wealth of wildflowers in that corner of Wales. When at the end of the summer Harry was transferred to Winchester, Mary went with him; but it was not long before he went out to the battle-front in France, leaving Mary to return to Caerynwch. There she helped to look after a few wounded soldiers of the Royal Welch Fusiliers who had been sent there to recuperate.

Caerynwch had been offered to the War Office as a military hospital but had not yet been accepted. So Mary, anxious to serve, went on a six-month course in London to train as a nurse. She then worked at a military hospital at Englefield Green, Surrey, and while there she heard from the War Office that they were now able to accept Caerynwch as a convalescent hospital for other ranks. So there she returned as matron of a hospital with fifty beds—quite a responsibility for one so inexperienced. Caerynwch was to remain a hospital right through until May 1919. And although in theory a convalescent hospital, it had to cope with many serious cases and there were even a few deaths. There were also difficult cases of shell-shock, a condition not understood at that time, those afflicted often being accused of malingering. In later years Mary often spoke of the wonderful support she got from her team of V.A.D.s, many of whom were her personal friends like, for instance, Sophie Blathwayt, who had been a fellow-pupil at the school in Belgium. In 1916 Mary Richards received what she always valued as her greatest honour—the Royal Red Cross Medal awarded for her capable management of Caerynwch's wartime hospital.

Early in the war Harry Richards was badly wounded while serving with the British Expeditionary Force in France and though he recovered he was lame for the rest of his life. After the war Caerynwch was redecorated and restored for domestic use and while they waited for these repairs the Richards family lived in a bungalow, now demolished, which overlooked the Cregennan lakes in the foothills of Cader Idris. This delightful property now belongs to the National Trust but at that time it was owned by the Richards' close friends, Major and Mrs Wynne Jones who in after years gave Cregennan to the Trust in memory of their two sons, both killed fighting in the Western Desert in the Second World War. By the time that family life was resumed at Caerynwch in 1919 there were two children, a second daughter, Kate, having been born in the previous September. Because Mary had had a difficult time with the birth of her first child, her second baby was born in a nursing home in London.

An anecdote that has come down the family relates to the year 1918. In Kate's words:

> Around this time there was a General Election. My mother, always enthusiastic, decided to canvas my father's tenants. (I don't know which party she supported, probably Conservative at that time as my father detested Lloyd George. In fact my mother was extremely liberal-minded). A much-respected family named Pugh lived at Fronolau. My mother called at the farm and delivered a passionate political speech directed at an elderly Mr Pugh across the kitchen table. He heard her in silence and then said: 'Mrs Richards, your job is not politics. You go back to Caerynwch and make an heir for the Major.'

And in due course Mary did just that. Their only son, Richard, was born in 1920 at Caerynwch. (There seems to have been a family tradition that if a son was badly wanted the baby must be born in the family home!)

*   *   *

Throughout her life, Cader Idris was Mary Richards' favourite mountain. On her childhood visits to Dolserau, then during her time at Caerynwch, and in later years when she lived in a cottage on the estate, this shapely range beckoned to her from four miles away. Sometimes she walked to the three summits along its ridge—first Mynydd Moel, then Cader itself, then on to Tyrau Mawr. Just as often she went the botanists' way, exploring the cliffs and corries that surround the mountain's flanks. Cader Idris is botanically interesting because its soils, though mostly sour, are here and there rich enough in calcium to support a good range of lime-loving plants. And from Cader these better soils extend north-east to Brithdir and beyond, including on the way the common land called Tir Stent, a wild, undrained area of marshland, rocks and scattered trees only a mile or so from Caerynwch. At Tir Stent Mary Richards was familiar with a fine community of plants like globe-flower, water avens, marsh hawksbeard, creeping willow, lesser clubmoss, various sedges, the locally rare frog orchid and the even rarer small white orchid.

At its eastern end Cader falls abruptly into the Tal-y-llyn Pass where there was a small, very shallow pool now largely filled in by road-widening and reduced to a marsh. Yet though so insignificant in size, it was a pool that had a place in legend as Llyn y Tri Graeanyn—the Lake of the Three Pebbles—so named from three massive blocks that lie nearby. They were hurled into the pass, legend assures us, by the disagreeable giant, Idris, whose *cader* (fortress) was on the summit and who, in his frequent bursts of bad temper, threw rocks in all directions. This lake in the pass was a frequent spot for Mary to bring the children to on nature walks in the 1920s.

East of Tal-y-llyn Pass the land rises again to grassy slopes below Mynydd Ceiswyn. Gone now, because of excessive sheep-grazing, is the heather which once clothed much of these hills and was a home for red grouse. From up there you look east into the vast gulf into which the A470 plunges from Bwlch Oerddrws. The cliffs on the right are Craig Portas and Craig Maesglasau; and

34

opposite, across the valley, are the Dinas Mawddwy hills which hide the spectacular Cwm Cywarch. The heights march on northwards above the upper reaches of the Dyfi till you come to the narrowing valley called Llaethnant at whose head rise the dark crags of Aran Fawddwy. It is all a delightful, rather secretive land of cliffs, screes, gorges, waterfalls and plunging hillsides with scattered outcrops of limy rocks well clothed with mountain plants. Mary Richards got to many of these botanically rich localities in her early days.

The peak of Aran Fawddwy looks north-east into the valley of the Wnion river which hastens under hills and woods down to Dolgellau. The Wnion had a special place in Mary Richards' early days because, flowing along the edge of the Dolserau estate, it was her childhood's first river. Her second was a tributary that comes in from the south, the Clywedog, which hastens down through the grounds of Caerynwch to create the fairyland of the ever popular Torrent Walk which keeps high above the Clywedog stream as it splashes or, after heavy rain, roars down its shadowy, wooded ravine, falling and cascading over rocks all the way. Among the flowers of spring are bluebells, bilberry, cow-wheat, woodruff and white sheets of wild garlic. But in so shady and moist a place it is ferns, mosses, liverworts and lichens that are dominant. So in the days of the Victorian fern-collecting mania, Torrent Walk (where there is today a Mary Richards memorial seat) was one of the places that drew fern-enthusiasts to Merioneth. Yet even in Victorian times, fern-gathering was not universally approved of. We read in Jenkinson's *Practical Guide to North Wales* (1878) that 'Mrs Richards, widow of the late R.M. Richards, Esq' had set up a notice at the bottom end of the path saying: 'Private Walk. Visitors are admitted on the condition that they do not touch the ferns and mosses; and do not injure the trees, seats and fences.'

Who can say what famous botanists may have visited the Torrent Walk at some time? One we know of was C.A. Johns (1811-74), a Hampshire schoolmaster whose classic *Flowers of the Field* was a best-seller. Wherever they went botanising, Victorian ladies had a copy of it in their reticules and it was still popular well into the next century. That Mary was brought up on it was inevitable: her grandmother, Mary Edwards, was a friend of C.A. Johns and gave Mary a copy of *Flowers of the Field* for her twelfth birthday. In it is her signature, 'Mary Stokes 1897'. C.A. Johns stayed with the Edwardses at Dolserau; and Mary has left it on record that he collected mosses down the Torrent Walk (having got permission, let us hope, from Mrs Louisa Richards at Caerynwch!).

North of Dolserau the land rises to the Nannau estate and two shapely hills, Foel Cynwch and Foel Offrwm, both crowned by the remains of Iron Age hill-forts. Nearby are the far-seeing Precipice Walk; the fishy lake, Llyn Cynwch; a former deer-park; and the tree-surrounded pool, Pwll y Gele. This superb estate was a playground for Mary Stokes because of the close links between the Vaughans of Nannau and the Edwardses of Dolserau. Further north the land goes on climbing to Rhobell Fawr from whose rocky summit there is a magnificent panorama not only of Cader Idris but also of the whole exciting profile of the Rhinog range. From her childhood Mary loved the Rhinogydd and in later life often spoke of youthful adventures exploring Cwm Mynach, the Clogau gold mines (which she knew as a nesting place of choughs) and the manganese mines of the uplands. At Bont-ddu her family were friendly with the Beales of Bryntirion who enthusiastically combined field sports (they had a grouse moor on the Rhinogydd) with an interest in natural history. The Beales also lived in Birmingham where Charles Gabriel Beale was a distinguished alderman. At the City Museum and Art Gallery there is the Beale Memorial Collection of nesting groups of British birds created in his honour in 1913.

Between the Rhinogydd and Cader Idris lies a scenic masterpiece—the estuary of the Mawddach which Mary Richards loved for its fishing, its birdwatching, its plant-life; and for the sailing the family had long enjoyed at Barmouth. And alongside the estuary there were the woodlands at Abergwynant and the peatbog at Arthog—all good country for naturalists. But of all this region within easy reach of Dolgellau, it was probably the coast that appealed to her most strongly in those happy days before the present ugly sprawls of permanent caravans had arrived. Along that coast her favourite spot in the 1920s and '30s was Mochras (Shell Island) and the nearby dunes, now Morfa Dyffryn National Nature Reserve. Here she often came with the family or with naturalist friends like James and Mrs Backhouse of Arthog. In spring and summer she enjoyed the spectacular displays of wild orchids in the damp dune hollows; and the burnet roses with their showy white flowers and shiny black hips. The Mochras area is no longer what it was in her day. She knew it as a breeding place for many redshanks, oystercatchers, ringed plovers, shelducks, black-headed gulls, skylarks and wheatears. Today the ground is far drier, the summer pools she was familiar with have mostly gone, there is infinitely more disturbance by people and adjacent to it there is today a military airfield. In her later years, if she went to the coast, she preferred the botanically rich, less disturbed dunelands of Morfa Harlech, five miles north.

While the children were young in the 1920s, Mary relived her own childhood, encouraging them in nature study just as Fraulein Wahl had inspired her in the 1890s. They did all the things children had been brought up to do since nature studies began in Victorian times. They sprouted oaks from acorns, reared newts and frogs from tadpoles and produced butterflies and moths from caterpillars. They kept sticklebacks in an aquarium and watched them guarding their nests and bringing forth their young, They had a whole zoo of other creatures: guinea pigs, hedgehogs, water snails, water spiders and the larvae of caddis flies and dragonflies. They learned about predation from seeing how, in the aquarium, the larvae of the great water beetle could kill lampreys and elvers.

They noted the wildflowers in their seasons, beginning with celandines, dog's mercury, pussy willows and hazel catkins. Along the Clywedog stream below the garden they found mosses in abundance, sheets of Wilson's filmy fern and, on the trunks of waterside oaks, the large and beautiful leafy lichen, tree lungwort. From the shore they brought home seaweeds and pressed them. In autumn they collected fungi, some mushroom-shaped, some finger-like, some like jellies, some strangely formed like the brown Jews-ears they found on dead elder branches. They laid the caps of toadstools on sheets of paper and marvelled at the patterns of spores they found next morning. In the family log there are hints of more serious lessons in botany, as on 20 August 1927, when 'between the Gwanas Drive and the Lodge' at Caerynwch, they picked a large bunch of wildflowers. These they then listed systematically: rose family, borage family, figwort family, thyme family and so on, 75 species in all. But Mary made a point of never forcing botany down their throats.

Sometimes the children contributed to the daily log. On 6 October 1926, Kate, aged eight, wrote:

> Nannie found a glow worm in Coed Lane. Although called a glow worm, it is not a worm for no worms have legs. It looks very like a grub, but is in reality a beetle. As it has no hard wings, it doesn't look like one. It is soft skinned and very helpless, but to make up for these things nature has given it the glowing light.

Next year they learned about birds' nest tragedies. On 27 May Kate wrote:

> Found blackcap's nest near the tennis lawn. The tennis ball hit it and put it crooked. There were four eggs, a deep cream colour with brown markings.

Two days later, despite this mishap: 'Birds hatched in blackcap's nest.' But on 29 May: 'Found birds in blackcap's nest tipped out of nest and dead.' Another nest is reported the same day along the stream:

> Popa found a sandpiper's nest under a dwarf elder bush, a deep nest of moss lined with grass. The egg was greenish with brown marks.

A month later Jonnet is the scribe. On the hill above the house they saw a 'beautiful little moth called blue forester'. Next day she wrote:

> Went to Three Pebble Pool and caught a huge discucis [*Ditiscus*] beetle and a laver [*larva*] and many dragonfly lavers.

On 28 July 1928 Jonnet reports on a visit to the wilds of Arthog Bog:

> We went for a picnic on the estuary with Mr and Mrs Backhouse. We explored marshes by Barmouth Junction, heard the lesser redpole and found nest with hen bird on it. Nest in young birch tree, small but deep. She did not mind us and continued to sit. When disturbed she returned immediately, evidently sitting hard. We also heard and saw the grasshopper warbler and stonechats and another kind of bird we were uncertain of.

A gale on 29 October 1927 was reported by Jonnet:

> The storm brought nearly all the branches off the big oak tree in the meadow and a huge oak on the drive snapped clean off its trunk. Along the back drive trees have fallen all over the electric wire cables and there is a big bit taken out of the dam. Along the road to Barmouth the railway line was carried away. All along the road the walls were laid flat and all the telephone and telegraph wires were blown down. On Barmouth front the shelters had been

torn up like bits of brown paper. The sea had been right on to the front, leaving it in a most terrible mess of stones and rubbish.

It was Kate who chronicled a February snowstorm in 1929:

> Had an awful blizzard. Some of the drifts are ten feet high at Gwanas and Dinas Mawddwy road. The storm started at 9 a.m. and ended at ten at night.

All part of the children's education were Mary's pets and for many years before the Second World War, Caerynwch had quite a menagerie of assorted creatures, so much so that one part of the garden came to be nicknamed 'Whipsnade'. From 1927 onwards Mary's diaries have copious references to this plethora of pets, many of which came from dealers in London. On 20 February 1928 there was a delivery of 'six golden orfe, four American dogfish, four red snails'. Other transactions brought goldfish, ale fish, sunfish, catfish and rainbow trout. Local fish were sometimes brought back from angling expeditions: perch from a pool in the deerpark at Nannau and from nearby Llyn Cynwch; and on 23 September 1929 we read: 'Caught 14 pike at Cregennan Lakes, some of which were put in the garden pond at Caerynwch.'

Small fry included minnows from Tal-y-llyn, three-spined sticklebacks from a stream near Caerynwch and ten-spined sticklebacks from ditches near the coast. Among fish purchased in February 1930 were two popes, two thunder fish, two bitterling and various tropical species. A month later she buys some angel fish. Next year she goes in for paradise fish which are soon spawning prolifically. In March 1932 there is a delivery of sunfish, catfish, mirror carp, leather carp, gudgeon and dace.

So life no doubt went on year after year but a long gap in the diaries of the 1930s deprives us of further information. Such a diversity of fish called for a variety of places to keep them in. As well as the garden pool there were several aquaria with warm water, cold water and salt water, their correct maintenance calling for much ingenuity by F.A. Drinkwater who for many years was the Caerynwch gardener. The sea aquaria were made from slabs of Aberllefenni slate and fitted with glass fronts. Sand and sea water were frequently fetched from Barmouth and there were outings to the coast to get seaweeds, sea anemones, prawns, shrimps, hermit crabs, starfish and other rock-pool inhabitants.

For the tropical fish, consignments of water-fleas came regularly from London and were collected from Dolgellau station.

In a tropical house half-filled by a bougainvillea lived tree frogs, geckoes, Dalmatian lizards, wall lizards and edible frogs, along with terrapins, turtles and black and yellow salamanders as well as those curiosities of nature, axolotls, which are young salamanders capable of breeding in their immature stage. The children soon decided that these sluggish, unprepossessing axolotls made completely unattractive pets. Mary even acquired a young alligator but as it grew up it developed such sharp teeth that poor Drinkwater, whose job it was to feed it, could no longer cope and it was transferred to other owners. Mammals, apart from cats, dogs, rabbits and ponies, are little mentioned in the annals. But to have taken delivery of as many as a dozen guinea pigs one day seems a risky venture in view of their well-known enthusiasm for reproduction. White mice escaped and crossed with house mice, producing piebald offspring. A hedgehog called Timothy lived in the schoolroom.

There were also the aviaries which, like the aquaria, housed a wide range of species both exotic and native. Budgerigars and canaries are frequently mentioned in the log. There were also cardinals, weavers, waxbills, Modina pigeons, diamond doves, bronze-winged doves, cut-throats and zebra finches. There were golden pheasants, Reeves pheasants, Amherst pheasants, brent-geese, carolina ducks, mandarins, mallard, shelducks and ruddy shelducks. For a touch of originality there were usually a few black-headed and herring gulls; and at one time great black-backed gulls strutted about the terrace like peacocks. Rooks too: occasionally young ones fell out of nests in the Caerynwch rookery and had to be reared.

From time to time, throughout her life, we hear mention of a cousin of Mary's to whom she was obviously devoted. Captain Stephen Stokes, M.C., a life-long bachelor, lived in Staffordshire as Mary had done, and was long in the leather business at Walsall. He and Mary had two strong interests in common: gardening and pet-keeping. At his house at Longdon near Rugely, Stephen had an outstanding garden, specialising in rhododendrons and other plants of limeless soils. He also had tropical houses complete with hummingbirds. As well as his garden, cousin Stephen also had a collection of ornamental waterfowl and other fauna and for many years he supplied not only plants for Caerynwch's garden but also various creatures for Caerynwch's 'Whipsnade'. When he retired he went to live at Paignton on the coast of south Devon where he had a friend, Herbert Whitley, the proprietor of Paignton Zoo. Stephen soon got involved with the zoo's gardens and animals, acting in an advisory capacity and helping to add to the collections of fauna and flora. And as he had from Rugely, he continued to send or bring plants to Caerynwch.

CHAPTER FOUR

Enough of her diaries have survived to give us a fair idea what Mary Richards was up to in the field of natural history in the late 1920s and much of the 1930s; but of the early twenties no records now exist apart from a few from Switzerland in 1921. Back in 1912 Mary had received from her godmother, Clipsie King-King, a copy of Correvon's *Alpine Flora*; and when she got to the Alps in June, 1921, she noted her botanical finds in the margins of the book. On the list are soldanellas which no doubt she saw peeping out of the melting snow; *Lloydia serotina*, the little treasure that we in Wales so parochially call the Snowdon lily; yellow whitlow-grass which in Britain grows only on the cliffs of Gower; and giant butterwort, hardly known in the British Isles outside south-west Ireland. Other British plants she found were mountain everlasting, hutchinsia, bird's-eye primrose, moss campion, alpine saw-wort and round-headed rampion. Among non-British species were *Clematis alpina*, *Anemone alpina*, *Primula minima*, *Androsace lactea*, *A. carnea*, *Gentiana punctata*, *Erinus alpinus*, *Daphne cneorum*, *Anthericum liliago*, *Phyteuma betonicaefolium* and many others including the 'King of the Alps', *Eritrichium nanum*, whose bright-blue forget-me-not flowers so enraptured Correvon: 'High, very high on the desolate Alps, on ridges beaten by the most savage fury of the storm, a wonderful jewel sparkles in the sun . . .'

Except that Mary and Harry were in the Canary Islands in January and February, 1925, as is still attested by 79 sheets of pressed plants, we do not pick up anything of Mary's life again till 1927 when her diaries resume. Though she had joined the Botanical Exchange Club (later the BSBI [Botanical Society of the British Isles]) five years earlier, we still find her daily log more concerned with birds than botany and at that time she was regarded as the local ornithological expert, so much so that when T.P. Ellis wrote his *Story of Two Parishes: Dolgellau and Llanelltyd* (1928), the chapter on birds was entrusted to Mary Richards, the one on plants being contributed by the eminent botanist, D.A. Jones, the Harlech schoolmaster. There is no

42

evidence that Mary Richards and D.A. Jones ever met. This may have been because Mary did not get seriously into botany until D.A. Jones, who died in 1936 aged 75, had largely switched his attention from flowering plants to mosses and liverworts, a group which Mary never tackled.

Even on days devoted to field sports Mary always kept an eye on nature. So though she went hunting on 24 and 25 September, all she logs in her diary is that she found a new locality for lesser bladderwort near Tywyn and saw seven caterpillars of the buff-tip moth feeding on sallows. She was, after all, very close to nature when hunting. We must not imagine her galloping across the landscape on horseback. All her hunting was done the hard way, on foot, up and down rocky slopes and across rough wooded hillsides with the Ynysfor pack in Snowdonia or the Machynlleth hounds further south.

Her botanical finds in 1927 included yellow mountain pansy on the moors above Lake Vyrnwy, upright vetch by Cregennan Lakes and 'a dark form' of marsh hawksbeard on Rhobell Fawr; but her best plant was marsh clubmoss at Cann Office, Montgomeryshire, a declining species no longer known in the county. Staying with friends in Devon in September she saw wild madder at Dawlish Warren, a plant she had not yet found in Merioneth where it is rare. Also that month she was let into a great secret by James Backhouse, a leading authority on the rarer ferns. He showed her a very hush-hush locality of the Killarney fern hidden behind a waterfall on one of the Merioneth streams.

In May 1928 Mary was in Hampshire. At Beaulieu she saw dwarf furze 'all over the Heath', greater spearwort, wood goldilocks and petty whin. Under a hedge at Exbury was a particularly robust specimen of green-winged orchid with a larger than normal lip. It was submitted to the great Dr Druce who declared it 'variety *churchillii*'. (In those days there was a fashion for splitting this orchid into various forms now long discarded.) Her best find in the south of England was the rare, today even rarer, purple broomrape which she saw growing on chalk near Lewes in Sussex.

In June she describes an unusual encounter with a hostile buzzard when she was botanising on the cliffs of Cader Idris above Llyn Aran:

> I must have been near the nest, as one of the birds swooped down within three yards of my head, I waving a stick to keep her off.

43

She repeated the manoeuvre over and over again, circling up in the air, dropping her legs and spreading out her claws, hunching up her wings and dropping with a swoosh, then turning to look back and making a shrill cry, the other bird circling overhead and crying.

Starry saxifrage, mossy saxifrage, lesser meadow-rue, roseroot and mountain sorrel are among the plants she found up there that day. On the calcareous marshes of nearby Tir Stent she found moonwort, frog orchid (always a good find in Snowdonia) and a profusion of common butterwort. When she got home she was annoyed to find that house sparrows had seized possession of one of nine house martins' nests built with much labour under Caerynwch's wide eaves. Happily, by the end of June she was able to report that the evicted martins had repossessed their property.

In Herefordshire in August she first met with common wintergreen: it was in Orleton Woods near Leominster. Also that month she got to Llanymynech Hill near Oswestry, famous for its calcicole plants among which she particularly rejoiced in the abundance of pyramidal orchids.

In the Dolgellau area she notes extraordinary numbers of peacock butterfly larvae on the nettles; a multitude of galls on oaks and alders; and the finding of a pale-yellow, marsh-loving snail, *Succinea putris*. Butterfly of the year was a clouded yellow in September. In autumn there was a sad event: when chickens began to disappear from the Caerynwch poultry run, a stoat or a weasel was suspected; but what was caught was a buzzard. This was a shock to Mary who had always been an admirer of buzzards, frequently noting them in her diary. On 10 July she had written: 'The Habenarias are magnificent everywhere this year.' It was just a casual observation but how poignant for us today! She never dreamt when she saw all the many fields around Dolgellau rich in Habenarias (greater butterfly orchids) and other delights, that pretty well all those flowery meadows were doomed to disappear in the next few decades, to be replaced by 'improved' but unbeautiful, botanically boring grasslands.

1928 was also the year when Mary made an interesting new friend. John Henry Salter, one of the best all-round naturalists of his day, had long resided at Aberystwyth where (1891-1905) he had been the first Professor of Botany at the University College. He was, as he described himself, 'a naturalist of the old style, knowing something of all branches and not being an authority on any . . . My ideas are mid-Victorian.' He expressed no admiration at all for politicians but he liked Prime Minister Neville Chamberlain much better on learning that he was an expert on moths. Though devoted to the flora of Cardiganshire, Salter had long been interested in the plants of Cader Idris; and in September, 1928, he wrote to Mary Richards, whom he had never met, inquiring about several Cader species.

His letter was one of old-world formality, beginning: 'Dear Madam'. He wanted to know about rarities like alpine saw-wort, bog orchid and oblong woodsia; and then: 'But the plant I especially want to inquire about is *Genista pilosa*. Following directions received from Mr D.A. Jones, I made a careful search of Cwm Gau Graig a week ago but failed to meet with it'. Hairy greenweed (*Genista pilosa*) is probably Cader's most distinguished plant. To most botanists it is known as a rarity of the mild coasts of Pembrokeshire and Cornwall. So it is very strange to find it flourishing on the heights of Cader where winters can be so harsh.

So it came about that the hairy greenweed drew together two botanists in a friendship that was to last till Salter's death in 1942. Occasionally he was invited to lunch at Caerynwch which he reached by train to Dolgellau (he never had a car) and then two miles on foot up to the house by way of the Torrent Walk. But though arriving for lunch he always brought his own food so as not to deviate from a lifetime of strict vegetarianism. His friendship with Mary Richards was, on the face of it, an improbable one. He was a Quaker and a pacifist; she was High Church and a soldier's wife. He was no lover of hunting and she revelled in it. Yet they always greatly respected each other and had many a happy day together in the pursuit of natural history, often with their mutual friends, James Backhouse of Arthog and E.H.T. Bible of Aberdyfi. For Mary's children, their mother's friendship with these staid, middle-aged to elderly naturalists was a source of amusement. 'Mummy's young men', they christened them. They also called them 'the bottoms up brigade', a name suggested by a frequent posture of botanists.

On 4 April 1929, walking from Caerynwch to the Precipice Walk by way of Dolserau and the Nannau deerpark, she noted 'a great absence of birds'. All she saw were buzzards over Moel Offrwm and 'yellow ammers' (note her Victorian spelling) by Llanfachreth. If she could go that way today she might do even worse, for the yellowhammer is now in serious decline. On 15 May at Caerynwch there was a squirrel 'with very long fur on his ears'. It is a reminder to us now that every squirrel in those days was a native red one, characterised in the breeding season by long ear tufts. It would be decades before the American grey squirrel would take the place of the red squirrel in the Dolgellau area. Fishing for trout in the stream below the house, Mary remarks on the extreme tameness of a pied flycatcher which sang on a branch just above her head. A big day for eleven-year-old Kate was 18 May: she got to the top of Cader for the first time—up by the Pony Track and down by the Foxes' Path. Next day we hear of a pair of goldfinches building a nest in an apple-tree in Caerynwch's walled garden. It was decorated with lichens and 'almost concealed in apple blossom'.

Two bird observations of historic interest come at the end of May. Mary walks the Merioneth shore at Tal-y-bont and is mobbed by three pairs of terns (no doubt little terns) which were obviously nesting there along with an equally agitated pair of ringed plovers. Ever increasing human disturbance has long since driven away most shingle-nesting birds along that coast. Incidently, Mary's name for the ringed plover was 'dotterel' which, like 'yellow ammer' was a hang-over from her childhood. Similarly on 30 May on the streamside at Caerynwch she saw a wader she called a 'summer snipe' though by then the name common sandpiper was well established. As well as the little terns, the other historic bird of 1929 was the red-backed shrike she saw at Penmaenpool. In those days this was still a regular breeding site for this now vanished bird, probably the last place for it in Merioneth before it disappeared about 1940. Yet earlier in the century it had been a common spring and summer bird in the coastal region. Unlike that of the little tern, the shrike's decline had nothing to do with disturbance and has never been convincingly explained.

On 1 June, Mary was at Mochras with two of the children, Kate and Richard (Jonnet being by now away at school), and we get a vivid cameo of life in the wet dune hollows among the creeping willows and the spreads of colourful wildflowers like bird's-foot trefoil, ragged robin, orchids, spurges and burnet rose. There was also that sinister plant, henbane; and angular Solomon's seal at its only Merioneth locality. About ten pairs of nesting oystercatchers yelped all round; there were two pairs of lapwings, each with four eggs; wheatears were breeding everywhere; there was a colony of black-headed gulls; and there were many pairs of 'sheldrakes' (Mary hardly ever called them shelducks). 'Further on, near the sea, we put up many pairs of redshanks nesting in clumps of rushes in the saltmarsh. The water was above our ankles.'

Three days later Mary was at another coastal spot then known for its breeding birds—the mouth of the Dysynni River with its wide spread of sea-borne pebbles. With her was Margo Masters of Petersfield, Hampshire, who in the 1920s and 30s was Mary's most frequent field companion, often staying at Caerynwch. On Aberdysynni's shingle they found ringed plovers, lapwings, oystercatchers, redshanks and little terns all nesting in tranquillity, a totally different scene from today when the place is overrun the year round by people and their dogs. The Dysynni was always one of Mary's favourite streams, not only because of its birds and its many otters, but also for the the interesting flora at its mouth—including quantities of sea-holly, yellow-horned poppy and autumn lady's tresses. In late August, 1929, Mary took the children camping at Tonfannau. The holiday began with two days of heavy rain and floods but the weather improved from then on. In the sea they watched seals and on the wide muds of the Broadwater there were flocks of small waders. Butterflies were many and on sallows they found a caterpillar of the eyed hawkmoth.

CHAPTER FIVE

The sun was unseasonably hot on 3 March 1930, when Mary and Margo were in the Rhinog range scrambling up Craig y Saeth which towers above the lake at Cwm Bychan. The year's first lizard was sunbathing and the heather was lively with spiders. A fox turned to look back at them as he made off over the rocks. Then, above the mountain-reflecting waters of Gloyw Lyn, they had that frustrating experience many naturalists have sometime in their lives—the not quite certain sighting of a rare creature: 'Near the top,' wrote Mary, 'we saw a wild cat, but whether marten or pole, we could not see.' Amid the wild crags of Rhinog a pine marten was indeed possible and it is regrettable that this was not a firm record of that most elusive of all Welsh mammals. Later, returning along the road by Cwm Bychan lake, they looked up to Craig y Saeth and Margo said she could see 'people' on the top. But 'looking through glasses we saw seven wild goats, two he-goats with magnificent horns and five females. They jumped and climbed down the precipitous face of the rock.' So, for the first time Mary saw the famous 'wild' goats of the Rhinogydd, the descendants of former domestic goats which long ago took to the rocks and the heather.

Mary Richards' severely impersonal diaries of the period rarely give us any hint about her own personality or ideas about life, nor about her social activities, many though these were. When she goes away she seldom says why she went, how she travelled or whom she stayed with. Without explanation she is somehow there. So with total abruptness her diary for 1930 says: 'Windsor, April 11.' And here she suddenly is, 150 miles from home, in Windsor Forest with the ever faithful Margo, admiring the leafing trees, watching a stoat that came close, noting redstarts, nuthatches, willow warblers and tree creepers and listening to a tree pipit parachuting down in song. Just as unexpectedly, five days later, she is back at Caerynwch. No mention of any journey, only an entry in the diary saying: 'Cold day. Snow on Cader.' How very often she notes the coming and going of that snow! The peak of Cader was an out-door thermometer to be glanced at many times a day.

On 3 May 1930, ever fascinated by ravens, their aerobatics, their remarkable voices, the fortresses of sticks they build among the high rocks, Mary was on the south end of the Rhinog range hoping to observe a pair at their nest. With her she had Jonnet, the younger two children having gone back to school. They walked up Cwm Mynach to the Beales' grouse-shooting box and on up the ridge past Y Llethr to Rhinog Fach. Looking up the cliffs above Llyn Hywel, they could see a raven's nest made of heather twigs but when they climbed above it they could not quite see into it because, as so often with ravens, it was cleverly hidden under an overhanging rock. Though they retreated and watched from a far distance, they could not conceal themselves, and the wary ravens, demonstrating noisily, would not come back to the nest.

Two days later they were watching ravens again, this time on Cader where they spotted a nest in the cliffs above Llyn Aran 'just above where I found the skeleton', says Mary's diary in a reference to an incident a few years earlier when she had been in Cwm Aran with her friend Florence Bristow and Florence's husband, the orthopaedic surgeon, Walter Bristow, of St Thomas's Hospital, London. While the Bristows rested by the lake, Mary went scrambling up the rocks in search of plants but what she found was a heap of bones. Picking one up she brought it down to show it to Walter who said: 'By God, Mary, it's a human arm-bone!' 'I know,' replied Mary, 'the rest is up there.' The identity of the skeleton still remains a mystery but it was presumably that of some luckless hill-walker who had fallen off Mynydd Moel.

On 23 May Mary achieved an ambition she had long nurtured: she got to Bardsey, that small, much cherished island which on clear days is visible across the bay from much of the coast of Merioneth. The morning was fine as she and Margo Masters set off in a sailing boat with Bardsey islander, Thomas Pritchard. Once under Bardsey's cliffs they were greeted by a mixed crowd of seabirds including one lone puffin. Landing at noon, they set off to explore, beginning with a walk to the top of the mountain. There they looked down on colonies of guillemots, razorbills, herring gulls, jackdaws and starlings nesting in the cliffs. Then down to the lighthouse at the low-lying south end, seeing on the way stonechats and rock pipits and hearing a voice no one is likely to hear there today—the rasping of a corncrake which no doubt they took for granted as a common country sound. The wildflowers that most caught their eyes were sea campion, sea pink and bird's-foot trefoil. They were also struck by the 'wonderful yellow lichen' (*Xanthoria parietina*) which so loves Bardsey's rocks.

They slept in the house called Plas Bach and 'heard birds calling all night, a curious sound, not like seabirds'. After breakfast, Miss Roberts, their hostess, told them her brother, Jack, had some eggs for them to see.

> He showed us a peregrine's egg, several guillemots' eggs varying very much in colour and a white egg of what he called a mackerel cock. After looking through 'Coward', we found it was a Manx shearwater. He told us the calls we heard at night were these birds who do not appear in the day, staying in their holes with their egg. He also said there was one pair of choughs.

So up the mountain again, this time to see a shearwater taken out of its burrow. 'The bird did not make a sound and hardly struggled. We photographed it and it went back onto its egg.' They ventured gingerly round Bardsey's steep eastern slopes, looking in vain for choughs. The narrow path high above the sea was not to Mary's liking, for she never had a head for heights. They found a bulky raven's nest of gorse twigs and looked on shags at their nests. They heard a cuckoo, then saw it being pursued over the sea by a pipit. Three herring gulls joined in the chase but the cuckoo flew much faster and dodged back to the cliffs. In a strong north-east breeze they left Bardsey that afternoon and after tea at Aberdaron went to see St Mary's chapel and well on the cliffs where, Mary's diary reports: 'The farmer who was watering his cows told us that there were many mackerel cocks about at night, so I suppose they also nest on the part of the mainland opposite Bardsey.'

Three days later Mary and Margo were on an island fourteen miles east of Bardsey. There was a warm south-west breeze as they crossed by motor-boat from Abersoch to St Tudwal's East Island.

> As we got near, we could see thousands of puffins circling round and flying from sea to land and back. The air was thick and the sea black with them. We landed on the island and sat to watch. The ground was riddled with their burrows. They soon got used to us and settled only five yards away. Many had bits of dried grass in their mouths and were evidently building. Some were billing each other like love-birds. Others had fierce fights and rolled over and

over down the slope. Every now and then, for no reason one could see, the whole lot took fright and flew into the sea but soon came back. They darted in and out of their burrows and were extraordinarily silent. Their only noise was a grunt and they seemed to make this when in their burrows.

This picture of St Tudwal's makes almost unbelievable reading today. There are still seabirds on the island but no sign of a puffin. For some unknown reason this once great puffin commune, estimated in 1907 to number 'some hundreds of thousands', fell on bad days and had quite abandoned St Tudwal's by 1951.

Next day Mary and Margo left for Anglesey where they walked across the Newborough dunes, seeing redshanks, sheldrakes, lapwings and curlews; and cuckoos being chased by meadow pipits. They slept that night in one of the old pilot cottages on Llanddwyn which is, as Mary says in her diary, 'a rocky island connected to the mainland by a causeway . . . rocks all round and sandy coves and small islands just off the coast.' They could see arctic and common terns nesting on those off-shore rocks but could not be sure whether there were roseate terns as well. From Llanddwyn, beautiful with sea-pink and blood-red cranesbill, they crossed Anglesey to South Stack whose cliffs were thronged with razorbills and guillemots. Then, after a night in Rhosneigr, they had a guided tour of Bodorgan headland, walking among the crowded nests of herring and lesser black-backed gulls built in long grass, sea-pinks and bracken. Further on, cormorants sat on nests of dead heather stalks and there were about two dozen pairs of great black-backed gulls on nests made almost entirely of chickweed.

When they got back to Caerynwch Mary was pleased to find her pet young gulls were thriving, her budgerigars hatching and that spotted flycatchers had a nest 'in the wall by the fruit room.' In hot and thundery weather on 4 June they went to Tal-y-llyn Lake and found a reed bunting's nest with beautifully marked eggs in rushes at the water's edge. The shallows of a stream running into the lake were 'alive with minnows' the males brilliant with their 'green and red gills and white spots on sides and fins'.

Major Harry loved the Mediterranean and on 27 September 1930 he and Mary left London by rail at 9.00 a.m., had a good breakfast on the train and got to Folkestone to find the sea smooth but the weather wet. At Boulogne they got into a luncheon car and were in Paris by 4.00 p.m. At the Gare de Lyon, Cooks had reserved window seats for them on the train to Italy but an elderly Turk and his wife had torn down the reservation notices and occupied their seats. So the conductor had to be summoned to sort things out. But, as Mary reports, the conductor's intervention was not altogether successful:

> We settled for the night, having fights at intervals about windows and heating which we opened and turned off and they shut and turned on. They ate queer food out of a large, black oil-skin bag . . . fish (niffy) and cheese (ditto). We woke at 6 a.m. near the Swiss frontier.

So across Switzerland and through the Simplon Pass. Veils of rain spoiled their views of Lake Maggiore and Stresa as the train took them on to Milan, Padua and finally Venice where, still in pouring rain, they went by gondola along narrow canals to their hotel on the Grand Canal. In four days they saw everything in Venice that it was *de rigueur* for tourists to see. Then a gondola took them to join the S.S. *Diana* which steered a leisurely course down Italy's east coast as far south as Brindisi where they were charmed by the old town, its palm trees and its harbour full of picturesque fishing boats. Overnight they crossed the Strait of Otranto to the Albanian port of St Quaranta. Soon they were landing on Corfu and hiring a taxi for a quick look at the lovely island before they were back on board and sailing south past the Ionian Islands and into the Gulf of Corinth amid a gorgeous sunset then moonrise. Next morning they were up early to see the view as the ship reached the eastern end of the Gulf and stopped to pick up a pilot to guide them through the Corinth Canal. And so to the port of Piraeus and a distant glimpse of the Acropolis high above the houses of Athens. For several blazing hot days they examined the archaeological treasures of Athens in the greatest detail and were particularly moved by the National Museum's collection of finds from Mycenae and Knossos.

For three exciting days they explored the remains of ancient life in the eastern Peloponnese: Mycaene, Tripolis and Argos. Then they sailed on a rolling sea to Canea in Crete and along the island's north coast to their hotel at Candia (Iraklion). Here Harry was not on such familiar ground as he had expected: 'The whole place has changed since H. was here. They have built breakwaters and made a harbour with a good road and good houses.' They went for a nostalgic walk along the shore to the ramparts where the Royal Welch Fusiliers had had their camp and Harry saw some of his old haunts. Next morning they were up early and after a walk of one and a half hours, 'we saw Knossos before us. We went through a wicket gate and came to the west court of the palace. Here we found a dear old guardian who went round with us.'

At Candia Harry and Mary had the adventurous idea of walking west along the Cretan north coast to Canea, a trek of about 90 miles. An ancient bus got them out of the town, then they took to the road, such as it was, with two donkeys and an old man as guide. As Mary says, they must have looked a rather bizarre party as they slowly made their way along the dusty, zig-zag trails that struggled over ridge after ridge above the coast, taking them from village to village. On the uplands, with their panoramas of mountains and sea, the country was 'all heath, arbutus and myrtle'. Between the ridges the valleys were often thick with olive-groves and vineyards. A fact of life they discovered on this six-day safari was that Crete in 1930 was still almost as primitive as in the days of ancient Knossos. In those pre-tourism days they had to put up each night at whatever makeshift accommodation they could find, including at one place a down-at-heels monastery which had 'appalling sanitary arrangements—a hole in the floor!' Some days they had donkeys, some days mules; these were mainly for carrying their luggage (spare clothing, blankets and food). Harry, because of his lameness, quite often rode while Mary walked and kept her eye on the wayside flowers, especially the autumn-flowering cyclamens. There was one exciting moment when two golden eagles, 'huge brown birds with yellow heads', came very close, one landing near them with a snake in its talons.

On their fourth night, glad to get under any roof after walking and riding miles through heavy rain, they again had to accept a lodging at an antiquated monastery. They dined, or tried to dine, off a boiled chicken but it was 'very, very tough! Then up to bed—outside pouring with rain—and a terrible sanitary arrangement miles away in the garden! Upstairs we found the beds with beautiful old embroidered covers and pillows but oh! so damp and dirty.' One bed they found to be crawling with bed bugs, the other sodden because it was under a hole in the roof. Eventually, having treated the one bed with insecticide which they had resourcefully brought with them, Harry slept in it while Mary slept on the floor. 'During the night there was an awful thunderstorm, torrents of rain and continuous lightning. However, we slept well, except for a flea which bit me badly.' At 4.00 a.m. a bell rang, the monks started service in the church next-door and Mary enjoyed listening to it in the darkness. It was light by six and they got up. That day they found that what had been a parched and dusty countryside had been transformed by forty-eight hours of rain: 'It has become green, trees all perked up, the hills all with a tinge of green, it's almost unbelievable.' The heavy rain persisted and they sought refuge in a house to eat their lunch.

> Three brothers evidently lived in it, and all their animals, in one room like a very dirty barn and the roof leaking. We sat on what I suppose was their bed—a settle by the wall . . . The sun came out and it was quite hot. A few miles on we saw a lovely sandy beach and had a heavenly bathe.

So in due course they reached Canea and sailed back north to Athens. There Mary went down with suspected food-poisoning, was critically ill for days, then made a quick recovery and was soon out sightseeing again.

On 10 November they went by hired car north-west to Thebes and on to Delphi under Mount Parnassus. Delphi was a delight:

> Woke at 7 o'clock, a perfect morning. It's a glorious place. My room has a balcony and I look down nearly 1800 feet into the valley, a narrow gorge with a river in the bottom and mountains rising the other side. On the right the valley widens and beyond a sea of olives is Itea on a bay opening into the Gulf of Corinth and beyond again the mountains of Peloponnesus with a powdering of snow. After breakfast we started for ancient Delphi.

Happily they explored Delphi's delights, making detailed notes of everything they saw, the highlight of which was the temple of Apollo where the Oracle was consulted in ancient days. Near the Stadium, on the path up Mount Parnassus, Mary found 'fascinating mauve crocuses'; and there were eagles planing above the nearby cliffs. Next morning, called at 4.00 a.m., they hurried by hired car down to the little port of Itea and sailed into a beautiful sunrise. In a tiny boat they crossed the Gulf of Corinth to the busy port of Patras where, two days later, they boarded a Serbian ship that took them up the coasts of Albania and

Yugoslavia. From Ragusa (Dubrovnik) they were the only passengers on this little cargo boat as it sailed past hundreds of islands with 'lighthouses everywhere. The place is lit up like a street with them at night.' So they reached Fiume where they left the ship and took a train round to Venice. Then on to Verona whose art and architecture they explored with their unfailing thoroughness before doing likewise at Milan. And there the chronicle ends.

CHAPTER SIX

2 March 1931 was ominous in the annals of local natural history: it brought news of the first American grey squirrel in the Dolgellau area. Another had been shot on the Palé estate at Corwen a few weeks before. These were warning signs of an invasion which had already swept across much of England. But there was no thought of alien squirrels a fortnight later when Harry and Mary were eating their lunch in very warm sunshine, sheltered in the dunes at Mochras. It was a day full of birds: the sea covered with scoters and wigeon, the mudflats lively with knots, lapwings, redshanks, curlews, ringed plovers, swans and shelducks.

> In the sandhills a lot of water with teal and wigeon and a beautiful pair of pintail . . . a perfectly lovely day. The big sharp rush has beautiful brown seed cases which look as if they had been polished.

By mid-April the children were home from school and Mary led them up Cader. It was warm and sunny as they struggled up the difficult scree of the Foxes' Path to discover snow and ice on the summit. Mary notes the abundance of stag's-horn clubmoss on the way up, a trivial enough observation at that period, yet significant today when, through excessive sheep-grazing, this attractive clubmoss is not nearly as common as it was. Spring was late that year but it came at last. Wood warblers sang near the house; goldfinches and pied wagtails nested in the garden; grey wagtails and sandpipers (Mary was still calling them 'summer snipe') came back to the stream; and Kate saw 'a pair of golden crested wrens building under a branch high up in the Douglas fir on the tennis lawn'. Then Kate went back to school and Mary was soon on the move, this time south-west to Pembrokeshire where she found the spring much more advanced than around Dolgellau. She got to the coast at Tenby where she was much impressed by St Mary's, the largest medieval parish church in Wales and with the tallest spire. The fine chancel roof and the medieval tomb of John White especially caught her eye. Then west to one of her favourite buildings, St David's Cathedral, rejoicing on the way at the colourful displays of roadside gorse, blackthorn and primroses.

On 4 July 1931, fishing at Cregennan Lakes, she noted long-leaved sundew (*Drosera intermedia*) in a waterside bog. In October there was a curious dog incident. The day was so glorious that Mary could not resist the call of Cader. With her went her spaniel, Squire, and she enjoyed perfect views from the top. On the way home she was given tea by the Pughs of Penrhyn-gwyn, one of the Caerynwch estate farms. Squire meanwhile was shut up in a stable but during tea he escaped and, not knowing where Mary was, ran away towards Cader. By dark he had not shown up and Mary went home without him. She was also without her rucksack which, she now remembered, she had left on the top of Cader. Next morning in a gale of rain, farmer Pugh, who held a Royal Humane Society medal for mountain rescues, went up Cader. There on the summit was Mary's rucksack and Squire quite fiercely guarding it.

1932 was full of variety. In early May, Harry and Mary had a fortnight in the south of France at Mentone where roses and geraniums were all in flower. They came home to find they had managed to avoid a spell of snow and frost and now the river was swollen by two days of rain. Then on 13 May, Harry saw a pied flycatcher in the drive, an event worth recording because this flycatcher was still not the familiar bird it now is. A fortnight later Mary was in Anglesey, being conducted round Bodorgan's gulleries by a gamekeeper, as she had been two years before. These great breeding colonies fascinated her and this year they were more populous than ever. The lesser black-backs, nesting amongst the bracken, had spread further inland, keeping aloof from the herring gulls. The great black-backs were nearest the sea, right at the end of the headland. Mary remarks on the diversity of shape, size and colouring of the herring gulls' eggs. Next day she was at Llanddwyn Island:

> The terns have changed their breeding place. Two years ago they nested on a spit of rock covered with sea-pinks, beyond the white tower landmark. They were guarded by Eliz Jones, the woman pilot, who allowed no one to go beyond the tower. She died last year, so it's possible they have been disturbed . . . The big island which was covered with herring gulls' nests two years ago has been taken by cormorants who have made a horrid mess and you can smell them from the lighthouse.

On 10 June she and Margo were listening to a nightingale and what she called 'goatsuckers' (nightjars) at Lindfield near Haywards Heath, Sussex. Then for two hot days they rowed on the Thames in the Henley and Pangbourne area, botanising a little but mainly birding. At Mapledurham a pair of black swans was an unexpected sight. A few weeks later they were on the Kent coast at Dungeness where they identified roseate terns for the first time and found two good plants—shepherd's cress, which is very rare in Merioneth, and the hemp-nettle, *Galeopsis ladanum*, a casual wanderer from the Continent.

It has long been a dream of botanists in Snowdonia to find a new site for the very rare Killarney fern which usually grows on perennially wet rocks in shaded gorges or behind waterfalls. So it was on 16 July 1932 that Mary Richards and James Backhouse searched for this fern up a stream that cascades down the northern flank of Cader. Finding no Killarney fern, they went on climbing till they reached the rock-band that geologists call the pillow lavas where they made a good list of plants including purple, mossy and starry saxifrages, Welsh poppy, early purple orchid, hairy rock-cress, lesser meadow-rue, burnet saxifrage, water avens and stone bramble. Among the ferns were green spleenwort and brittle bladder fern. Then at 4 o'clock torrential rain ended the expedition. But Welsh mountain botanists are quite used to summer drenchings. Mary's diary for the rest of 1932 is unusually scrappy but she manages to record that 22 August was her and Harry's silver wedding and was a lovely hot day; and that on 9 October an oil painting of Harry was finished and placed in Caerynwch's dining room where it hangs to this day.

Meanwhile pets of many sorts continued to keep Mary busy. In November two pairs of axolotls were sent from Paignton Zoo. In December the mildness of the weather was cause for comment. Christmas Day was 'glorious, warm enough to sit out on the terrace in the morning'. And on 29 December: 'Lots of flowers out in the garden—violets, roses, primulas, alyssum, veronica; and the Christmas roses this year are wonderful.' The unseasonable mildness went on well into January, 1933. On the 9th Mary foot-slogged over the hills above Forge with the Plas Machynlleth foxhounds, first having to drive her car through one of those famous floods at Dyfi Bridge. They didn't see a fox all day but the sun shone, the air was gentle, the views magnificent and the hazel catkins and pussy willows already in flower. Three days later, the weather still soft and fine, she was again at

Machynlleth. This time the hounds met at Garthgwynion and worked their way across the Llyfnant Valley to Glandyfi, all very rough going for people on foot. A fox was chased a long way but eventually vanished into the depths of a badger sett.

Such mild weather could not last for ever and it was soon displaced by weeks of heavy snowfalls, the worst being on 24 February:

> Woke to a dull roar and found a terrific blizzard going on. Wind N.E. and fine powdery snow so dense it was impossible to see beyond the terrace wall. By 9 a.m. there was a foot of snow and deep drifts beginning. We rescued the golden pheasants and the mandarin ducks and put them in the stables. The wind was so strong you could hardly stand against it and the air so full of snow it blinded and choked you. It went on till 5 p.m. The postman, for the first time in forty years, he told me, was unable to go beyond Brithdir post-office. The drifts on the Brithdir road were terrific. The river frozen over and covered with snow. The birds came in flocks to be fed. More snow fell during the night.

A few days later it was thawing and raining and this brought disaster to the railway which feels its way gingerly along the Merioneth sea cliffs. Mary wrote: 'A tragic railway accident by Llwyngwril—a landslide fell on the train.' This was the 6.10 a.m. from Machynlleth. The engine fell into the sea, killing both stoker and engine driver.

In 1933 Mary Richards joined the Alpine Garden Society and on 10 June drove north to Llanberis where the society was meeting to investigate the flora of Snowdonia. On their first morning (Monday) they went up Snowdon on the train, just for the view. Coming back down they got off at Clogwyn station for a scramble into the depths of Cwm Glas Mawr where they saw a good selection of mountain plants like alpine meadow-rue, moss campion, mountain sorrel, green spleenwort and many others. Mary also notes ravens, buzzards and ring ouzels. Tuesday was spent in Cwm Idwal in thick mist but that did not prevent them from spotting six plants of the rare Snowdon lily high in the Devil's Kitchen. Up there they also found prostrate juniper and mountain everlasting; and water lobelia and awlwort in the lake below. Next day they had a change from mountains as they examined the limestone flora of the Great Orme. On Thursday it was back to the heights—up Snowdon again on the train, finding least willow and alpine saw-wort near the summit. Again down into Cwm Glas Mawr looking especially for the arctic saxifrage but failing to find it. After a day along the Llŷn peninsula they revisited the Devil's Kitchen but now the mountain gods afflicted them not with mist but 'terrible rain' and all that Mary reports is northern bedstraw, hairy rockcress and a few more Snowdon lilies. Alas, the gale and rain went on all that night and much of the following day, washing out a scheduled visit to the Carneddau. Rather than sleep in a hotel, Mary had chosen to camp but evidently her tent weathered the monsoon all right. The next locality was Clogwyn Du'r Arddu, a classic site visited by many of the early botanists from Thomas Johnson onwards. Along the skirts of Clogwyn's great precipices they soon found plenty of seedlings of Snowdon lily along with northern rockcress, arctic chickweed and other alpines. Next day they were among the mountain ferns, adding the rare holly fern and the ultra-rare oblong woodsia to their tally. Then a third day in the Devil's Kitchen in a last desperate attempt to find the arctic saxifrage. But again they failed.

That day ended with a typical Mary Richards idea. Who else, at the end of a gruelling scramble in Cwm Idwal, would have suggested they should walk up Snowdon by night to see the sunrise? She had only one taker for this frolic, George W. Temperley, a well-known naturalist from Newcastle-upon-Tyne. So, 'on a lovely warm night', they set off at midnight from Llanberis and reached the summit at 3.00 a.m:

> Such a still night. A match burned steadily on the top. Mist lay in the valleys with the mountain tops emerging. The mists cascading over the rocks of Lliwedd. Got down by 7 a.m.

Strangely she fails to mention whether they saw the sun come up or not! Next morning, after two hours sleep, they were off yet again to Cwm Idwal but this time climbing up past Llyn Bochlwyd to the Gribin where they were delighted to see one of Snowdonia's very rare localities for mountain avens. Mary thought the flora up there 'very rich indeed'. Then they went on up into the Nameless Cwm and found two new plants for their list—alpine bistort and three-flowered rush. Their Snowdonia experience ended with another visit to Clogwyn Du'r Arddu where Norman Woodhead of Bangor showed them mosses and lichens as well as a distinctive form of the brittle bladder fern with finely divided fronds. Choughs, with their musical calls, flew round this majestic cwm where they have long nested safely in the depths of old copper mines.

Mary followed her midnight walk up Snowdon with a similar nocturnal venture up Cader Idris in July, presumably with the ever faithful Margo Masters. From the top they saw a 'wonderful sunrise' which lit up the Irish mountains a hundred miles away in the west. On the way down they bathed in Llyn y Gader, normally a very cold lake but presumably just then a littte less frigid than usual because of a heat wave which a few days before had taken the shade temperature up to 95°F in the walled garden at Caerynwch. The very hot weather persisted. On 20 July Mary was at a royal garden party in London. Next day she was camping by the Thames near Oxford, the start of four days of rowing on the river and enjoying every minute, for no sunshine in Britain was ever too hot for her.

On the first day she and Margo rowed upstream from Folly Bridge to beyond Godstow Lock, admiring the riverbank flowers, including two not common in Wales—arrowhead and fringed waterlily. Next day, the weather still hot, they came back downstream to Abingdon where they pitched their tent in the lock-keeper's garden. On their third day, which was hotter than ever, reed and sedge warblers were still in good song and the banks below Abingdon were flowery with 'gardens of wildflowers, teasel, loosestrife and masses of inula and valerian'. They had lunch at Shillingford Bridge, tea and a bathe at Moulsford and camped that night by Basildon Farm. As every evening, mist lay on the river, to be burnt off early next morning. On their last day:

> Off by 9 a.m. Very hot row to Mapledurham. Lunched in backwater above lock by old mill—a great many fish. Yellow water-lilies lovely. Tea Sonning. Henley by 7.30. A lovely trip. Two kingfishers seen. Many plants collected.

Several of these are now in the herbarium of the National Museum of Wales.

At the beginning of September, 1933, Mary took the children off camping for a week along the Llŷn peninsula. They pitched their tent on the Warren at Abersoch in dunes just behind the beach where they could bathe every day. Mary's friend, Martin Williams-Ellis, took them out in his boat round the St Tudwal's

Islands but it was just too late to see the puffins—they had gone to sea a week before. One day they visited the foundations of St Mary's tiny medieval church high on the majestic headland of Braich y Pwll that looks across two miles of often turbulent water to Bardsey Island. A good find on Braich y Pwll that day was the beautifully aromatic chamomile, not at all a common plant in Wales. Next day (Tuesday) they went across to Bardsey Island where they had a guided tour of the lighthouse. On Wednesday they were given tea at the fine old house of Nanhoron near Botwnnog where Mary was impressed by the tender plants growing out-of-doors and which could never survive the winter up at Caerynwch—tenderlings like myrtle, lemon-scented verbena and balm of Gilead. On their last day they fished from a boat near the Gull Islands off Aberdaron and caught 89 mackerel. From the boatman they learnt that professional collectors came every year from Liverpool to take seabirds' eggs. It was a trade that was to last until Bardsey and the Gull Islands became nature reserves twenty years later.

It is on a rhapsodic note that Mary concludes her log for 1933: 'It has been a wonderful year; bad droughts in England but here wonderful weather, a year to remember. The garden has been a glory.' She was now 48 and in tip-top condition after so many days on the hills fox-hunting on foot or simply walking to various summits. She went twice up Snowdon from Pen-y-pass; several times up Cader; and on 5 October she (and presumably Margo) tackled the Aran ridge from north-east to south-west. They took a train from Dolgellau and got off at Carnedd Wen Halt ten miles away. From there they 'walked up Sir Watkin's moor and saw quite a lot of grouse'. So they came up to the top of Aran Benllyn amid fine views and cloud effects and looked down on the corrie lake, Llyn Lliwbran. Then higher still to the rocky peak of Aran Fawddwy where they looked in vain for the least willow, a failure not at all surprising because by autumn the leaves of this two-inch willow would have fallen, leaving it extremely inconspicuous. Immediately below them they saw the source-lake of the Dyfi, with the infant river going away down its first moorland valley. Then they walked back across country to Caerynwch.

At this time of her life, Mary Richards' perennial restlessness and excess of energy were, if anything, increasing. And athough she threw a great deal of herself into a wide range of social and family duties, she still found plenty of time for outdoor activities. We can picture Major Richards feeling a little bewildered at times by the whirlwind way his wife was so often out for the day or for several days at a time. Because of his lameness he could never have kept up with her in the field, whether she was hunting, birdwatching or botanising, even had he wished to. As it was, he had plenty to occupy him in the running of the estate.

Mary Richards' diaries, because they are preoccupied with the great outdoors, give a quite unbalanced picture of her life between the wars. Only rarely do they give a hint of the immense amount of social and public work both Harry and she performed. Major Richards was a magistrate for many years and a member of the Joint Police Committee. He was on the governing body of the Church in Wales and was also involved in running the Territorial Army in north Wales. For eighteen years Mary Richards was a county councillor (most of the time the only woman member), her specialities including health, particularly the fight against tuberculosis which, because of bad housing, unemployment and malnutrition, was especially bad in the slate-quarrying area of Blaenau Ffestiniog. At one meeting she held forth on the need for all milk to be pasteurised, whereupon the chairman rose and declared: 'Mrs Richards is quite right. We should have clean milk. We must have clean milk. And if we cannot get clean milk, we must take the bull by the horns and demand it!'

Mary was also prominent on various committees to run and raise funds for the county's hospitals. She was involved in organising Ranger and Girl Guide groups, the Girls Friendly Society, the Mothers' Union and Brithdir church. And for some time she was a keen Women's Institute member. Courageously she helped to pioneer family planning in north Wales and 'as a result,' reports Kate, 'she suffered much criticism from close friends. It was not thought at all a suitable subject for a lady to be involved in.' Bravery of a different sort was called for when she took her Girl Guides camping at Tonfannau. As Kate narrates:

> A large group of nubile young ladies attracted the lusty young men of Tywyn who attempted to surprise the young ladies in their tent at midnight. They fled in terror when the fearsome and furious figure of my mother in blue pyjamas, brandishing a peg mallet, appeared out of the gloom. They could not face such a virago.

In the mid-1930s Caerynwch was known for its lively parties and by chance an account of one of them has been preserved. It speaks of Harry Richards as 'a retired army man who seemed very good-humoured'; and of Mary as 'a kind and hospitable hostess but slightly formidable'. (The writer, be it said, was only nineteen.) Mary is also described as 'very well acquainted with the country and an ardent ornithologist'. Then there comes this extraordinary final touch: 'One Caerynwch custom I remember was that of ascending the eastern part of Cader Idris in evening clothes at dawn after a dance.'

*   *   *

January 1934 was notable for the large number of bramblings and red squirrels about Caerynwch. And for a great flood at the head of the Mawddach estuary. On 4 March, Mary notes the contact calls of curlews passing over in the darkness. It is a sound the hill people love to hear as the birds move up from the coast to their moorland breeding places—a much welcomed first sign of spring. On 2 April, Mary walked to the rocks of Creigiau Llyn Gafr, the only site on Cader for the purple saxifrage. This early-flowering alpine is Cader's Easter flower-show, sometimes in bloom amid snow and icicles. Mary speaks of 'brilliant patches of magenta on the grey rocks'. On other days she walked to Moel Offrwm, Torrent Walk, Aran Fawddwy and Llyn Cynwch. Failure to catch any trout in the hot sunshine of 12 May at Cregennan Lakes was more than compensated for by the butterflies—'a very large number of green hairstreaks'. On 26 May came her annual spring pilgrimage 'to Portmeirion, Mr Haig's garden—rhododendrons and azaleas a wonderful sight'.

CHAPTER SEVEN

In the summer of 1934, Mary and Harry took themselves off on a fishing and birdwatching tour of the Shetlands, with Mary's old friend, Sophie Blathwayt. Their route to the Shetlands was not one that would readily occur to anyone these days. From Wales they motored leisurely across to south-east England, staying with friends on the way. On Tuesday, 19 June, they sailed from London Docks on the S.S. *Copeland* of the Clyde Shipping Company.

> It took a long time to get out of the dock into the Thames. Very interesting seeing the shipping of all nations going down the river. A good deal of wind and colder. Southend by 11 p.m. Fare from London to Glasgow is £2.15.0. and food paid for as you have it.

So along the south coast in cold winds and choppy seas, passing close to the Isle of Wight. On the Thursday they rounded Land's End and raised the coast of Ireland in early afternoon. Off Dublin the sea was calm and gannets, gulls and shearwaters followed the boat. They got into Belfast early Friday morning, had a few hours ashore visiting the Belle Vue gardens and sailed at 3.00 p.m.

> It was lovely going down Belfast Loch. A stormy day with scuds of rain and beautiful gleams of sunshine between. As soon as we were out of the loch we saw Scotland, Wigtownshire on the right and the Mull of Kintyre on the left. And then the Isle of Arran. The sea full of gannets, gulls, fulmars, razorbills, guillemots, shearwaters. Soon the huge mass of Ailsa Craig came in sight. We passed fairly close and could see thousands of gannets on their nests, the cliffs white with them. Soon we were going up the Firth of Clyde with islands on each side and lovely scenery made lovelier still by the changing play of sun and rain. At 11 p.m. we tied up at Greenock, quite light still and the sunset reflected in the still water like an opal. Terns fishing all round. It is sad to see so little shipping and the shipyards grass-grown.

From Greenock by train to Edinburgh, then on the S.S. *St Rognvald* to Aberdeen. A few hours ashore then north again to

Orkney, finally disembarking at Scalloway on Mainland, Shetland. Using Lerwick as a base for five days, they got to Loch of Spigie and Loch Tingwall; over on Bressay they went to Loch Brough, Loch Grimsetter and the Isle of Noss. Throughout their stay in Shetland they contrived each day to leave Harry fishing happily at a promising lake while the two ladies went off birdwatching. On 1 July they left Lerwick by sea to carry on north past Whalsey Island to Fetlar. After five days there they moved north again to spend three days on Unst, staying at Buness on Balta Sound. While there they had two days at Hermaness and also managed to get to Muckle Flugga, Britain's most northerly lighthouse. From Unst back to Fetlar for another six days before returning to Lerwick where they took the opportunity of getting to the most southerly tip of Shetland, Sumburgh Head.

Everywhere the birds of Shetland amazed them by their variety and numbers. Often under the guidance of paid watchers they were shown breeding colonies, some huge, of gannets, fulmars, puffins, guillemots, razorbills, terns, shags, kittiwakes and other gulls. They saw eiders, black guillemots, golden plovers, whimbrels, mergansers and merlins. They were impressed by the abundance of skylarks that filled the air with song and were delighted to find the nests of dunlin and twite. But of all Shetland's birds what fascinated them most were divers, skuas and phalaropes. Divers, both black-throated and red-throated, they watched on many lakes and listened to their strange wailing songs. On the breeding grounds of great skuas and what they called Richardson's (now arctic) skuas, they were dived at by birds very bold in defence of their young. Most precious of all, because the rarest, were the several little colonies of red-necked phalaropes. They saw them best on Fetlar:

> We went to a small loch with reeds and grass in the middle. Here we saw three pairs of phalaropes which came quite close to us, feeding and catching flies and preening, sometimes flying round and settling on the water or on the shingle. The males were much shyer than the females.

Amid this preoccupation with the birds, the flora was distinctly neglected. There are a few remarks on the extra colourfulness of the common wildflowers; and on the abundance of moss campion, alpine meadow-rue, mountain everlasting, moonwort and lesser clubmoss.

66

They said a reluctant farewell to Shetland on 19 July, returning to Wales by train from Aberdeen. Caerynwch, they found, was suffering from drought: 'All drinking water springs have been dry for weeks and the house supply is very dirty. River abnormally low. Garden is getting dried up.' 23 July was a day for rejoicing when they heard that Richard, aged 13, had passed into the Royal Naval College at Dartmouth. They had been home only a few days when they were off again, on a family holiday to Brittany, at first staying at an inn in a forest owned by their friends the de Clervilles, a forest which had wild boars and swallowtail butterflies. They learned a lot about history by visiting most of the Loire chateaux; and about prehistory at the stone monuments at Carnac.

Back at Caerynwch on 26 September 1934, Mary noted the abundance of red squirrels: 'They seem to be everywhere, taking all our filberts.' In November she added '*nobleanum*' and '*thomasonii*' to the rhododendron collection. And there was excitement when, with her friends Backhouse and Bible, they found a ferruginous duck on Tonfannau pool, the first record of this rare bird in Merioneth. On 21 November, there was an interesting botanical experiment. Mary, James Backhouse, Dr Owen Morris and the Caerynwch gardener, Drinkwater, planted six Killarney ferns by the Clywedog where it flows past the house. They were carefully placed 'in the rocks on each side of the waterfall above the dam, and by the Cefn Coch bridge. We know of only one plant in Merioneth and want to re-introduce it.' No doubt these ferns were supplied by James Backhouse whose family had long been in the nursery trade in Yorkshire. We next hear of these Killarney ferns on 12 January 1935, when Mary reports: 'All are doing well.' But we hear no more and the assumption must be that the little ferns soon died. In the absence of diaries for 1935-8, much of what we know of those years has to be gleaned from Mary's botanical records. In July 1935, the year of her fiftieth birthday, she collected a few plants in Guernsey including common dodder (growing on gorse), purple broomrape, greater broomrape and spotted medick. On Sark she found subterranean clover. In June 1936, we find her botanising with great enthusiasm when she got to Teesdale and saw spring gentian, shrubby cinquefoil, twisted whitlowgrass, alpine bistort, bird's-eye primrose, mountain avens, Scottish asphodel, pink stonecrop, alpine bartsia, bearberry, lily of the valley and mountain melick. Two months later there was a family holiday in the west of Ireland. The main object was to fish for sea-trout but Mary managed to record a few choice plants like great sundew, St Patrick's cabbage, lax sea-lavender, frog orchid and various pondweeds.

In July 1937, she got to the Ben Lawers district of Scotland for the first time and in that botanical Mecca saw some of Britain's rarest plants: alpine gentian, alpine fleabane, netted willow, alpine pearlwort, purple mountain milk-vetch, drooping saxifrage, two-flowered rush and several good carexes like *atrofusca, saxatilis, atrata* and *capillaris*. Down on the shores of Loch Tay she found strikingly tall specimens of the bird's-nest orchid.

The diary for the whole of 1937 is missing but Kate remembers an amusing incident from the autumn when she, her mother and an aunt holidayed in Italy and then went on to Yugoslavia:

> We took a small boat from Venice down the Jugoslav coast, stopping at small ports including Split with its remains of Diocletian's palace. We left the boat at Dubrovnik which in those days was a quiet, intensely beautiful and unspoilt little walled city, only occasionally visited by cruise ships. There was only one hotel and we were offered, as a great honour, the rooms recently occupied by King Edward VIII and Mrs Simpson. My mother and aunt strongly disapproved of the liaison and haughtily declined these rooms and asked to be accommodated at the other end of the hotel! Mother botanised vigorously and when I left with my aunt to go to Paris, she journeyed on alone to Mostar and Sarajevo.

Mary's diary for 1938 brings her back into focus after a gap of three diary-less years. On Thursday, 24 March, we are reminded of her passion for horse-racing as she, Major Harry, their two daughters and M. de Clerville from Brittany take the 2.00 p.m. train from Dolgellau to Liverpool for their annual visit to the Grand National. Back home on 27 March she reported: 'Daffodils fully out, hazel in leaf, garden a mass of hyacinths, polyanthus, forget-me-nots, wall-flowers, azaleas and Himalayan rhododendrons.' On the 30th, as she drove to Worcestershire for a wedding, the cherry blossom was coming out, the hedges were green and many trees were in leaf: 'The earliest spring I have ever seen.' Then on to Devon where Richard was leaving Dartmouth College and where primroses were everywhere and bluebells were opening weeks before their time. At home again on 8 April she ritualistically observed the purple saxifrage in good flower on Cader Idris. Then almost inevitably in mid-April there were a couple of frosty nights which would not have worried the purple saxifrage but which blackened all Caerynwch's precocious rhododendrons, magnolias and fruit blossom.

On 12 May Mary was in London to present Catherine (Kate) at court but characteristically all the mention this great family occasion gets in her diary is: 'London. England looks so dried up. Not a blade of grass . . . Warm day. Presented C.M.R.' On the way home a visit to a fish-farm receives fuller coverage:

> To Oakroyd. Heard turtle dove. Went to L. Haig's fish-farm. Bought crayfish, Italian newts, edible frogs, salamanders, turtles and mussels. Rain at night. Watched searchlights spotting aeroplanes in defence of London.

This is the first mention of the war shadow that in 1938 began to darken people's lives. From now on there was to be increasing talk of air-raid precautions, shelters and gas masks.

Mary had long been in the habit of making a spring visit to the Happy Valley rock garden at Llandudno and on 19 May she was as enthusiastic about it as ever, judging it 'a very fine sight', mentioning especially the rock-roses and the bellflower *Edraianthus pusillus*. Next day she was off to Shropshire to have lunch with her friend, N. Stevens, who lived in some splendour near Lydbury North at Walcot Hall, described by topographer Bagshaw in 1851 as

> a spacious and elegant mansion, the occasional seat of the Earl of Powis. It contains a fine collection of paintings and Indian curiosities collected by the first Lord Clive. The pleasure grounds are very beautifully laid out and the park is richly wooded.

The lake there, when Mary visited, was thickly populated with waterfowl from all over the world, many of them free-flying. Visitors were often greeted by a delegation of stately cranes, while squadrons of tree ducks and other exotics passed frequently overhead.

A mishap Mary never forgot was when a party including herself, Margo Masters and two old Forestry Commission friends, Frank Best and Arthur Cadman, attempted to cross to Bardsey Island in the evening of 10 June 1938. It was very rough weather but the boatman decided to chance it. They had just got aboard the motor-boat when a wave caught them sideways and the boat capsized, leaving them in water up to their waists. All their kit was soaked and there was irreparable damage to binoculars and cameras. They dried out in the Ship Hotel, Aberdaron, had an early supper and spent the evening looking for choughs on Braich y Pwll headland. Next day, in calmer seas, they managed to cross to the island. They spent a day looking at the seabirds on the cliffs and ringing some of them; and they found the nests of chough and peregrine. Mary collected a few plants, the most interesting being lesser meadow-rue which, in some miraculous way has found its way to one of Bardsey's very few outcrops of limestone. Then they stayed overnight to get acquainted with the nocturnal shearwaters:

> At 11.30 we started out to hear and see the shearwaters. There was a very wetting fine rain and mist on the mountain. We climbed to the far end from beyond the old abbey and soon heard the birds. It is an extraordinary cry and is pitched in so many different keys. The mist was so thick it was difficult to see the birds but the whirl of wings was all round us and every now and then they landed close to us with a plop. Twenty shearwaters were ringed altogether. We were soon soaked and got in at 1.15 and they gave us hot tea and excellent sandwiches.

From Bardsey they went north to Anglesey, going via Nefyn to see the splendid commune of cliff-nesting birds at Craig y Llam—kittiwakes, razorbills and a huge number of guillemots. They found a hotel at Rhosneigr where, strolling along the shore after their evening meal, they came upon a nesting colony of a dozen or so little terns, something quite unimaginable these days when beaches everywhere are thoroughly disturbed by people. Next day they went to see the birds of Bodorgan headland near Newborough where the lesser black-backed gulls were nesting amongst the bracken as usual, while the herring gulls, hugely increased since Mary's last visit in 1930, kept to higher, rockier ground. At Llanddwyn Island next day they were allowed to see a protected colony of terns; a new Mrs. Jones was in charge.

> The island has now been taken over by the RSPB with Mrs Jones as watcher. She met us at the causeway and took us to see the terns. They have increased enormously since I was last here.

Near Malltraeth Mary collected a specimen of chestnut sedge (*Blysmus rufus*) which is always a good find so far south. They spent their last morning on Holyhead Mountain observing the seabirds of South Stack but their best find was that exquisite little treasure, the annual rock-rose, each tiny yellow petal neatly marked with a dark-red spot at the base.

*   *   *

The last week of September 1938 was a time of universal unease. Even Mary Richards, normally so determined to limit the scope of her diaries to natural history, the weather, the great outdoors, her garden or her many pets, could not exclude current political anxieties from her daily log:

Sept. 17	Country anxious over Czechoslovakia question.
Sept. 21	Chamberlain flew to Berchtesgaden. War scare bad.
Sept. 24	Chamberlain went to Godesberg. Impossible terms. War seems inevitable.
Sept. 26	Roosevelt appeals for peace.
Sept. 27	Situation seems hopeless. Chamberlain goes to Munich with Daladier and Mussolini to meet Hitler.

From Munich Chamberlain came home waving his famous piece of paper and Mary's diary continues:

Sept. 30	Cold day. Stormy. Immense relief that peace agreement has been reached at 2 o'clock this morning.
Sunday, Oct. 2.	Thanksgiving for peace in all churches. Gentiana sino-ornatas are covered with flowers.

So she quickly recovered her composure, helped perhaps by a day in the field with Sophie Blathwayt who was just then staying at Caerynwch. They went to look for plants on Craig Maesglasau, a spectacular corrie that hangs above the A470 near Dinas Mawddwy. Maybe she nurtured a hope of finding Killarney fern behind the waterfall there; but what she did find were lots of parsley fern, beech fern and oak fern along with much golden saxifrage, mossy saxifrage and some 'very large rosettes' of starry saxifrage. Then they went to the top to enjoy all the heart-lifting panoramas of that deeply folded upper Dyfi landscape. They walked through the heather and put up ten grouse to round off 'a really lovely day'.

After the Munich crisis, life settled down to being as normal as possible in a world resigned to the probability of war sooner or later.

That Mary went all the way to Corwen to attend a lecture on air-raid precautions was symptomatic of the prevailing atmosphere in the winter of 1938-9. But all was not gloom. Her diaries go on telling us about the natural world: how a turtle was washed up on the beach at Harlech on 29 November; how the weather turned so cold that they skated on Gwernan Lake and on a pool at Nannau just before Christmas; and how in January she scrambled for hours through snow-drifts on the southern slopes of Snowdon and Lliwedd to see the Ynysfor hounds chasing the agile mountain foxes.

She got to many good places in 1939. Staying at Sophie Blathwayt's house, Dyrham Park (now National Trust), near Bath, she found a patch of yellow Star-of-Bethlehem in a local wood. In mid-May near Bracknell, Berkshire, she and Sophie admired fields full of fritillaries: 'They are in two damp meadows and are partly preserved. People pay 3d and may gather 18. Part of the field is uncut to allow them to seed.' From there they went to see the Royal Horticultural Society gardens at Wisley followed by three days at the RHS show in London. Then on to the coast of Kent at Dungeness where the RSPB warden showed them a vast colony of common terns nesting on the shingle with nearby small groups of little terns and common gulls. They had hoped to see a Kentish plover but that rare bird had entirely disappeared 'owing to the building of bungalows', according to the warden. Another ambition was to see a stone curlew and this they achieved when the warden showed them a nest which was 'a depression in the shingle close to a patch of sorrel and had two eggs. The stone curlew slips away from the nest without fuss very quickly, is difficult to see and does not fly round eggs or young like the curlew.' Back home on 27 May, Mary had a day at Portmeirion: 'Mr Haig's garden is beautiful beyond words. The *Rhododendron fragrantissimum* is perfect and every kind of rare and lovely azalea and rhododendron.' Next day she was at Tywyn admiring her friend Mrs Kettle's garden at Rhowniar: 'Very beautiful but she has lost a good deal last winter. Her *Lithospermum* was wonderful; also primulas and azaleas.' On 31 May she led her girl-guide troop up Cader Idris from the south side. They saw a peregrine chasing two ravens and found that a new hut had been erected on the summit. On 4 June, a very hot day, Mary, Frank Best and others hired a motor-boat at Abersoch and crossed to St Tudwal's East Island to see the birds, especially the puffins which were 'as usual flying back and forth like swarms of bees. I think they are on the increase. It struck us how tame all the birds were.'

A fortnight later, in bad weather, Mary was in Cwm Idwal looking for the Snowdon lily (*Lloydia serotina*):

It poured with rain and the water was coming down in lovely falls from the top, flooding the path which is bad and washed away. Flowers to the left of the Kitchen as lovely as usual and in as great a variety—moss campion, Welsh poppy and globeflower. Hunted every rock for Lloydia . . . then we climbed to the top of the Devil's Kitchen and it cleared and the sun came out. After scanning every rock and crevice with glasses and telescope, we finally spotted one Lloydia in flower, its tiny white bell blowing in the wind. It had been a hard hunt and we were very pleased to find it. In the bog close by, I found Juncus triglumis; a lovely evening. Two ring ouzels seen going down.

They spent the rest of the evening at Frank Best's house in Betws-y-coed where he showed them his considerable collection of butterflies—all very exciting to Mary. She was, after all, a Victorian.

At the end of June, 1939, Mary went off for a long weekend near St David's in Pembrokeshire: two days for birdwatching, when she particularly noted the abundance of 'yellow ammers'; and two days for botanising with a Botanical Exchange Club party led by John Chapple. Among plants she collected were saltmarsh sedge (*Carex extensa*) and small-flowered catchfly (*Silene gallica*) and she made an elegant sheet of specimens of one of the smallest plants she ever pressed—all-seed (*Radiola linoides*) which was only half an inch tall. From Pembrokeshire she drove to the Royal Agricultural Show at Windsor, then to Henley Regatta. She spent Sunday, 9 July, boating on the Thames from Pangbourne to Mapledurham. Next day she got back to Caerynwch where she found: 'it has rained all the time'. A few weeks later, botanising, birdwatching and all other frolics came to a sudden halt with the outbreak of the Second World War on Sunday, 3 September. Mary's diary entry is brief: 'War declared between England and Germany. House cleared to receive 30 evacuated children.' Only 25 came and were moved in five days to Corris.

Almost throughout the war Mary's diary is extremely meagre. Though she plunged into a maelstrom of voluntary work for the Red Cross and the WVS, we hear practically nothing about it. But something she could not ignore was the arctic weather of early 1940.

January an extraordinary cold month—snow, ice, skating, 30 deg. of frost on 20th. Saturday 27th it poured with rain. Saturday night it began to freeze and wind went to N.E. Sunday 28th: Woke to amazing world all white. Freezing wind had coated everything with ice. Conditions got worse all day, till by 3 o'clock the trees had up to an inch of ice on everything and the branches were weighed down by the weight of ice. The wind smashed into the trees and great branches cracked off. These conditions went on all week. Birds in crowds on the bird table. A great quantity of redwings eating holly berries. Monday 29th: Still freezing and roads blocked. Wednesday 30th: Roads still impassible. The estuary frozen over and ice floes a wonderful sight. The Clywedog also frozen over. The coldest winter for many years. All the same the daffodils were out by March 25th.

War or no war, on 5 April she and Harry went to Liverpool for their annual visit to see the Grand National. It was to be Harry's last National, for the race was not run again until 1946, by which time Harry had been dead four years. Mary's diary for 28 November, 1942 says simply: 'Henry Meredyth Richards passed to his rest.' At the start of the war, too lame to be a serving soldier, Major Harry had struggled into his old uniform and joined the Home Guard. He died after a very brief illness and was buried at Brithdir. But this was not the first family grief of the war. In 1940 Kate Richards had been married in Brithdir church to Sub-Lt John Seyton Kyffin, of Devon, but he was posted to HMS *Formidable* in the Mediterranean in November, 1940. She never saw him again as he was killed in action in December 1941.

The war years went on. Mary remained extremely involved in her duties, seeing her children only at rare intervals when they got home on leave: Jonnet from nursing at the Westminster Hospital, London; Kate from her job in the Foreign Office at Istanbul; Richard away at sea. But the Dolgellau countryside, far from the scene of hostilities, remained peaceful enough. One day, early in the war, as spring came in with great beauty, Mary was moved to write in her log:

Whitsunday May 14th—a glorious hot day, the garden a mass of rhododendrons and azaleas. Gentians wonderful this year. Most of the tropical fish have lived through the winter. The canaries are nesting. Golden, Amherst and Reeves pheasants and Caroline ducks all laid and their eggs are under hens. One cannot believe that all Europe is at war.

That vignette from May 1940 is the last we ever see of the old life at Caerynwch. Things changed quickly as wartime restrictions increased. It became unpatriotic to devote precious food and heating to keeping alive exotic animals and plants. All over Britain tropical aquaria were abandoned and many an orchid house was turned over to the production of tomatoes and lettuces. Caerynwch's tropical fish died of winter cold. The wildfowl and ornamental pheasants survived for several years but were eventually sold in 1943. It was the end of Mary's long pet-keeping phase. From now on she turned her attention more and more to wild nature.

A few rare glimpses of wildlife survive from those bleak years of war. On 14 June, 1943, Mary wrote: 'A red-backed shrike noted as usual by Penmaenpool bridge.' How astonished she would have been if she could have known that this was to be the final record of a red-backed shrike at this their last breeding place in Merioneth. Not many years later they had gone from most of Britain. 18 June 1944 brings another breath of fresh air. After years of very scrappy records Mary's diary suddenly blossoms into a long description of a walk from Caerynwch to the village of Llanfachreth. On the way she chanced upon the small white orchid (like the red-backed shrike, a declining species). It was growing in a meadow along with fragrant orchids and 'very beautiful specimens of *Vicia orobus*—a lovely, reddish purple-pink'. There were also 'quantities of globe-flowers which are not as common as formerly' (as the herb-rich meadows steadily vanished under a vigorous, Government-led ploughing and reseeding programme). She reported sadly on 30 December that her old friend, James Backhouse, had died—'a fine botanist and ornithologist'.

January 1944 had brought a complete change of existence at Caerynwch. On the outbreak of war, the house had been offered to the Government as a military hospital, as in the previous war, but it had been declined. But now bombs were raining down on many cities; and on 11 January a crowd of evacuee children and staff, sent by Birmingham Education Committee, occupied most of the house, the furniture being stored in the attics. With her gift for organisation Mary would have run things at Caerynwch very efficiently but was debarred from doing so as she had no paper qualifications. But, as her daughter Kate has observed: 'She did not think much of the capabilities of those in charge and, although she never interfered, they invariably appealed to her for help in a crisis.' These children remained at Caerynwch until well after the end of the war.

The spring of 1945 brought disaster to the garden. Nearly the whole of April was unseasonably mild and everything was flowering magnificently on 24 April when Mary's children were all home together for the first time since their father's funeral two and a half years earlier. But the idyllic weather did not last. On the night of 27 April the thermometer plummeted and the world woke next day to snow and a severe frost that went on for days. On 30 April we read:

> Garden a complete wreck. All rhodos frosted; young shoots all killed. Maples—all young shoots and leaves killed. All primulas and spiraeas frosted. Currants, apples, cherry plums, most of the pears and plums killed. Lilium regale brown and dead. Strawberries which were in full flower frosted. Young shoots and leaves on oak, beech and sycamore killed. Never here has anything like it been seen.

Her gloom soon evaporated. The next entry in her diary reads: 'Wonderful news from Europe—peace at any moment—we can hardly believe it.' On the following Sunday, 12 May, she was at a peace parade in Cardiff representing Merioneth's WVS. A week later Richard came home on leave and announced his engagement to Pamela Watson of the WRNS, from Bridge of Weir, Scotland The marriage took place at Kilmacolm Church on 3 July 1945; and for Mary this was an opportunity not to be missed: after the wedding she set off on her second pilgrimage to the Ben Lawers area, staying at Killin at the south-west end of Loch Tay, with her daughter, Jonnet.

Because of petrol rationing, they had no car at Killin but explored as far as they could with the help of local buses. Most of their nine days they spent on the shores of Loch Tay or the nearby slopes. Without a car, Ben Lawers was too remote but they came near to it when they walked up the road that climbs from Loch Tay towards Glen Lyon by way of the narrow lakelet, Lochan na Lairige. Among the plants they found in the cliffs above the lake, Mary notes arctic saxifrage, mountain everlasting, least willow, netted willow, grass of Parnassus, alpine cinquefoil, mountain avens, alpine mouse-ear, alpine pearlwort, mossy cyphal, alpine bistort, Scottish asphodel, spiked woodrush and hair sedge.

CHAPTER EIGHT

As far as Mary's diary is concerned, 1946 began on 18 May when the year's first entry reports that her daughter Kate (so cruelly widowed by the war) married Captain G.B. Heywood of Haresfield Court, Stonehouse, Gloucestershire. Three days later Mary was off with friends to Yorkshire to enjoy the botanical delights of Upper Teesdale. They wandered far over Widdybank Fell and Cronkly Fell, finding flowers for which the area is so famous: spring gentian, alpine bartsia and shrubby cinquefoil. At one place they 'walked through a field which was a sheet of *Primula farinosa*'. Back in Wales on 1 July, Mary got to Mochras (Shell Island) for the first time since the war began. For years the dunes had been used for military training and that day, though the war was long over, the troops were still firing and she had to walk along the shore from Tal-y-bont. She found the dune-hollows nearest the sea as colourful as ever with pansies, houndstongue, viper's bugloss, Solomon's seal, spurges, bog pimpernel, marsh orchids, twayblades and burnet roses. But all along the landward side former bird-rich wetlands had been drained to make way for a military airfield.

Five days later, also for the first time since 1939, she walked, with Jonnet and others, over the Rhinog hills. They climbed the Roman Steps, seeing whinchats, wrens and ring ouzels. The day was beautiful, the panoramas superb and in one place there was a wide, green carpet of beech fern. From the top of the Roman Steps they curved southwards round Rhinog Fawr and came down into the Nantcol valley through the Pass of Ardudwy, relieved on the way to see that at least five 'wild' goats had survived all the years of disturbance caused by the firing of heavy guns on the nearby Trawsfynydd military range.

On 31 July 1946 Mary heard of the birth of her first grandchild, Marguerite Ann Richards, at Woking, Surrey, and by next day she was at nearby Byfleet. Having paid loving tribute to her grand-daughter, she moved to Bishops Waltham, Hampshire, where she was much impressed by the wealth of the downland flora, notably frog orchid, musk orchid, yellow-wort and various campanulas. She came home to find Wales wet. And that is how her weather record went on through August and September, punctuated by anguished remarks like: 'Corn and hay spoiling'; 'Violent rain and gale'; 'A very wet day and floods'; 'A week's rain'; 'Another hopeless wet day'; 'Prayers for fine weather in church on Sunday'; 'Another wet day and gales'; 'Cold and showery but got hay carried in the afternoon when the sun came out'; 'They say there has not been a summer like this for a hundred years'. Despite the weather she and Jonnet got to the top of Cader Idris from the south side on 11 September: 'A tearing gale and very cold. Mist came down and it was lovely to see it sweep over the crags and give sudden vistas through vents in the mist.'

Mary enjoyed writing about the weather and we are given full coverage of the great snows of 1947 which began on 21 January and went on for many days without stopping. On 30 January she could not get to Lichfield to see her mother by road but managed to get there by train. There she was snowed in for a week. It was the same story on 12 February. The only way of getting from Caerynwch to Gloucestershire was also by rail. The occasion was the birth, on St Valentine's Day, of Kate's first child, Sarah. Meanwhile snow fell almost continually, drifting deeply over the Cotswold Hills.

The blizzards raged, on and off, for yet another week and when Mary got back to Caerynwch on 10 March she found the snowdrifts lying really deep.

> The sheep are dying of a disease called snow fever. It is tragic to see them trying to find food. Owing to the bad hay harvest last year there is hay for cattle only. I am afraid there is a great deal of harm done to dwarf rhododendrons and azaleas—the sheep eat every leaf they can reach.

The bad weather continued:

> March 10 and 11: a freezing blizzard raged and the fine snow drifted. On Wednesday night it turned to rain and on Thursday there was a tremendous thaw. The rivers came down in big floods. Late on Thursday night it again turned to hard frost and the roads were icy . . . Saturday, March 15: another terrific blizzard raged all day and turned to rain as the wind went to south-west on Sunday. Another thaw, very rapid, and a gale and tremendous rain. I heard

a chaffinch sing and this evening curlews flew over. It seems extraordinary that they should come when the moors are still covered with snow.

When she motored to Lichfield on 18 March there was one-way traffic from Bala to Gobowen because of banks of snow alongside the road. The drifts were deepest at Llangollen. When, on 5 April, she helped to decorate Brithdir church for Easter not a daffodil was yet out and they had to use snowdrops!

*   *

The rest of 1947 was very eventful and at, one point, momentous. On 21 May Mary was admiring rhododendrons at the Chelsea Flower Show, the first to be held for nine years. On 3 June she found alpine saw-wort on the top of Snowdon. Three days later she was at Marlborough, Wiltshire, for a weekend with the Botanical Exchange Club. The leader was Donald Grove who took them to Knowle Down, Spye Park, Bowood, Walkers Hill and other good spots. Of the many plants they found, Mary was most thrilled to see her first burnt orchids. She was also pleased to see bird's-nest orchid, white helleborine, sweet flag (*Acorus calamus*) and thin-spiked wood sedge (*Carex strigosa*). On 13 June she enjoyed the International Eisteddfod at Llangollen. On 18 June she found five species of orchid in the corner of a meadow on the Caerynwch estate: early marsh, fragrant, greater butterfly, heath spotted and small white. At the end of the month she was out with the BEC again, this time at Ashbourne, Staffordshire, to explore the botanical treasures of the Manifold valley where she especially enjoyed seeing Nottingham catchfly, spring cinquefoil, wood vetch ('a lovely sight with its pale-mauve flowers climbing over rocks and shrubs') and masses of Jacob's ladder so endearing with its blue flowers and yellow anthers.

The most crucial turning points in our lives are often quite unrecognised as such at the time. So it was with that BEC gathering in the Manifold valley. It was on that occasion that Mary first met Edgar Milne-Redhead of the Kew Herbarium. They became life-long friends and so was forged a link between Mary and Kew that was eventually to transform her life. Though she had a very long interest in plants behind her, it had never really developed much beyond dilletante levels, except sporadically. But now in 1947, in her sixty-second year, the

79

botanist in her truly began to assert itself, as she got ever more involved with the BEC which became the BSBI in October 1947. She was out with them again in August, as happy to meet new friends as to see new plants. This time they were at Cambridge to be shown the treasures of Wicken and Chippenham fens, among them milk parsley, marsh pea, fen orchid and Cambridge parsley.

1947 was a memorable butterfly year with an unparalleled abundance of clouded yellows in Britain. Wave after wave of them came up from south Europe and Mary noted many from 18 August until the end of October. After that the most memorable natural history event came when she spent Christmas with Kate at Haresfield, Gloucestershire. On 27 December, she and some of the family were taken round the wildfowl collection at Slimbridge by Peter Scott who also showed them the many white-fronted geese which had been wintering on the salt-marshes, the New Grounds, for over a hundred years.

Reading Mary Richards' log of what she was up to in 1948, no one could say her life lacked variety. On 4 January she was watching waders in Chichester harbour; and on the fifth she was in London, looking at Van Gogh pictures in the Tate Gallery. In February she was bemoaning the ruination of Caerynwch's early-flowering rhododendrons by frost. In March she reports 38 fallow deer in the park at Nannau, a valuable record because it could have been the last count made of these deer before they escaped from the park. Their descendants have lived in the nearby plantations of Coed y Brenin ever since. She also got to the Grand National at Aintree that month. In April she was again in London, this time for a botanical conference on 'The Study of Critical British Groups'. Next day she had a happy few hours in Kew Gardens. On 23 April she was in Bath for several days of festival music. And while there she managed to find yellow Star-of-Bethlehem in a local wood. On 15 May she was at a garden party at Buckingham Palace. A week later, near Caerynwch, she had a successful hunt for what is in Wales a rare herb—spignel (*Meum athamanticum*). Then to Chelsea Flower Show before going off by train from London to Switzerland with Jonnet to see the alpine plants and birds of the Kanderstag area.

Her big moment of 1948 came on 25 June when thirty-two members of the BSBI came to Dolgellau to be taken round the region under her leadership. The visit lasted ten days and among those present were three distinguished botanists from Kew—Edgar Milne-Redhead, Peter Taylor and V.S. Summerhayes.

Desmond Vesey-FitzGerald, a distinguished naturalist with a special knowledge of African wildlife.
(*Anon*)

North Rukwa Plain, Tanzania, in the late 1950s. It became a lake soon afterwards.
(*Photo by Mary Richards*)

Flooded trees: the transition from plain to lake. The North Rukwa Plain may become a lake for many years but sooner or later it dries out and is a plain again. Mary Richards knew it as a plain in 1954 but ten years later it was a lake sixty miles long.

North Rukwa
Lake, 1963,
seen from the
Mbisi Forest
on the western
escarpment.

By 1963 North
Rukwa Lake,
though only
recently formed,
already had a
thriving fishery.

Lake Rukwa:
marabou
storks and
crowned
cranes.

In woodland by Lake Rukwa Mary Richards marvelled at the skill with which a pair of white-crowned shrikes had attached their nest to an acacia twig.

Close-up of the white-crowned shrikes' nest.

Topi were the commonest antelopes of the Rukwa Plain. Their habitat was destroyed by the change from plain to lake.

Puku were another Rukwa speciality. They were described as abundant there in the early 1960s though scarce elsewhere in Tanzania.

Houses built for the locust-control service by the Tumba River on the North Rukwa Plain. Mary Richards often stayed there on safari.

Ndundu, the bungalow near Abercorn where Mary Richards lived from 1958 to 1968.
(*Anon*)

Mary in the garden at Ndundu.
(*Anon*)

The aloe garden at Ndundu. (*Photo by Mary Richards*)

Chameleons were often in the garden at Ndundu.

This African thrush nested close to the house at Ndundu.

A well-camouflaged fiery-necked nightjar on her nest amongst fallen leaves just outside Ndundu garden.

The green-headed sunbird was one of several kinds of sunbird to be seen daily in the garden at Ndundu.

Outsize caterpillars formed conspicuous clusters on the trunks of *Brachystegia* trees around Ndundu.

Gladiolus psittacinus. Its pale-yellow flowers were a frequent adornment of the *dambos* (marshes) around Abercorn.

Alpine enchanter's nightshade. Mary Richards found this rare plant on a scree in the upper Dyfi valley, north Wales, in 1955.

The trimaran *Triton* which Vesey and Mary often used for botanising on Lake Tanganyika.

Mary on the summit of Rungwe (9,700 feet) near Mbeya, Tanzania, with David Orr of the game department and a ranger, 24 October 1956. 'I had set my heart on climbing Rungwe,' Mary wrote in her diary.

(*Photo by D. Vesey FitzGerald*)

Giant lobelias in the Poroto Mountains, near Mbeya, Tanzania, 1956. Vesey-FitzGerald with butterfly-net.

(*Photo by Mary Richards*)

A section of the archaeological excavations at Kalambo Falls near Abercorn. Mary Richards supplied the project with botanical information.

Mary Richards pressing plants in camp.

Plant-collectors on safari: Mary Richards and Ali Omari, Poroto Mountains, Tanzania.

Another notable was Eleanor Vachell, a leading Glamorgan botanist. The main object of this BSBI meeting was to try and add to the number of species known to occur in Merioneth as no complete list for the county had ever been published. Possibly it was during this BSBI meeting that Mary began to think about writing a county flora, an idea that may well have been suggested to her by Milne-Redhead.

On three of the days she led them to cliffs on the north face of Cader Idris where they saw four kinds of clubmoss, green spleenwort, oak fern, mountain sorrel, roseroot, lesser meadow-rue, Welsh poppy, various saxifrages and Cader's speciality—hairy greenweed (*Genista pilosa*). Other places visited were the southern slopes of Rhobell Fawr (mountain everlasting, upright vetch [*Vicia orobus*], globe-flower, small white orchid); Aberdyfi (bee orchid, marsh orchids, narrow-leaved helleborine); Mochras (marsh helleborine, marsh orchids, burnet rose); Cregennan Lakes (water lobelia, lesser bladderwort, long-leaved sundew); Tir Stent (greater butterfly orchid, frog orchid, marsh orchids, fragrant orchid, small white orchid); the Mawddach estuary (tassel pondweed, white beak-sedge, other sedges); and Arthog Bog (sweet gale, bog rosemary, royal fern). The social highlight was the afternoon they had tea at Caerynwch with Cader Idris rising majestically in the west.

1949 brought a huge break with the past. Family life at Caerynwch was now only a memory and the house was too big for Mary on her own. For the first time in the diaries we have a mention of Tynllidiart, a cottage on the Caerynwch estate which enjoys even wider views of the mountains than Caerynwch itself. To this humble abode Mary had resolved to move; but not before she had pretty well rebuilt it by converting it from a single-storey to a double-storey house. That summer Caerynwch was let as a hotel and Mary moved into a caravan at Tynllidiart while the builders carried out the conversion. Meanwhile her son Richard and his family came to live at Coed, the house near Caerynwch which had been the home of Richard Richards who in 1785 had married the Caerynwch heiress, so uniting the two estates.

With her usual energy, Mary immediately set about making a garden at Tynllidiart by enclosing a large piece of meadow which in spring was a joy of greater butterfly orchids and globe-flowers. Cousin Stephen Stokes of Rugely came and designed a rock garden and a bog garden. Karl Keiderer, a German ex-prisoner of war who had opted to stay in Britain when peace came, worked on the cottage and in the garden. Meanwhile Mary did not allow this upheaval in her life to interfere at all with her usual round of activities. In February, 1949, she had a week's walking holiday in one of her favourite haunts, Hampshire's New Forest. On 19 March she was in Gloucestershire at the christening of her new grandson, Mark Heywood. On 20 May she went to Taunton, Somerset, for a meeting of the BSBI. On 9 June she attended a concert in Gloucester Cathedral. A few days later she was botanising at Cheltenham and Temple Guiting. In mid-July she joined a BSBI weekend at King's Lynn, Norfolk. In October she was at the BSBI annual meeting in London. On 24 December, 1949, her mother, aged nearly eighty-eight, died in a nursing home at Church Stretton.

Mary moved into her delightful new home, Tynllidiart, on 14 March, 1950, and it was not long before it became an open house for friends old and new, especially some of the botanists she had got to know recently. But before she could begin to entertain people she had to learn how to cook because till then she had probably never so much as boiled an egg in all her life. She was off with the BSBI again in early April, this time in Essex, looking at primroses, oxlips, cowslips and their hybrids. From Essex she went to stay with a friend, Mrs Farquharson, who lived near Salisbury, Wiltshire, and who took Mary on a round of the choicest local wildflowers, among them yellow Star-of-Bethlehem, toothwort, asarabacca and green hellebore. Most exciting to Mary was wild tulip:

> We went through a farmyard down a bank to a stream. Here we saw quantities of *Tulipa sylvestris*. Unfortunately the hens from the farm had scratched all round the plants and many flowers were broken off.

Back home, Mary spent 13 May in the dunes at Harlech. The spring flowers were at their best ('burnet rose just coming out and the place blue with *Viola canina*—a lovely bright blue with very wide flowers and yellow spur and the leaves narrow'). She also found spring vetch (*Vicia lathyroides*)—commenting: 'I think this is a new record for Merioneth.' She got close to a party of migrant whimbrels bathing in a pool and she even had the luck to flush a short-eared owl. On her way back to the station she passed through a fine array of green-winged orchids.

Not content with being a member of the BSBI, Mary also

belonged to the Wild Flower Society; and in June, 1950, she joined them when they came to Llandudno for a few days:

> June 16. By car—petrol rationing having finished!—to Llandudno. Got to Penrhyn Old Hall Hotel at 4.30, a lovely old place and garden. Other members of the WFS arrived and Miss Frost, leader, took us up the Little Orme.

In the next two days they explored widely (maiden pink and spiked speedwell among the finds) and they finished with a trip up Snowdon where they were too late to see the Snowdon lily except in seed. On 8 July Mary went to Arthog to see the bog rosemary but none of it was in flower. What she did find was greater spearwort, which she had not seen in Merioneth before. When pteridologist Peter Taylor came from Kew to stay at Tynllidiart he managed to find twenty-seven different ferns in Snowdonia despite having to battle against continual gales and heavy showers. Their best finds were Killarney fern, royal fern, forked spleenwort and its hybrid with maidenhair spleenwort. In the whole week the rarest thing they saw had nothing to do with botany. It happened on 3 September:

> On the way home, crossing Llanelltyd Bridge, we saw an extraordinary phenomenon—the sun, very large and bright blue. At first we thought it was the moon. It was seen all over the British Isles and one theory was that it was caused by dust.

Although 1951 was to be a year that would completely change the course of Mary's life, there was no suggestion of it at first. On 28 April, she went to the Cricieth district to a meeting at Glasfryn, an estate with a beautiful lake, owned by Rupert and Cecily Williams-Ellis. It was a meeting to discuss the possibility of forming a North Wales Field Society modelled on the very successful West Wales Field Society on whose behalf Ronald Lockley had come up from Pembrokeshire. One of the earliest results of this meeting was the establishment of the bird-observatory on Bardsey Island. In May, Mary was in London to see the Festival of Britain opened by the King; she visited the herbarium at Kew and went to Chelsea Flower Show. Back home, on a day out at Portmeirion, she reported: 'It is sad to see it so neglected and fine rhododendrons and azaleas being overgrown.' On 2 June, she went to Bodnant and had lunch with its owner,

Lord Aberconway, who presented her with a particularly hardy form of embothrium which had been raised at Bodnant.

One of the first to be welcomed to Tynllidiart in 1951 was Dorothea Eastwood, described by a fellow member of the BSBI as 'young and very charming'. Dorothea was not only a good botanist but also a talented artist and writer whose book, *Valleys of Springs*, gives us some vivid glimpses of Mary Richards in the field. Dorothea was met off the train at Dolgellau by Mary and her yapping little corgi, Taffy. Then up to (let Dorothea take over)

> her small house which she has built out of an old stone cottage. It is full of old and beautiful things and every window looks out over the mountains. We had tea on the little terrace. The garden was full of the scent of azaleas. The air was very sharp and fresh . . . we went down across the meadow to fetch milk from the farm below. The grass was full of orchids, mauve and magenta. There were globe-flowers, too, filling the moist, peaty hollows with their yellow lamps, butterworts digesting the midges stuck on to their leaves, and sundews and cotton-grass and sweet vernal grass . . . We had supper out as well as tea. The mountains changed from gold to sapphire in a cloudless, lucent sky. The dreamy scent of the azaleas strengthened. A yellowhammer sang to his nesting mate.

They had a day on Snowdon, going up on the mountain railway which crawled so slowly that they could have picked parsley fern from the carriage window. They alighted half-way up to go and see the Snowdon lily. Then up to the summit where it was bitterly cold and 'the trippers stood shuddering in cotton frocks and high-heeled shoes' as they sought shelter behind the then disused café.

> There was no sheltering for Mrs Richards . . . she sped feverishly up and down the rocks in search of the Alpine Saussurea which she had searched for and failed to find last year . . . The bitter wind whined and squealed, whipping up the cloud and dashing it over the summit, giving by its force a hint of its winter rages.

Dorothea, detailed to look after the corgi, waited and watched from the summit cairn:

> Mrs Richards was still dashing hither and thither; I could see her grey tweeds and bare head fleeing among the rocks.

Then triumph:

> I heard her crying in one of her shrillest screams which must have startled the trippers . . . I hurried down to where she stood under a pinnacle, gazing in exultation at the Alpine Saussurea as yet only in leaf.

On 9 June 1951 they had a day on Cader Idris which Dorothea thoroughly enjoyed but which was to be an even more significant date for Mary. The occasion was an outing of the Montgomeryshire Field Society to Cwm Cau, the spectacular, lake-floored corrie which time and erosion have gouged out of the south side of the mountain. The day was organised by Mary's friend, Janet Macnair of Welshpool, and it was led by Evan Price Evans who had devoted much of his life to studying the ecology of Cader but whom Mary had not previously met. Dorothea Eastwood is again worth quoting:

> Llyn Cau lies at a great height under the crests of Cader and the path to it is rough . . . the clouds began to come down and soon it was pouring steadily and implacably as it well knows how among these mountains. Half the society had come in cotton dresses without mackintoshes and were very wet indeed in no time. Half of this half trailed down again to the bus, the rest wrung out their hair and clothing and plodded lugubriously on, their interest in natural history ebbing fast. Mrs Richards and I were fortunate in the possession of mackintoshes, thick shoes and the consoling presence of a real expert, a delightful, massive, white-haired old gentleman who knows all so far to be known of the geology and plant ecology of Cader. He discoursed as we climbed, on rocks and soils . . . and on Cader's first eruption from the sea when its peaks were 23,000 feet high and its rocks fiery.

When Mary Richards and Price Evans met on Cader that day, they immediately became friends, united in their enthusiasm for mountains and plants. Mary, now sixty-six, but still skipping across the screes like a goat; Price Evans, five years older, but still reaching the heights despite being out of condition, overweight and subject to attacks of palpitations. Soon Price Evans joined the procession of botanists who were regularly entertained at Tynllidiart, for although no longer actively studying Cader Idris, he was always glad of an excuse to come back to Dolgellau from his home near Llandudno. And Mary was ever grateful to him for widening her horizons by his ecological approach to mountain botany. It was Price Evans who first saw the need of a wildlife conservation society in Merioneth and it was he who put the idea up to Mary Richards. Her competence quickly impressed him: 'Mrs R. replied that she would undertake the work if I helped. She's more than fulfilled her promise and got on like a house on fire with little or no help on my part.'

On 10 June we get a rhapsodic line from Mary about the flower-rich meadows that surrounded her new home—various orchids, milkwort, globe-flower, water forget-me-not, butterwort, sundew and an assortment of vetches and grasses, nearly all of which would disappear in the next few years as the meadows were 'improved' by ploughing, fertilising and reseeding. But Mary had no such gloomy thoughts as she set off to stay with Kate at Haresfield in Gloucestershire. While there she and the family had a walk up Painswick Beacon where they soon found a few good things like musk orchid and purple milk-vetch. On another day she went to see one of Gloucestershire's great rarities—adder's-tongue spearwort, whose watery site had been fenced round to protect the plants from the cattle. As Mary discovered, the fence did more harm than good:

> We found the pool where the *Ranunculus ophioglossifolius* grows. The pool has been enclosed by a fence and barbed wire but *Glyceria fluitans* has grown into such a thick tangle of matted grass that nothing else will grow. After searching I found the *Ranunculus* in the wet meadow outside the enclosure—there was a fair quantity of it.

That evening, 15 June 1951, she motored from Cheltenham to Monmouth for a BSBI weekend which took them to well-known botanical places like Lady Park Wood, Reddings Inclosure, the Wyndcliff, Undy and Trelleck. They saw an impressive variety of plants, among them narrow-leaved bittercress, wood vetch, lily-of-the-valley, Tintern spurge, cranberry, water-fern (*Azolla filiculoides*) and narrow-leaved woodrush (*Luzula forsteri*) which is rare or quite absent in much of the rest of Wales. Good finds among the sedges were hair sedge, fingered sedge and thin-spiked wood sedge (*Carex strigosa*). Trees of which Mary had had little experience were wayfaring tree, wild service and large-leaved lime. Dorothea Eastwood wrote about that meeting:

I walked round with Mrs Richards, who was staying at the Ivy Bank Hotel. Her room was a shambles of various specimens, botanical books and bundles of pressing paper and her tooth glass was stuffed with carices. It is, of course, an understood thing that no botanists clean their teeth on expeditions owing to the absolute necessity of using the tooth glass for cherished specimens. We sat happily on the bed sorting the carices while we discussed tomorrow's plans.

On the evening of 20 June, Mary and a friend went to Arthog Bog to see the royal fern and the greater spearwort but they soon got more interested in birds:

Sat for a long time and watched a pair of grasshopper warblers. They did not mind us at all but flew about, especially the male bird, catching flies and dropping into the same place in the undergrowth where the nest undoubtedly was. They came quite close to us. Coward says they are shy but we found them quite otherwise. They did their delightful reeling call and a good deal of twittering as well.

Mary's weekend with her botanist friend, Mrs Farquharson, of Salisbury in April 1950 had been so rewarding it is not surprising to find her there again in 1951, this time in August. Mrs Farquharson clearly knew her plants and once again Mary had an exciting time. In three days they covered much ground, ending up in the New Forest, among their best finds being round-headed rampion, wood vetch, moth mullein, Saracen's woundwort, greater dodder, shepherd's rod, yellow bird's-nest, pale butterwort, pheasant's eye, heath lobelia and Hampshire purslane.

At the end of August, Dorothea Eastwood came to Tynllidiart again and was taken up the Rhinogydd. As Mary's diary puts it:

By car to Cwmbychan. Walked up Roman Steps and down towards the Pass of Ardudwy. D. Eastwood wished to see the wild goats and we were lucky to see five on Rhinog Fawr. Then the mist came down and it poured. We got very wet.

Dorothea's report on the day gives us a picture of

Mrs Richards springing ahead of us, eager and energetic, absorbed in the moment and asking no more than to be able to enjoy a day's walking on her beloved hills . . . she has a great gift for excitement which time seems unable to diminish.

It was not only botanists but also Mary's family who sometimes stayed at Tynllidiart. An amusing cameo from those days cannot be left out. It comes from Mary's grand-daughter, Sarah, who has a happy memory of a day on the beach at Barmouth:

> Granny changed into an extraordinary, hand-knitted bathing-dress with yellow and black horizontal stripes. She looked just like a bumble-bee. Where on earth did she pick it up? From some Red Cross jumble sale? We were fascinated.

Back in 1950 the fates had begun to meddle hugely in Mary Richards' life. An old friend, Freda Davies, had gone to live more or less permanently in south-central Africa with two spinster sisters, Marian and Hope Gamwell. These ladies had formerly lived at a house called Aber Artro near Llanbedr, a village near the coast south of Harlech. Restless and energetic and wanting a completely new life, they had sold Aber Artro in 1928 and had gone off to south-central Africa looking for somewhere to settle. Along hundreds of miles of rough roads they motored adventurously westwards from Nairobi in their search for a place that appealed to them and eventually they arrived at the little Northern Rhodesian (now Zambian) town of Abercorn (now Mbala). That the Gamwell sisters fell immediately in love with Abercorn need surprise no one: it has been described as 'the town with the most beautiful setting in Central Africa'. Freda Davies, on a visit to Wales, had got in touch with Mary and suggested that she would enjoy a holiday in Africa where life was an idyll: gardens alight with tropical flowers and brilliant sunbirds, the bush full of strange wildflowers, the weather continually warm and sunny. Mary knew and admired the Gamwells who had greatly distinguished themselves in both World Wars by their services to the First Aid Nursing Yeomanry. 'Why don't you come out there?' Freda had said. 'You have no real ties in Britain now. You'd love it. It's just the life for you.' Mary had not been convinced: 'It sounds heavenly but I've just built Tynllidiart, my travelling days are over and I'm settling down to a peaceful old age.' And she had quite forgotten this conversation when out of the blue she received a letter from Marian Gamwell just before

Christmas, 1950, saying: 'Freda tells me that you would like to come out to us. We shall be delighted to have you but you should come for six months. It is not worth it for a shorter time.' When Mary's daughter, Jonnet, at Tynllidiart for Christmas, had been shown this invitation, her unhesitating advice was: 'Accept at once and go next autumn.' So Mary had accepted and was soon in London booking a passage to Dar es Salaam.

CHAPTER NINE

She could have gone to Abercorn by air. But flying had never been her way of travel. She was, after all, a Victorian for whom the only way of going abroad was by ship. Besides, she wanted to see as much of Africa as possible. So on 2 November 1951 she sailed from King George V dock, London, on the Union Castle ship *Dunrottar Castle*. This was the sort of journey she most loved, sailing with a ship that lingered at port after port, enabling the passengers to go ashore, perhaps even sleep in hotels and go sightseeing for a day or two. The journey from London to Dar es Salaam took thirty-six days, calling at Gibraltar, Marseilles, Genoa (rough seas and heavy rain nearly all the time) and Suez. They found no warm weather till they were in the Red Sea and the air got ever hotter as they came to Port Sudan where they had two days ashore and saw strange birds and butterflies. Then past many islands and through the narrows to Aden and more sight-seeing and shopping. Next stop Mombasa in Kenya. Mary got up at 5.30 a.m.

> . . . just daylight. We were coming into Mombasa harbour. It is lovely, so green and tropical. The channel is narrow with Mombasa on the left and the mainland on the right. We got in about 9 o'clock. Very, very hot and a deluge of tropical rain.

After six pleasant days in Mombasa their next port of call was Tanga. Here the passengers had a lazy day on a bathing beach where 'delightful little crabs simply flew about over the sand'. They sailed at midnight and were in Zanzibar early in the morning. A day there, and then at last they were negotiating the narrow entrance to Dar es Salaam harbour. Mary got ashore at midday and the next stage of her odyssey had begun—600 miles by train and bus into the heart of Africa

At first things went badly wrong. She had a train to catch at 10.00 a.m. but as the hour approached there was panic because not all her luggage had been transferred from the boat, the missing item being what she called her Kew box. At a BSBI meeting during the previous summer Mary had again met Edgar

Milne-Redhead of Kew Herbarium and when she told him of the forthcoming Africa trip he had urged her to collect plants for Kew. Mary's first reaction had been emphatically negative. She wanted a holiday free from the bother of collecting, drying, pressing and posting off plants. But Edgar used the persuasive argument that the Abercorn district was botanically unknown and that to collect plants from there would make her an explorer of uncharted country. So Mary had given in and had agreed to collect a few plants, provided that Kew would pack her a collectors' kit (presses and drying papers) to take with her.

Leaving her missing Kew box behind at Dar es Salaam docks she caught the train at the last minute, having arranged for the box to be sent on later. The train steamed out on time, passing through plantations of coconut palms and then into the bush, climbing steadily. Mary was aware that this was one of the world's most historic railways in the sense that it followed ancient Arab caravan routes and the trail of Livingstone, Stanley and other nineteenth-century explorers. At first she had planned to go all the way to the rail-head at the north end of Lake Tanganyika and thence by boat down the 400-mile-long lake to Abercorn. But that route was impossible because the lake steamer was just then out of action. So after a journey of some 340 miles, she left the train at Itigi, a small place from where a road went south to Mbeya and along which a bus ran once a week. Mary and a fellow rail passenger got on the bus at sunset and off they went into the endless bush country that was to be a huge part of Mary's world for years ahead. She began to pick up impressions of inland Africa. There was not only the seemingly limitless *miombo*, which is woodland of deciduous trees mostly of the genus *Brachystegia*. There were also breaks in the bush giving views to distant mountains—the Southern Highlands of Tanganyika:

> A lovely evening and the usual beautiful sunset. Mrs Browning and I sat together on the front seat. As dusk came I saw some baboons and, just beyond, five giraffes feeding on the trees. Then one of our back tyres burst and we all got out and wandered into the bush. The flowers were lovely.

So she encountered her first African plants among which she recognised a thunbergia with white flowers. The bus drove on through the night to avoid the *tsetse* flies that infested the area by day. The road climbed and climbed up to the Lupa goldfield

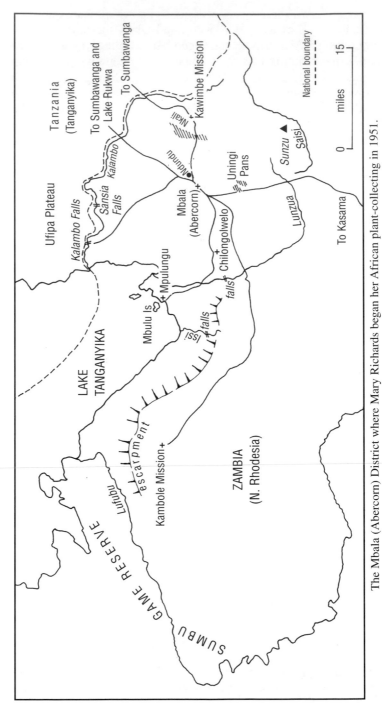

The Mbala (Abercorn) District where Mary Richards began her African plant-collecting in 1951.

country, reaching the mining town of Chunya at dawn. 'It was very, very cold and I was glad of my jersey and thick winter coat.' Here Mary picked up her first African word:

At the Goldmine Hotel no one was up but I got in and a boy finally appeared and gave me some tea—called 'chi' in Swahili. I had a very good breakfast. We left at 9 a.m. and began to go through very hilly country—the most wonderful motor run I have ever had. We started to climb up the mountains. The road, which is an earth road, was bumpy but good and wide and very well engineered. We went up and up. The grassland on each side was like a brilliant alpine meadow but the colours more vivid. As we got up, we could see for hundreds of miles. Below us was an endless plain, on the right a high range of hills. Down the sides were gullies filled with palms and tropical creepers and flowering trees. The top is about 9,000 feet. Then we began to go down to Mbeya, down a steep zigzag road.

On the floor of a detached fragment of the western arm of the Great Rift Valley, Mbeya is a town deep between high mountains, some of them extinct volcanoes. There, with still about 200 miles to go, Mary changed buses. They left at 4.00 p.m., climbing slowly up the rift escarpment. She was now really getting the feel of the *miombo*, the savanna woodland defined by Leslie Brown in his magnificent book *Africa—a Natural History* as:

one of the greatest expanses of uniform vegetation in all Africa, or in the world. Stretching sixteen hundred miles from east to west and from eight hundred to twelve hundred miles from north to south . . . It fills all of southern Tanzania, most of the southern Congo, Angola, Zambia, Rhodesia and Nyasaland.

They reached the border between Tanganyika and Northern Rhodesia at 8.00 p.m. and stopped for the night. Next morning came the last 100 miles to Abercorn.

About 12.30 we saw hills in the distance and black rain clouds. The road varied; sometimes it was wide and not too bad, at others a narrow track and fearfully bumpy and we had to make several diversions where the rains had made the road impassable. We got into the rain and it came down in sheets. It was almost impossible to see ahead and it was chilly and damp. This went on till we got into Abercorn at 1.30 and the bus dropped me at the hotel. There was no one to meet me as we were in early. So I had lunch and soon after 2 o'clock Freda Davies and Hope Gamwell arrived. They had shopping to do, so we walked about Abercorn which is a delightful town with many Government buildings and European houses and two big stores. Freda and I walked down to Lake Chila which has no crocodiles.

So, on 11 December 1951, forty days after leaving London, Mary reached Abercorn. By air she could have got there in less than two days but in going by road she had managed to see enough of Africa to make her feel it was a place she might well fall in love with.

From Abercorn at about 5,000 feet the main road north goes gently downhill, dropping 3,000 feet in twenty-one miles to Mpulungu, the little port at the south end of Lake Tanganyika. A dozen miles down this road was the Gamwells' estate, Chilongolwelo, reached by turning left up a narrow, winding track through the bush until it ended with sudden surprise in a colourful and unmistakably English garden. As an article in the Rhodesian magazine *Horizon* put it:

> Across the garden, where one might expect the Thames at Maidenhead, is a breathtaking African vista—the blue waters of Lake Tanganyika framed by high green hills. Overlooking the garden is the homestead, a collection of thatched buildings snuggled together and providing not only home for the Gamwell sisters but detached rooms for their guests as well.

So Mary was established in a little house on her own but with a sort of cloister leading to the main sitting room and dining room. She was amused to find small lizards (geckos) scuttling up the walls after insects at night. By day they hid behind the pictures on the walls. She soon found that out of doors the nights were loud with the ceaseless trilling of cicadas, the shrill piping of tiny frogs, the harsh voices of large toads and the songs of several different kinds of nightjar.

On her first morning at Chilongolwelo, Mary was up at dawn, eager to get acquainted with this Arcadia sheltered under steep escarpment slopes and watered by the perennial streams essential for growing bananas, lychees, citrus fruits, pineapples, aubergines, avocados, guavas, paw-paws along with peas, beans, lettuces and cabbages—everything guarded all day long from very persistent monkeys. The main crop was a large field of coffee; the most specialised was a local wildflower locally called *nindi*, a labiate (*Aeolanthus*) from which an essential oil was extracted in a still built for the purpose. That first afternoon Mary spent helping Marian Gamwell to plant a new field of *nindi*. But much of the gardening and farm work was carried out by a sizeable team of Africans who, along with their families and others, lived in a compound on the estate.

Seeing unknown plants everywhere she went, Mary soon itched to start collecting; but her box of equipment from Kew was still lost at Dar es Salaam. Happily Hope Gamwell was able to help. She had at one time sent a few plants to Kew and had even had one named after her—*Gamwellia flava*, a pretty little yellow pea-flower that grows on the Chilongolwelo escarpment. So with papers, presses and labels provided by Hope, Mary took her first steps into African botany:

> Thurs. Dec. 13th. Marian took the tractor to plough and I went with her to a stream where I started collecting. I found a quantity of curious plants and did a good morning's collecting. In the afternoon I went out with Hope and collected some more.

It had been a good first day to which was added the delight of hearing by telegram that she had a new grandson, Henry Lloyd Richards, born in Hong Kong where her son, Richard, was then stationed. More botany next day: 'Went out plant-hunting with Hope who wished to see the old kitchen garden and pick mulberries. On the way home it came down in torrents and we got very wet.' On the Saturday she really got down to things.

> Hope and I started soon after 10.00. I was given a toto—(small boy), to carry my vasculum and press. We had a steep climb to the top of the ridge. It began to pour with rain and we got soaked but went on. At the top we had marvellous views over the lake and the port of Mpulungu. It cleared and the sun came out and we were soon warm and dry. The plants were most interesting—many flowering trees and shrubs and some lovely orchids. Collected till about 3.00 and then came down to tea. It took me some time to do my notes and press the plants and I didn't get quite finished before I had to bath and change as we went out to dinner with some people about six miles away. It was wonderful motoring at night— nightjars kept flying up in front of us.

This abundance of nightjars seen in car headlights was something she would soon get used to. On the Sunday morning she finished her plants and worked at her notes till lunch-time. Already, after five days, African botany had begun to dominate her life.

A long-settled region, the district immediately around Abercorn had long since been more or less cleared of large and dangerous wild animals such as lions, except for individuals that turned up occasionally. But there were still leopards, hyenas, hunting dogs and buffaloes in the wild, rocky escarpments above Lake Tanganyika and Mary was warned never to go out on foot at night. The Gamwells also told her about other perils of the bush such as puff adders, mambas and spitting cobras; and smaller creatures like scorpions, leeches and the very formidable driver ants which during the rains are ever on the move through the bush, hastening in military-style columns, killing and eating every small creature (chiefly invertebrates) in their path. All living things flee (if they can) before these advancing hordes which kill even birds and small mammals. People are easily routed by these hugely abundant ants called *siafu* in Swahili. Step into one of their columns and your whole body is quickly invaded. Then your only hope of getting rid of these fiercely biting ants is to strip off all your clothes and pick off your tormentors one by one. Even an elephant will stampede if *siafu* invade its trunk.

Mary's diary mentions another unpleasant insect: 'I have had two of those horrid putzies—i.e. a burrowing fly which deposits eggs in you—I had one on each arm and you have, when it is ripe, to squeeze the grub out—it's very uncomfortable.' Yet another scourge of the bush that she was warned against was the buffalo bean, also known as itchy bean and hell-fire bean. It is a liana that hangs from the branches of trees and whose large pendulous seed-pods are clothed with viciously irritant hairs. Even old Africa hands can fall foul of the dreaded buffalo bean (*Mucuna poggei*) as when the eminent botanist, John Hutchinson, came up from South Africa with General Smuts, another distinguished botanist, in 1930:

> Though the country from Broken Hill to Abercorn was very little known botanically, the part we were now to explore was almost untouched. This was the region between Abercorn and the south end of Lake Tanganyika, an inland sea I was eager to behold, for never in my wildest imagination had I ever expected to visit it . . . Our camp was pitched amongst rather high Brachystegia forest . . . Before dark I was badly pricked by the hairs of Mucuna hidden among the long grass; and scared out of the water whilst bathing in a small pool by a vicious-looking water-snake gliding over the surface.

A few days before Christmas, Mary got down to the shores of Lake Tanganyika for the first time. The drop of nearly 2,000 feet from Chilongolwelo meant a change of temperature from comfortably warm to very hot. But Mary, lizard-like in her tolerance of heat, was charmed by the little port of Mpulungu sweltering in its clearing in the lakeside bush, and by its group of tree-crowned, off-shore islands. Lakeside birds were many; egrets, lily-trotters, grey-headed gulls and various waders; and crowded, noisy colonies of black-headed weavers busy at their basket-like nests skilfully suspended from the ends of the arching boughs of trees close to the water. Mary was soon to develop a strong attachment to this wonderful lake 420 miles long and 20 miles across with an area greater than that of Wales, and whose bottom is as far below sea-level as its surface is above it and whose depths are home for a wealth of fish species found nowhere else in the world. Coming back from that first lake visit, Mary spotted her first antelope—one of the smallest species—a duiker that leapt across the road in front of the Gamwells' car.

The white population in and around Abercorn was a small community in which everybody knew everybody else. And as the Gamwell sisters had long been amongst its leading lights, Mary soon got acquainted with a wide circle of people. Dropping in for tea was a common Abercorn custom and Mary quickly acquired the habit, at the end of a long hot day in the field, of getting a welcome cup of tea from somebody or other on the way home. Her first African Christmas was convivial but, even so, botany could not be entirely neglected. As they drove home after a Boxing Day lunch, Mary notes: 'We were in party clothes and coming back I saw some plants. So we stopped and collected—not good for nylon stockings.' It is not easy to picture Mary or the Gamwells in party clothes; in their photographs they are almost invariably in bush jackets and trousers and with a knife in their belts.

Every day in those first weeks Mary saw something new; a snake up in a tree; ants' nests the size of footballs conspicuous on the branches of trees; little freshwater crabs scuttling about in streams; huge grasshoppers with scarlet wings she at first mistook for birds as they flew away; a butterfly which perfectly imitated the colours and patterns of another species of another family; magnificent fish eagles with their far-carrying, melancholy cries; pied kingfishers that hovered over the water in a blur of whirring wings; reed cormorants, a smaller kind than the cormorants she was familiar with back home on Craig y Deryn. She met with pink begonias, red *Gloriosa* lilies, green maidenhair ferns, yellow irises, white orchids. She soon got used to the idea that on many days her plants had to be gathered hastily between huge and frequent downpours, often amid spectacular thunderstorms. On 4 January 1952 she walked, or rather stumbled, all round Lake Chila which is roughly circular and about a mile across.

> I was given Isaac [one of the Gamwells' African staff] to carry my things and look after me. The soil was sandy and I found a lot of carex and juncus. Then we got into bog. Found bog orchids, utricularias and a vast amount of other interesting plants. Sat under shade and ate my lunch. Then went on through the bog to the end of the lake where we cut across the marsh, the orchids and other plants interesting but the going awful! Up to my knees in mud and falling into holes—Isaac having to pull me out! It got worse and worse and I was not sorry to reach firm ground. I found Marion and Freda . . . I was mud all over and very wet but we went to the Bredos—they are Belgian and he is head of the scientific branch of the locust-control centre. We had delicious coffee and got home about 7.00. It's a hard job getting one's finds sorted and properly pressed and I was up till midnight!

Next day she was taken north towards the Tanganyika border to look at the flora of a local marsh (a *dambo* in Swahili):

> Nkali Dambo is a lovely bit of country. You go quite a lot uphill and then have low hills to your left and the big dambo or marsh below you. The flowers were unbelievable, tall lemon-yellow gladioli and yellow arums and we found a dwarf protea with white flowers. We collected till about 4.30, then we went to Mrs Draper at Ndundu and she gave us very welcome tea.

This is Mary's first mention of Ndundu, a house that was destined to play a huge part in her life.

Termite mounds were a striking landscape feature Mary soon got used to, they were so abundant. There were endless miles of bush and plain where these mounds stood every thirty or forty yards in all directions, the size of small houses, rounded in shape and covered with vegetation. Mary soon realised their special botanical interest. Centuries old, many of them, and built of sand grains and termite saliva, they had greater fertility and sharper drainage than the land around them and often had their special flora, some blue with plumbagos, others pink with begonias. So over the years termite mounds (people often erroneously called them 'ant-hills') were often to be mentioned in Mary's daily log.

Despite persecution, baboons were common in the escarpment woodlands as Mary saw the day when, motoring along a bush road, they drove a pack of about forty in front of them. 'They were all sizes, some babies. They do the most awful damage, stealing fruit and digging up the gardens. They make an awful row.' Though they were reputedly harmless to people, Mary felt uneasy the first time she met with baboons while on her own. She was trying to reach the cliffs above Chilongolwelo but was frustrated by a dense barrier of creepers and undergrowth: 'The baboons were close to me all the time on the other side of a ravine. They had evidently been eating the huge beans from a big tree.' The next excitement was a pair of martial eagles which had a nest in a tree near the cliffs. They flew out of the trees as Mary came down from the escarpment. They were no more popular than baboons, Mary found, because they had lately been taking the Gamwells' poultry. So though they are amongst Africa's most magnificent birds they would be shown no mercy if their predations continued. Hearing the Gamwells talk like this, did Mary remember that day at Caerynwch in 1928 when a buzzard had been trapped while taking chickens?

Mary had been at Chilongolwelo only a month when she went down with a fever but she was soon on her feet again, stimulated perhaps by the arrival of the box of plant-presses and papers which had got mislaid at Dar es Salaam. Continually widening her range, she got to Kawimbe, a leper settlement fourteen miles north-east of Abercorn run by the London Missionary Society. Its director was Elsie Baker and she and Mary became immediate friends, Kawimbe becoming one of Mary's favourite places, sited as it was at the edge of the Lumi Dambo, a marsh hugely rich in plants and birds. In Mary's words (26 January 1952):

> Hope and I took the car right across the dambo to the leper mission. Miss Baker, who runs it, has just had an O.B.E. She has done fine work. We had lunch in the shade of the car—very hot— then went into the marsh—very wet—our ankles in water. Many interesting plants—one lovely orchid with the most delicious scent. It is such a lovely place—miles and miles of marsh. And distant hills, the colouring so beautiful.

On the way home they got a cup of tea from Mrs Draper at Ndundu. Next day, being Sunday, was a day of rest spent in

Chilongolwelo garden enjoying the bougainvilleas, the strelitzias, the blue and mauve water-lilies and watching amethyst sunbirds taking nectar from the flowers. Another endearing little bird was the African pied wagtail which is simliar to the European pied wagtail but is a size bigger, has a melodious song and is remarkably tame.

25 January 1952 was a moment in history for Mary Richards. It was the day she sent off her first packet of pressed plants (200 of them) to Kew. This she followed about a fortnight later by posting off some living orchids to the Royal Botanic Garden at Edinburgh. But how she had established a link with Edinburgh so early in her African career is something her diary does not explain. What is a happy thought is that at least one of those orchids of 1952, the epiphyte *Ansellia africana*, is still alive and flowering at Edinburgh.

When news came through on 6 February that King George VI had died, the English section of the Abercorn community held a memorial service. Mary found it strange to be singing 'God save the Queen' for the first time since her girlhood. Meanwhile, botany continued to lead her into ever wilder places like the gorge of the Lunzua River or the remoter parts of the escarpment above Chilongolwelo where she had 'a glorious scramble' and collected

> some orange orchids to send to Edinburgh . . . Then I went down the rocks to the Katula River—steep and rough and very thick bush with twining creepers and high grass difficult to get through. I wanted to find the waterfall but it was such dense vegetation one can't get through it. Then I turned and climbed up and it got worse and worse. I found quite a lot of plants. Finally I got out of the ravine into the bush above. Leopards lie up here but I saw nothing. I got on to the path again and got home to tea very very hot.

Besides Chilongolwelo there were other private estates below the Lake Tanganyika escarpment, one of them belonging to the Gamwells' close friend, old John Holgate, a coffee-grower whom they always called 'Uncle John'. They often collected his mail for him from Abercorn post-office and he frequently came to them for meals. He was a cheerful old boy full of reminiscences of the Boer War in South Africa and other events long gone. The moment he saw Mary with her vasculum and her presses he laughingly christened her 'the Kew marauder' and so he called her from that day on. She seems to have enjoyed the title.

Some days Mary was busy on the farm, usually helping to plant the *nindi*. But collecting was taking up more and more of her time and as she ventured further into the bush she increasingly had to have someone with her who knew the country and who could help to carry her heavy presses and also to hack a way through the undergrowth. Isaac was frequently given this duty, as on 24 Februay:

> Hope dropped me and Isaac at the Uningi Pans, a very wide stretch of marsh full of duck and some water buck. I wore puttees and socks as protection against leeches. I went down into the water which was full of scirpus and long grass. Soon the leeches were all over my puttees and Isaac's bare legs. He gave a yell and made for the bank and didn't come into the water again. I wandered about all morning and found a great many new plants and some lovely orange orchids which are nearly all over but must have been wonderful earlier on. Then a thunderstorm rolled up and rain came down in sheets, so we started for home . . . We walked for about another four miles then a car came and it was 'Uncle John' Holgate who took us to his house where I had a lovely hot bath and a huge tea. About 6 p.m., Hope and Freda appeared and we went home—a lovely day. On the way we saw two wild dogs cross the road. They are about the size of an alsatian and have white-tipped, bushy tails and rounded ears. They hunt in packs and are very savage.

Mary, always a butterfly enthusiast, was thrilled by the dazzling swallowtails everywhere:

> The butterflies are in clouds, every colour of the rainbow. There is also a huge carpenter bee which pierces the wooden beams of the house and lays eggs. There is every kind of praying mantis, grasshoppers, crickets and moths . . . beetles in profusion—every colour and size. There is a curious caterpillar all over the bush with brown and green hairs—it is most unpleasant when it stings. We saw a line of processionary caterpillars. It was three or four yards long and they all moved as one, head to tail and no space in between. They were about an inch long and grey with black heads. The whole place swarms with caterpillars. We saw one enormous fellow with long orange hairs.

On 30 March 1952 Mary first saw the Kalambo Falls. Twenty-one miles north of Abercorn (Mbala), the Kalambo River cuts a

101

deep valley across the Ufipa plateau, then falls over a mighty quartzite precipice into a gorge which in a few miles ends at the shores of Lake Tanganyika. Dropping 700 feet, this is the highest singe-leap fall in Africa, being twice the height of the Victoria Falls though only a fraction of the volume. The gorge below the falls is rimmed by cliffs where eagles have their nests along with peregrines, red-winged starlings, rock martins and, most spectacularly, a colony of marabou storks which can often be seen circling magnificently as they come into their cliff-ledge nests. Mary Richards was to come here very often over the years and always find new plants—aloes, euphorbias, nindi, gladioli and many others along with a great variety of trees.

The magic of Africa affects many who go there. Mary Richards went only for a holiday yet in a very few weeks we find her confiding to her diary that she longs to settle there in a house of her own. On one of the frequent visits to Lake Tanganyika she writes:

> Freda and I walked up to the delightful little house built by the Northern Fisheries which they now want to sell as the Fisheries are closing down. It has a lovely view of the lake. One could make a delightful garden and I long to buy it!

What appealed to her about that part of Africa, apart from the richness of the wildlife, was the wilderness reaching all round: 'It's a wonderful feeling to be in the bush, miles away from everything.'

A letter on 10 April gave her much satisfaction—it was the first communication from Kew Herbarium since she had begun sending them her specimens. With relief she reports in her diary:

> They are pleased with my plants, especially the milkweed (*Asclepias*) and want seeds. Also the plant I got on Mbulu Island in Lake Tanganyika is unknown and seed is wanted. At this moment a pair of buffaloes are on the island. They are not pleasant animals to meet!

Encouraged by Kew's first letter, she went on collecting with ever greater zeal—utricularias both yellow and blue; gladioli, hibiscuses, acanthuses, osmunda ferns, commelinas and 'a curious parasite which grows on *Isoberlinia* trees and looks like red coral'. Almost every day there were new encounters with wild creatures. In the bush she saw huge, noisy hornbills which she could not name. Down by the lake she met with her first crocodiles, her first green-backed herons and startlingly scarlet bishop birds. She was stung on the face when she walked into a nest of hornets; suffered from sweat-flies, 'a kind of tiny bee', which crawled into her eyes and ears; and had to retreat from a menacing snake: 'It turned and went for us in big bounds. We all got rapidly out of the way. It is not often snakes go for you. This one may have had young.'

Some days in the field were an ordeal, as when she explored one of the local streams with Laski, one of the Gamwells' men:

> As we got well down the stream it began to thunder and we had a terrific storm and Laski and I were wet through in a few minutes. It was a very rough walk. The river goes down a steep rocky gorge with huge rocks. I was hunting for the leguminous tree Kew wants flowers of. It was hard work on such rough ground and in soaking slacks and tunic which clung to me . . . Laski plunged us into fearful long grass which was saturated and was an awful business to get through. Then we came to the bank of the Inono with one log crossing. I stepped on to it into a seething mass of *siafu* [driver ants]. They got all over me and, wet as I was, I had to plunge into the bush and undress to get rid of them. Then we plunged on, the long wet grass making going slow. It began to get twilight and I knew Marian and Hope would fuss, so we strode on as fast as possible. When we got nearly home, Hope appeared in the car, looking for us.

After 'a huge tea and a strong drink', Mary quickly recovered and next day was botanising as usual.

CHAPTER TEN

On 1 June 1952 Mary said farewell to all her Abercorn friends and headed for home by a very circuitous route. She had come into Abercorn from the south but she now departed towards the north, by way of Lake Tanganyika, determined to see as much of Africa as she could, lest she never came again. All the same, she had every hope of returning: 'It has been a truly wonderful six months. I am asked to come again. I wonder if I shall?' She sailed on the *Mwanza*, the one vessel then available, and although she had booked a cabin there was none to be had; and instead of a bunk she had to make do with a chair on the bridge. The journey up the lake took three days, calling at several villages. Despite discomforts she enjoyed the trip and the company of her few fellow passengers who were all white sisters from local missions.

> The lake was rough all day but the sun was heavenly in the middle of the lake, the shores on both sides a long way off . . . We got to Kigoma at midnight and I slept on till 6.30. It is wonderful how comfortably one can sleep in a deck chair but I am very tired of my clothes and I long for a good wash.

Having booked in at the Stanley Hotel, she walked in the midday sun the few miles to Ujiji, the village where Stanley had so famously found Livingstone eighty-one years earlier.

Kigoma being the terminus of the railway from Dar es Salaam, Mary now boarded a train for Tabora, 220 miles east. At Tabora she changed to the line that goes north to Mwanza on the southern shore of Lake Victoria. She slept a second night on the train and on 9 June her diary begins:

> Woke up to the most fascinating country, undulating and growing millet and rice and a certain amount of cotton; then very wild country with low hills and the most extraordinary rocks—huge boulders weathered smooth, piled up into fantastic shapes and other rocks balanced on them. This country went on till we came to Lake Victoria.

From Mwanza in Tanganyika she went north across Lake Victoria to Entebbe in Uganda, a journey of a day and a half. From Entebbe she went to nearby Kampala where she had booked on a two-week tour of western Uganda and part of the Belgian Congo. The tour was an experience of famous lakes (Edward, George and Albert), high mountains (the snow-capped Ruwenzori) and equatorial rain forest. By the lakes Mary saw her first hippos along with flocks of pelicans, storks and cranes. And she saw pygmies in the Ituri Forest. But the high spot came in the Parc Albert National when she went off on her own and hired a guide to take her part way up the slopes of the Ruwenzori:

> The path led almost at once into dense tropical forest, very slippery, wet and steamy. We came first to great masses of wild bananas, their leaves 12-14 feet long. The mountain was a series of deep ravines and as we got further up, the path became very narrow and slippery. The trees were very tall, thick with creepers, masses of ferns and a few orchids. The tree ferns were 30 ft. high. I slithered up and down the ravines, getting very hot and very blown. As we got higher there were big tree heaths and grey moss hanging from the trees and a huge composite in seed, possibly a tall senecio. There was a thalictrum, a buttercup and an alchemilla very like an English one. I went on till, just at 1 o'clock, I got to the Rest Hut where you sleep the first night on the climb to the summit. I had hoped to see the summit and the glacier but the guide intimated that we had to get back before sundown. Going down was very slippery. The forest on Ruwenzori is a gorilla sanctuary but I am not sure which part. I saw no animals and only heard a very few birds—it was much too thick to see any.

The trip ended back at Lake Victoria:

> At Kampala we parted. The tour has been a success. My two female companions were nice, our one male polite but frigid. I think that, being a bachelor, he thought we might be 'Designing Females'. I spent a week at Kampala which, like Rome, is built on seven hills.

Then by boat to the Kenya side of the lake at Kisumu after a rough night crossing. From there by bus through the Kenya Highlands to Nairobi which she left ten days before the Mau Mau trouble erupted. She went by train to Mombasa, then sailed in the *Durban Castle* via South Africa; and on 14 August 1952 she got to London where she lost no time in getting to Kew to learn that she had added about 100 new species to the Abercorn plant list. And so, after ten months absence: 'home to my Welsh cottage and my corgi'.

At Tynllidiart she soon settled into her old routine of entertaining, gardening and natural history. That was the autumn when Atlantic gales killed thousands of Leach's petrels. With her neighbour, Mary Cox, Mary went to Harlech and found the corpses of several of these little seabirds along the tide-line. She spent Christmas with Kate in Gloucestershire and began 1953 with a visit to Slimbridge to see the Russian white-fronted geese. On 7 March she was at a meeting in Aberdaron where it was resolved to rent a house on Bardsey Island for use as a bird observatory; and a fortnight later she convened a well-attended meeting at Dolgellau to form a Merioneth group of the West Wales Field Society. In making her opening address, Mary was in a somewhat awkward position. Here she was, a well-known participant in field sports, now taking a lead in nature conservation. Not that fox-hunting was any problem: in sheep-country foxes are generally accepted as vermin. But it was impossible to justify otter-hunting when otters were getting scarcer every year. Mary gave an assurance that her otter-hunting days were over and that otter conservation would be high on the agenda of the new society. That month she also went to a meeting of the BSBI council in London. In April she motored to Rhandir-mwyn in Carmarthenshire to stay with her new friend Mrs Irene Vaughan whom she had met at BSBI meetings; and during that weekend she had the thrill of seeing her first red kites in the upper Tywi valley where a tiny population of them had survived although throughout the rest of Britain this beautiful bird of prey had long been exterminated.

In 1953 her interest in the flora of Merioneth received a fillip. As her diary of 21 February put it: 'Mr Benoit, botanist from Barmouth' spent the day with her. She had not met him before but they had corresponded. When he came to Tynllidiart on that first occasion she expected a middle-aged, perhaps even elderly man, who had taken up botany as a retirement hobby. So we can picture her surprise when Peter Benoit turned out to be a very young man but with prodigious botanical knowledge, all self-taught. They quickly became friends and were soon exploring the county's flora in Mary's car.

On 16 May came the first outdoor meeting of the newly formed Merioneth field society. It was a thoroughly wet day led by Price

Evans up the northern slopes of Cader Idris where, despite the weather, he spoke at length about the ecology of mountain plants. Mary's diary reports:

> I started a Field Club into which I enticed various people with glowing pictures of lovely days out on the hills birdwatching and botanising. Our first meeting on the slopes of Cader Idris could hardly be included in the category of a 'lovely day'. Twenty wet and bedraggled objects crawled up the foot-hills of the mountain, buffeted by blinding rain and wind. We took shelter under a wall while our delightful and enthusiastic leader discoursed on Cader, its rocks and plants. He tried to get us to go higher up the mountain but we very thankfully took ourselves back to the Gwernan Lake Hotel where hot tea, scones and cakes were disposed of. The lecture was continued there in more favourable conditions.

In finer weather a few days later she enjoyed a BSBI meeting based on Bangor and led by Professor Paul Richards (no relation). They saw the rarer plants of Newborough Warren, Anglesey, including the little annual grass, *Mibora minima*; then at Cors Goch they were shown sedges as well as the pale heath violet and carpets of mountain everlasting. Next day, led by Inigo Jones and that greatest of all Snowdonian botanists, Evan Roberts, they went to the cliffs of Ysgolion Duon on the Carneddau where, among other alpines, they saw 27 Snowdon lilies. 'It is a lovely amphitheatre of rocks, very grand and wild,' says Mary's diary.

At the end of May, Mary was introduced to one of Britain's rarest though most unspectacular plants—the tiny annual called Welsh mudwort because it grows nowhere else in Europe. It is, however, known in eastern North America. This modest plant, which creeps across bare mud, had been found by a Birmingham BSBI member, Christine Goodman, while on holiday near Tywyn. Mary's diary reports: 'Miss Goodman showed me *Limosella subulata* in the tidal mud at the entrance to the Broadwater.' On 2 June, botany was put aside for the coronation of Queen Elizabeth. There were sports in one of Caerynwch's fields and in the evening Mary had the honour of lighting a bonfire on the top of the Foel. Then several days of botanising with Peter Benoit included a scramble up steep slopes near Dolgellau to see the rare little fern, forked spleenwort, and its even rarer hybrid with maidenhair spleenwort. This hybrid 'formed a very fine clump and there is a good deal of it on the rocks'. From there they went to the Nannau estate to see the touch-me-not balsam (*Impatiens noli-tangere*).

The whole of July, 1953, Mary spent in Shetland with Jonnet, taking part on the way in a BSBI meeting led by the well-known botanist, Mary McCallum Webster, who showed members the treasures of the country around the Findhorn estuary and Forres. Among good plants seen were common wintergreen, serrated wintergreen, wood stitchwort, chickweed wintergreen and yellow bird's-nest. Dragonflies were demonstrated by the expert Cynthia Longfield.

Next day:

> By car to the Culbin Sands and Buckie Lake. The Culbin Sands have been planted by the Forestry for hundreds of acres to control the blowing sand but there are still miles of sand hills and marshes with a lovely flora.

Among their finds were lesser twayblade, greater wintergreen, field gentian and smooth cat's-ear. They went to tea at Moy House, 'a lovely old Georgian house full of furniture and pictures but in bad repair and with the sad remains of a lovely garden.' Creeping lady's tresses was growing in masses on an outhouse roof. On the way back from Buckie Lake they went up a steep bank among the pinewoods and saw a whole bank of one-flowered wintergreen.

From Forres they went off on a bus for a day on the Cairngorms, a distinguished member of the party being J.E. Lousley, general secretary of the BSBI. Mary writes:

> A long run to Aviemore where we turned off along a rather rough road through lovely valleys of old Scots pine and juniper to Loch Morlich. The party divided into two. Some went to the Coire an Lochan and some to the tops. I went with the Coire an Lochan party. We had 1½ hours fast walking along a good path but a fairly steep climb. We could see a corrie above us with two large patches of snow which are more or less permanent. The last part was over very large boulders and we saw ptarmigan with young.

They ate their lunch by a lochan below the summit of Braeriach. Among the plants she mentions twinflower, Scottish asphodel, cloudberry, northern bilberry, spiked woodrush, arctic woodrush, alpine willow-herb, dwarf cudweed, alpine mouse-ear and alpine speedwell. The BSBI week ended with a day at the mouth of the Spey where on shingle beds they found mountain plants like northern bedstraw and northern rock-cress whose seeds had been brought down by the river. Mary's final comment was: 'It has been a good week and about 20 new records for Moray were found. Miss McCallum Webster has organised it well.' (A few years later she was to be less pleased with Miss McCallum Webster.) The BSBI week over, Mary and Jonnet went by sea from Aberdeen to Lerwick. This 1953 Shetland holiday was more or less a re-run of that of 1934—bird-watching on the remoter islands and trout-fishing in the lakes. Mary also collected a few plants, among them an extra-tall, large-leaved specimen of least willow and the distinctive Shetland form of red campion with thick, densely hairy stems and large, deep-red flowers.

During the rest of the summer Mary entertained a succession of botanists at Tynllidiart, among them J.E. Lousley, Christine Goodman and Edgar Milne-Redhead, taking them to choice localities in Merioneth. She sent specimens of upright vetch (*Vicia orobus*) to Stella Ross-Craig at Kew to help her illustrate Volume VII of *Drawings of British Plants*. The field society had a good day when Price Evans led them from Rhyd-y-main up to Craig y Benglog where there is an ashwood on a very local outcrop of limestone. Here they saw a community of plants— narrow-leaved bittercress, rock stonecrop, marjoram, mountain melick, common rockrose and others so different from the lime-avoiding vegetation that covers most of upland north Wales On 26 August there was the happiness of Jonnet's marriage to Jack Oldfield of Doddington Place, Kent. The ceremony was in Dolgellau, the reception at Dolserau Hall, Mary's birthplace.

The new field society had excellent local support. As well as local individuals, its members included the heads of two leading Dolgellau schools—Eurfyl Jones, headmaster of the grammar school for boys and Doris Lickes, headmistress of Dr Williams School for girls. Meetings were held at both schools and Eurfyl Jones became the society's first chairman. The first indoor meeting was at Dr Williams School where a large audience heard Ronald Lockley on seabirds. Next day Mary took Lockley to Aberdaron for a council meeting of Bardsey bird-observatory just installed at Cristin, a house in the centre of the island. On the following day they got across to the island:

> Walked up to Cristin which has been much improved—cleaned and furnished. Walked down to the Heligoland trap where first bird seen has been the rose-coloured starling. Saw goldcrest, ring ouzel, three chough pairs, ravens, whimbrel, shag. Saw Mrs Till,

wife of a lighthouse keeper, who has made a fine list of Bardsey's plants. Started back at 1 p.m., rough sea, very lovely.

In December the field society again held a joint meeting with Dr Williams School, this time to hear that eloquent speaker, John Barrett, who came up from Dale Fort in Pembrokeshire. His sparkling talk on sea-shore biology ended with him throwing armfuls of seaweed into the children's part of the audience. They loved it.

In February, 1954, Mary went to Kew Herbarium where she met V.S. Summerhayes, the expert on African orchids and E. Nelmes, an authority on African sedges. They went over her Northern Rhodesian plants with her and urged her to go back and continue her collecting. So she decided there and then to accept the Gamwells' invitation to stay with them again in September. Meanwhile she was getting more and more involved with conservation in Wales. Those were the days when the newly created Nature Conservancy, in deciding where to site its first National Nature Reserves, was heavily dependent on information supplied by amateur naturalists and inevitably Mary Richards, Price Evans, Peter Benoit and others were soon involved in advising on the boundaries of proposed reserves such as Morfa Dyffryn, Morfa Harlech and Cader Idris. The Conservancy's director in Wales was Dr Elfyn Hughes in Bangor and he and Mary Richards soon became firm friends. One of her chief anxieties was that the conifer plantations then being created by the Forestry Commission at Morfa Harlech should not be allowed to invade any of the plant-rich parts of the dunes and in the event they did not.

For the rest of 1954 she kept up with her usual busy schedule. In early April she was in a working party on Bardsey Island, helping to get the bird-observatory ready for the visitor season. In mid-April she watched blackcock dancing at dawn in a moorland forestry plantation high above Drws-y-nant. Two days later she was with the poet, R.S. Thomas, looking for kites in south Merioneth where they were just beginning to establish themselves. He managed to spot one but she missed it.

To have a daughter now living in Kent was a heaven-sent opportunity for Mary to get better acquainted with the flora of the chalk; and on 3 May (thanks to some friendly BSBI member?) she was able to see a plant which had long eluded her—the early spider orchid, growing 'in considerable quantities' on the Downs near Sittingbourne. Back in Wales she found another rarish calcicole, herb Paris, in one of its few Montgomeryshire sites about three miles west of Bishop's Castle. On 1 June she went to a famous north Wales garden in the Conwy valley, the Mill Garden, which she was shown by its celebrated creator, A.T. Johnson, who wrote three lovely books about it and who was described in an obituary as one who had 'assumed the mantle of William Robinson'. We now find in Mary's diary the first mention of the BSBI scheme to map the flora of the British Isles, a project on which she embarked with enthusiasm. On 16 June she was on the trail of the elusive small white orchid, always one of her favourite plants, and found several near Craig y Benglog with Peter Benoit and Edgar Milne-Redhead. Next day they found another along the ancient trackway that goes from Dolgellau up to the Tal-y-llyn Pass. There it grew near another Merioneth rarity, spignel, here close to the southern edge of its range.

By now Mary was in demand among visiting BSBI members wishing to be shown the plants of Merioneth. So on 25 June: 'Met Mr R.E. Abel and Mr Bannister in Dolgellau. Mr Abel very lame.' So he may have been but that did not stop her taking him up the rocks from Gwernan Lake to see the hairy greenweed (*Genista pilosa*) 'in beautiful flower' on Mynydd y Gader. 'Then walked across to Llyn Gafr. It began to rain a steady downpour. Things are very backward. Welsh poppy just coming out. Mr Abel delighted with the plants.' On 29 June, at the request of the Nature Conservancy, Mary listed some of the plants at Pistyll Cain, the well-known waterfall six miles north of Dolgellau. With her was the Kew fern expert, Peter Taylor, and down in the shadows of the gorge, below sheets of lemon-scented fern, they found Tunbridge filmy-fern which Mary had never seen before.

1954 was the year when the rabbit plague, myxomatosis, began to spread through Britain. Mary first saw it in Kent in mid-July: 'Very bad on the Downs, dead rabbits everywhere and a very bad smell. Several poor wretches crawling about half dead, it's a horrible thing.' Back in Wales after a garden party at Buckingham Palace, she was at the Royal Welsh Show at Machynlleth, an occasion memorable for the heavy rain that turned the show-ground into what she describes as 'a sea of mud'. The rain went on. When the distinguished botanist, N.Y. Sandwith, and his aged but very active mother, came to visit Mary, she led them to Llyn Cynwch to see what is rather a Welsh speciality, floating water-plantain: 'The lake was higher than I have ever seen it, the *Alisma natans* completely drowned! I waded in up to my knees and found a few leaves for Mr Sandwith.' August continued wet. In heavy rain and fog Mary surveyed the heather-clad, deeply fissured rocks of the wild northern end of the Rhinogydd for the Nature Conservancy, this time with her old Caernarfonshire friend, Cecily Williams-Ellis. They groped their way up to various little lakes—Eiddew, Tŵr Glas, Pryfed and Corn Ystwc, in search of the pondweeds, sedges and bur-reeds of acid waters, and they got soaked. Mary was on the range again a few days later in perfect weather:

> It is glorious, wild, rocky country—the precipitous sides of the two Rhinogs . . . We saw for miles—Moel Famma in Denbighshire, the Berwyns, Arrenig, Arans, Rhobell, Cader; and Plynlimon in the distance.

CHAPTER ELEVEN

On 22 September 1954 she was off on her second visit to Africa and this time she went by air. It was her first experience of flying and she enjoyed it. Her intention on this second visit was to resume the routine of the first—two or three days a week botanising in the Abercorn district, the intervening days being taken up with helping on the farm or in the garden at Chilongolwelo. But it was not to be quite like that. Her life was about to take on a new dimension as she got ever more deeply involved in plant-collecting. An important extension of her activities was her increasing involvement in the herbarium at the Abercorn headquarters of the International Red Locust Control whose chief, Dr D.L. Gunn, gave her every encouragement. And as no one used the herbarium anything like as much as she did she soon became its unofficial curator.

Returning to Abercorn in September meant going back to an Africa she had not seen before. Her first visit had been in the rains (which last from November to May) but now it was the dry season and coming up to the hottest time of the year. The land was not only droughted but also burnt where fires had swept between the flame-resistant trees of the *miombo*, turning huge areas of tall grass into a carpet of black ash on the woodland floor. She quickly settled down to life at Chilongolwelo. The birds sang beautifully at dawn and from her bedroom window she saw a new one—a very small bird with blue head and underparts, an orange back and with an immensely long red-brown tail streaming out behind—a paradise flycatcher. A few days later she met with another bird that trailed long ribbons behind it—the bizarre-looking pennant-winged nightjar. For this second visit she made two changes to render her less dependent on the generosity of the Gamwell sisters: she engaged an assistant to help with the collecting and she bought a second-hand car. Her helper was a young African called Leonard: 'He was asked if he could climb trees, could find his way about and knew the trees and plants; to all of which he said yes!' Next day when she went out with him, she was happy to report that 'Leonard climbs trees like a cat'. It

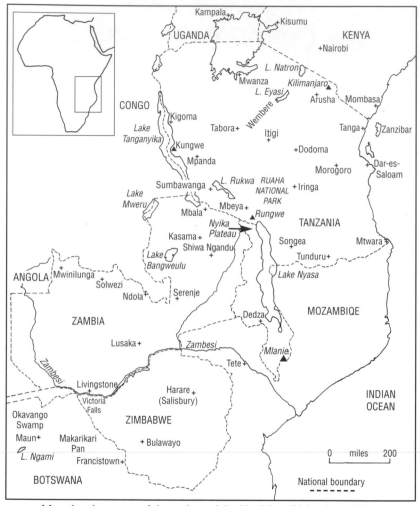

Map showing many of the regions visited by Mary Richards in Africa.

was an ability that would be invaluable whenever she wanted the flowers, fruits or foliage of the tree-tops.

Botanising in a burnt land was at first a frustrating experience but, as she explored around, Mary began to find a few plants in flower and especially deciduous trees blossoming before they leafed. The marshes called the Uningi Pans were quite dried up, causing her to marvel at the survival of the bladderworts and water-lilies she knew would be there in the rains. The Nkali Dambo, she found also desiccated but there was 'one lovely tree

114

with large, sweet-smelling, white flowers turning primrose as they go over'. From the dambo she walked back to Ndundu where she found Mrs Draper as happy as ever to give her a refreshing cup of tea. An exception to the general drought were the streams. Most were perennial and along one of them, the Inono, Mary must have felt quite at home when she found 'a lovely clump of *Osmunda regalis*', the royal fern she knew well in Wales and which is world-wide.

Almost everyday, as she botanised, Mary met with new birds, some of which she could name with the aid of her *Birds of South Africa* by Roberts; but inevitably she was foxed by the many small brown birds which the British settlers called grass warblers and which science knows as cisticolas, a group only experts can identify. Less confusing were some of the brilliant sunbirds common in gardens where they hovered in front of flowers taking nectar like the hummingbirds of America. Quite unmistakable was her first Ross's loerie (or turaco), a splendid, crow-sized bird of the tree-tops, raucous of voice, striking of plumage—body brilliantly purple-blue, face and beak vivid yellow, crest dark-crimson, wings opening to a startling bright-red in flight—every child's idea of what a tropical bird should look like.

On 12 November 1954 Mary reached one of life's turning points—she first met Desmond Vesey-FitzGerald and his wife, Octavia. 'Vesey' ('Bwana Vesey' to the Africans) as everyone called him, was in charge of the scientific side of the anti-locust work at Abercorn but had been away during Mary's first visit. A close friend of the Gamwells and a leading member of Abercorn's community of expatriates, Vesey was one of the best field naturalists in Africa, an entomologist of wide experience from previous appointments in South America, Arabia and the Seychelle Islands. A world expert on grasshoppers and locusts, he had a wide knowledge of other invertebrates, notably butterflies and dragonflies. He was also very good on mammals, birds and especially snakes. Now at 45, the author of many scientific papers, he had become a leading ecologist and conservationist. In his mind he was ever writing a work of eco-philosophy that would bring together all his ideas. This genial, humorous, quick-minded, forever pipe-smoking Irishman of a noble family but with never a trace of Irish brogue in his voice, was famous for his hospitality towards fellow naturalists. Nothing delighted him more than listening to their stories and in return he entertained them with a stream of anecdotes from his own experiences. He loved to recall eccentric characters he had met and was especially amusing at taking off the snake-man, Ionides, who had a very strange manner of speech.

Mary and Vesey hit it off at once. They both had an enormous enthusiasm for wilderness, exploration and the whole world of nature and they both loved camping and the challenge of the elements. And both were highly sociable and full of friendliness, laughter and fun. That first meeting was such a happiness that they decided there and then to go in a few weeks time to the Rukwa valley a hundred miles away in Tanzania, where Vesey promised to give Mary a taste of a wilderness rich in wildlife. Quite soon, off they went. As Mary put it in a letter home: 'He took me camping in December. His wife doesn't like camping so he and I went off together, to the mild scandal of Abercorn! We got our legs very much pulled!' Having reached her seventieth year, she felt she could safely joke about such things.

The North Rukwa valley, deep between the escarpments of the Great Rift, is a strange, chameleon-like place. If some maps mark it as a lake while in others it is a plain, this is because, at long intervals, it changes from one to the other. If the rains fail for years, North Rukwa becomes an arid plain; but sooner or later the drought ends, the lake is restored and may be there for decades. When Mary first got there in 1954 it was an uninhabited grassy plain and as such was of professional interest to Vesey because it was known to be one of the chief breeding grounds of locusts.

On their way to the Rukwa they camped on top of the valley's western escarpment at the edge of the Mbisi Forest, an impenetrable patch of evergreen rain-forest totally different in character, fauna and flora from the deciduous *miombo* and perhaps a relic from long ago when such forests may have covered much of the uplands. Mary was enchanted by the many plants that were new to her and her presses were soon full. Her diary mentions balsams, lilies, asclepiads, ferns and orchids, including a cream-flowered one with spurs over four inches long. Then they looked down into the Great Rift:

> We climbed up to the top of some rocks and the view was superb. We looked from the escarpment over the Rukwa—miles of flat plain with cloud shadows passing across. In the far distance we could see the opposite escarpment.

That first safari to the Rukwa plain was a great broadener of Mary's experience. Under Vesey's guidance she learned to recognise antelopes such as topi, puku and bohor reed-buck; and she got to know some of the huge number of birds for which the Rukwa is well known. In a long list of them named for her by Vesey, she mentions pallid harrier, black-winged kite, secretary bird, long-crested eagle, blue-cheeked bee-eater (catching dragonflies on the wing), black-winged stilt, red-winged pratincole, black vulture, striped kingfisher (nesting in a hole in a dead tree), harlequin quail, red-billed hornbill, European roller (eating locusts), black-bellied bustard, black coucal, red-shouldered widow-bird and a Rukwa speciality, the white-tailed bush-lark.

It was on the Rukwa plain that Mary had her first taste of bumping across intensely hot, trackless country in a Land-Rover, sometimes driving blindly through tall, dense grass that hid dangerous holes where elephants had been digging for water. It was also her first experience of collecting on a camping expedition. Over the years this collecting was to impose a daily test of her perseverence and self-discipline. At the end of each day, though she might get back to camp tired out and maybe not very cheerful, with the weather bad and mosquitos troublesome, there was the task of carefully placing each plant between sheets of drying paper and then putting them to bed between presses. In addition, each specimen had to be given a numbered tag which corresponded with a numbered description in a register in which were recorded details of where the plant was found. By next morning the specimens would only have begun to dry. All the damp sheets had to be exchanged for dry ones; and the damp ones had to be dried in the sun if it was shining. Only then would she be free to continue collecting and sometimes it would be noon before that happy moment arrived. Invariably she was up at first light, opening her presses before entertaining any thought of breakfast.

Her first safari she summed up as 'a wonderful ten days. Vesey-FitzGerald is a very fine all-round naturalist.' Crawling with difficulty in their Land-Rover up the zig-zags of the escarpment road they climbed back up into *miombo* woodland where Mary saw for the first time the colours of the *Brachystegia* trees just coming into leaf, going through a stage of colouring that in temperate climates is associated with autumn.

> In the intense drought of six months, all the trees lose their leaves; and now the rains have come they are coming out. The colouring is most extraordinary. The young leaves are every shade of rose, pink, red and a lovely golden-yellow—a blaze of colour.

Back at Chilongolwelo she resumed her collecting in the Abercorn district which happens to be exceptionally rich in plants, though she had no idea of this at first. She got soaked nearly every day by torrential downpours but soon dried out again. Once back home she would have a bath and some tea, change her plant papers and would then be ready for Abercorn's social round, perhaps dinner with the District Officer or an evening at a play put on by the local dramatic society. On 31 December she was able to look back on 1954 with satisfaction: 'A very good year. I think I have learned a good deal botanically and ornithologically.'

Zambia's highest mountain, Sunzu, rises about 16 miles southeast of Abercorn. Its height is 6,782 feet but since the Abercorn plateau is at about 5,000 feet the ascent of Sunzu is no more than the climb up Cader Idris from Caerynwch. Mary went up Sunzu for the first time on 9 January 1955 with Ken Bock, a visiting botanist. They collected in the woodlands that go up the slopes and saw klipspringers and wild pigs. Then they came up to a zone of rocks and ferns and could see the Rukwa escarpment very far away. Below them along the Saisi River stretched wide grasslands that were now cattle country but which had formerly been rich in wild animals. Summit birds were crag martin, martial eagle, augur buzzard and a peregrine. There was a thunderstorm but no rain. Yet when she got back home, Mary learned that Chilongolwelo had had an inch of rain in twenty minutes mid-afternoon.

From January to the end of May, 1955, Mary went on collecting around Abercorn, ever extending her range and regularly sending off parcels of plants to Kew. Young Leonard's tree-climbing skill was to prove invaluable one day in February when she was searching, as she had on many occasions, for an unnamed tree of the pea family that Kew particularly wanted. They had specimens of its leaves but had never seen its flowers. The break-through came on 14 February:

> Leonard and I had a long day collecting along the Inono River which for some miles runs through a steep, rocky defile with very thick vegetation difficult to force a way through. It had been a very hot day and we had had several violent thunder showers. I was very hot and very wet and by four o'clock I had had enough. I climbed out of the defile on to flat ground. Leonard was behind me. Suddenly he shouted: 'Memsahib, maua, maua! (flowers, flowers!)' I said: '*Maua* finished, I go home *chakula* (food).' 'No,

118

Memsahib, you come,' and he dragged me to the edge of the defile and there below me, hanging over the water, was my pea-tree in flower! We fairly hurled ourselves down that defile till we stood under the tree, its branches weighed down with flowers. Leonard seized my knife, climbed the tree like a monkey and cut down large clusters of the flowers. Then we looked at each other and danced with delight. It is the only time I ever saw that tree in flower. Kew were very kind and rewarded me by naming it after me—*Monopetalanthus richardsiae*.

On 16 March her diary makes the first mention of an exciting new venture: *Flora Zambesiaca*, which was to be a pioneer survey of the plants of what were then Northern and Southern Rhodesia, Mozambique and Nyasaland. When Mary went with Vesey to a meeting at the Abercorn Arms hotel on 28 March to meet a team of botanists to discuss the new flora she noted in her diary: 'The flora will take 20 years or more to complete and is to be started in London next year.' At her age, she could not hope to see the flora finished but she consoled herself that she was able 'to do a bit of collecting and so assist'. The project certainly gave an added purpose to her efforts if one was needed.

The *Flora Zambesiaca* team had arranged a trip to Kasama, nearly a hundred miles south of Abercorn, and invited Mary to go with them. Kasama, she found, was a pleasant little town 'mostly government officials in nice houses and nice gardens', among them Mr and Mrs C.W. Benson, he a leading ornithologist and his wife 'a keen botanist who collects orchids for the British Museum'. The party visited the nearby Chisimba Falls:

Left the cars below and walked up a path. We could hear the roar of the water. The falls are in three, the first is the biggest. It is very wide and the water comes over in a great mass on to the rocks below, causing clouds of spray which rises each side of the steep gorge, making all the vegetation wet and dripping—masses of vanilla hanging from the trees and many ferns. We went to the top of the first fall where the river runs between flat rocks and palm trees. I got a nice collection of crotalarias. There was a common sandpiper flying over the stream and I wondered which of us would be back in Europe first. The sun was brilliant and at the bottom of the fall was a lovely rainbow made by sun and spray.

In April, Mary was out of action for a fortnight with a poisoned leg caused by a sharp seed that penetrated her ankle. It was a painful experience but at least it was not the snake-bite she was always dreading and very nearly got on 18 May while botanising with a group on the Chilongolwelo escarpment. When they disturbed a Gaboon viper 'we all scattered quickly and the boys cut a stick to kill it but it went into a hole. They are one of the worst snakes.'

A last vignette from that second Africa visit comes from the Kawimbe leper settlement where she went to say goodbye to Elsie Baker, by now one of her dearest friends:

> I had a cup of tea then went off to the marsh beyond the fish-ponds. I walked right across to the Lumi River. It is a lovely spot—several miles of grassland and marsh. There were four lovely crested cranes and we saw the spoor of a lion in the mud. I saw three wattled plovers with long yellow legs and yellow and black beaks. The Lumi marsh and the termite mounds that rise out of the marsh were full of interesting plants. The water lilies were quite lovely—pale-blue and soft-pink, masses of them. I walked back close to the river which somewhere here is the boundary with Tanganyika. I found a beautiful orchid.

*   *   *

In early June, 1955, she flew back to England. After a day's shopping in London, where she 'found the pavements very tiring after Africa', she headed for Kew where she went over her plants with Edgar Milne-Redhead and Peter Taylor. Then to Wales to resume her open-house way of life at Tynllidiart. She took up her field-work where she had left off, going on surveys for the Nature Conservancy and pressing on with the flora of Merioneth with Peter Benoit. All the same she did not find it easy to adjust. It was one thing to look for plants in a botanically unexplored region of Africa where, any day, anywhere, you might come upon a species new to science and maybe have it named after you. But it was tame indeed to botanise in Britain, ticking off the names of well-known plants on a card for the new BSBI maps scheme. And though she did her best to enter into the spirit of the thing she was once heard to mutter that 'British botany is finished—it's all been done ages ago—there's only splitting into sub-species left!' Already she was planning to spend ever more time in Africa. Meanwhile, on 3 August 1955, she marked her 70th birthday by having her three young grandchildren (living at nearby Coed) to tea at Tynllidiart.

Her field activities that summer included a survey of Morfa Harlech with Peter Benoit and Hugh Chater. She had a day on Borth Bog and Ynys-las dunes when P.W. Carter, led members of the Merioneth field society and showed them three species of sundew and lesser bladderwort on the peatbog and thirty-three bee orchids in the dunes. She was with the Montgomeryshire Field Society when they went nearly to the source of the Dyfi and found Ordovician fossils and some interesting mountain plants including alpine enchanter's nightshade.

When Peter Taylor of Kew Herbarium came to stay at Tynllidiart he helped with a survey of the Rhinog flora, good finds being awlwort at Llyn Eiddew Bach and Tunbridge filmy-fern at Llyn Eiddew Mawr. On 8 August Mary provided flowers to decorate the luncheon tables when the queen opened an extension to the National Library at Aberystwyth. With Peter Benoit she surveyed the vegetation of the Presely Hills, Pembrokeshire, for the Nature Conservancy—an experience of great expanses of purple heather intermingled with the gold of western gorse. Her diary has two lines only for 11 October but they are enough to show us that even Mary Richards sometimes relaxed: 'Glorious day, brilliant sun. Gardened and sat on the terrace. Woodlark singing.' Those few terse words might have come straight out of Gilbert White's journals. He too was familiar with the beautiful carolling of the woodlark, one of the few birds to sing in October. On 10 October 1781 he noted: 'Woodlarks sing sweetly thro' this soft weather.'

For two days in late October, 1955, Mary was in the botany department of the National Museum of Wales, Cardiff, studying the manuscript list of Merioneth plants made in earlier years by D.A. Jones, the distinguished Harlech botanist. Through Irene Vaughan of Carmarthenshire she had become involved in the protection of the red kite and while in south Wales she attended a meeting of the Kite Committee on which she reports gloomily: 'It has been a bad year—only one young kite known to have successfully flown . . . interesting discussion as to whether myxomatosis or the cold wet summer has been the cause of the bad season both for kites and buzzards.' In November she was in Cardiganshire where in Cwm Einion she saw Tunbridge filmy-fern and hay-scented buckler-fern, 'both found by Mr Chater, junior'. And at Cwmystwyth she was shown colonies of forked spleenwort on roadside walls. Then to Tregaron Bog to crawl very quietly to within thirty paces of a wary flock of the dark-backed, yellow-beaked Greenland white-fronted geese that wintered regularly there in those days. That evening at Aberystwyth she gave a sparkling talk, 'Plant-collecting in Africa', to the recently formed Cardiganshire branch of the West Wales Field Society. She was a spontaneous lecturer, using neither notes nor illustrations, her clear, attractive voice easily holding her audience's attention.

There is good news and bad news in Mary's diary for January 1956. The good news is on the 16th: 'Very bleak and wintry, began to write list of Merioneth plants.' She had had lengthy discussions on this with Peter Benoit before Christmas and now the project was really beginning to take shape. The bad news is on the 21st:

> Left at 10.15 for Montgomeryshire. Went about seven miles beyond Welshpool to the Camlad meadows. Stopped by Hem Pool and saw 40 teal feeding and 40 wigeon; and 400 white-fronted geese flew over us. It was a really lovely sight, much more exciting than seeing them on the ground. They are being badly disturbed and shot at.'

Because of this Peter Scott came up from Slimbridge and at a meeting in Chirbury village hall, gave a lecture on geese and pleaded for their protection. It was of no avail and those Camlad geese are today only a fading memory.

In those years birdwatchers were encouraged to take part in monthly duck-counts. Mary took these very seriously on the Mawddach estuary, usually with her friend, Mary Cox. Sunday, 12 February, was special: for the first time she took her three young grandchildren, Marguerite, Andrew and Henry, to see the mixed assembly of mallard, wigeon, pintail and swans. The children were 'thrilled to be taught to use binoculars'.

In April, Mary was in London for a BSBI meeting that was followed by an outing to the Hitchin area led by Dr J. Dony. Among the sites visited were

> the remains of chalk downland. Miles of the downs are being ploughed up but there was a steep bank and the *Anenome pulsatilla*—pasque flower, was in bloom. I had not seen it in flower before and was delighted.

That week she also had a day in London buying camping equipment for Africa. That first safari to the Rukwa plain in 1954 had decided her that from then on her life in Africa would be lived under canvas as much as possible. To this end she was also arranging to take a Land-Rover to Africa.

There was no shortage of variety about her life during May. She discussed the conservation of Arthog Bog with the local farmers. She went to the Royal Horticultural Society gardens at Wisley and listed their rhododendrons; then the Saville Gardens in Windsor Great Park; then Chelsea Flower Show. Four days later she was in Cwm Idwal in splendid weather with twenty-nine members of her field society from Dolgellau. Dr Elfyn Hughes, head of the Nature Conservancy in Wales, gave a talk and Evan Roberts led them up to the heights of the Devil's Kitchen and showed them moss campion, arctic saxifrage and Snowdon lily high above them on the cliffs. Then to everyone's amazement a girl from Dr Williams School, Dolgellau, spotted a beautiful Snowdon lily growing on a rock just at the side of the path on the way down. Mary talked to the school about Africa a few days later.

The many outdoor frolics of that summer of 1956 included a memorable day among the birds and plants of Newborough Warren, Anglesey, where marsh orchids and round-leaved wintergreen were in superb flower and Montagu's harriers and short-eared owls were nesting. Another good day was when she got to Tir Stent near Dolgellau with Peter Benoit, the botanical Chater family and the ecologist, Price Evans. On the base-rich marshes there they made a long list of plants—not only many sedges and orchids but also moonwort, adder's tongue, globe-flower, lesser clubmoss and so on. Arthur Chater's diary for that day reads:

> We left the cars by Tabor chapel and then walked south up the marshy and rocky slopes. Mrs Richards on good form, talking all the time, clambering up rocks, darting from one lot of people to another, shouting, rushing off to see plants, quite the most energetic person there . . . and she is 71! . . . We all adjourned to Mrs Richards for tea—outside in the sun. Then we looked round the garden—a lovely sight—Azalias, Veronicas, Primulas, Roses, Rhododendrons and endless other fine plants.

Yet her life was not all botany. A few days later she was at a meeting in Dolgellau setting up a local branch of the Family Planning Association! Four days later she slept on a boat in Dartmouth harbour, Devon, where the Cadet Training sailing ships were in preparation for the race from Berry Head to Lisbon next Saturday. Twenty of them, all sizes. The Portuguese boats with four huge masts and sails, and several other big sailing ships—a unique sight. One will not see it again.

She felt 'wafted into another age.'

CHAPTER TWELVE

Mary's third trip to Africa began on 20 July 1956. By now she was fully launched into the lifestyle that was to be hers for many years—a split existence spent mainly in Africa but punctuated by longish stays in Britain. No talk of flying this time. Instead she went overland by train to Venice then by ship via Suez. Sailing down the coast of what was then Italian Somaliland, she spent her seventy-first birthday sitting on deck, the heat tempered by a very welcome breeze. At Dar es Salaam she picked up a new Land-Rover and two Tanzanians. One was Ali Omari (from Tukuyu) who had been trained as a plant-collector by Edgar Milne-Redhead of Kew during his work on the East African flora. Ali was not only to help with the collecting but also to act as driver and handyman. The other man, also recommended by Milne-Redhead, was Mhilu Abdalla (from Lushoto) who came as cook and house-boy. Both were to be pearls beyond price.

Via Morogoro, Iringa and Mbeya, Ali drove Mary and Mhilu the 600 hundred miles from Dar es Salaam to Abercorn but then they did not go to Chilongolwelo. Mary had decided that she should take advantage of the Gamwells' hospitality no longer and had arranged to stay at Kawimbe Mission with Elsie Baker. There she would have her own little house, would be independent and, possessing a Land-Rover, would be a useful means of transport for the mission and the leper settlement. And her rent would be a contribution to the mission's funds.

In August, Mary got to Kambole, a very isolated village and mission station in the bush only sixty miles west of Abercorn but of difficult access because the track was often underwater for miles, causing huge delays and detours. Mary wrote:

> It is a wonderful place on an escarpment,' wrote Mary, 'and Lake Tanganyika is 3,000 feet below with the Congo mountains on one side and the Tanganyika mountains on the other. I am camping about fifty feet from the edge of the escarpment and I look out over huge precipices. Rock martins are nesting in the cliffs and other birds sail over the forest below.

Quickly she realised how excellent Mhilu and Ali were in their different ways:

> Tents were up—bed, table and chair and a fire going—in under an hour. They are both most attentive. Mhilu is an excellent cook—bakes good bread and cakes—I live mostly on stews as meat is ages old and very tough.

She spent a week in that August of 1956 exploring the many gorges of the Kambole escarpment. She saw waterfalls leaping over colourful cliffs and taking the sunlight before they vanished into the forest below. One fall, the Nyonge, was especially beautiful, set in a horseshoe of red cliffs patched with orange orchids and masses of exquisite white-flowered sedges. Swallow-tailed butterflies sipped in clusters on bare, wet rocks. Aloes with long fleshy leaves hung down the cliffs, and below them, also cranny-rooted, scarlet gladioli waved in the mountain wind. Further down still wild bananas spread their broad leaves in the spray of the falls. Occasionally the shadow of an eagle, a buzzard or a vulture passed across the rocks.

$$*\qquad*\qquad*$$

At Kawimbe Mission she had got on to the trail of an earlier botanist, Alexander Carson, who had been a pioneer missionary in the district. It was in a spirit of archaeology that Mary and assistants from Kawimbe went off to look for Carson's former home in a valley a few miles away.

> Since Carson's day the valley has been cultivated and there are many more villages. All the same I did find a number of the same plants which he had collected. At the end of the valley the bush was dense. We were near the Saisi River. Sunzu Mountain rose on our right. We poked about among the thick undergrowth and Ernest found a pile of bricks and remains of old walls. This was the ruins of the old settlement where Carson had lived. Here he started the first Mission Station at Fwambo nearly seventy years ago and collected and pressed plants which he sent to Kew. Ernest picked up a brick which he carried back balanced on his head. It is to be built into the wall of the new Kawimbe church.

An interesting new feature was just now being added to Abercorn life. At Kalambo Falls an archaeological dig of world-wide importance had begun under the leadership of J.D. Clark, Professor of Anthropology at the University of California, Berkeley. In the next few years Clark was to excavate in a basin of the Kalambo River valley just upstream of the falls, his work providing one of the longest and richest records of man's activity so far recovered from a single site in Africa. The first Iron Age people are reckoned to have entered northern Zambia about 2,000 years ago, settling around a shallow lake of prehistory upstream of the falls. Always strongly attracted by archaeology, Mary lost no time in getting to Kalambo where she was shown round the dig by one of Clark's colleagues, Mrs Lilian Hodges, and soon became a frequent visitor to the site.

Meanwhile plant-collecting was taking her ever farther afield, enormously helped by the fact that Abercorn was a centre for locust control, being midway between two locust breeding grounds—the Rukwa plain in the north-east and the Mweru Wantipa in the west. As Vesey had to go to all known locust breeding places from time to time, Mary took every chance of going with him and having the great support he could give by way of vehicles, equipment, manpower, knowledge of the terrain and also accommodation. On 20 September 1956, she set off with Vesey on her first visit to the wilds of the Mweru Wantipa where she found herself in richly varied country full of promise. Right on the border with the Belgian Congo there was Lake Mweru, about 80 miles long and 25 across, the site of a great fishery that sent its fish down to the Copperbelt towns. Nearly forty miles east of this lake was the very much smaller Lake Mweru Wantipa and between the two were vast areas of marshland. Elsewhere stretched many miles of a woodland of small deciduous trees collectively known as *mateshi*. There were far-spreading grassy plains; and patches of evergreen forest, especially along the many small rivers. The land was generally much lower than Abercorn and much of it drained north-east to Lake Tanganyika where there was the Sumbu Game Reserve.

It was towards the end of the dry season and collecting was not at its best; but Mary enjoyed her first glimpse of this new country which was almost unknown botanically. As was to be the pattern of all her expeditions, the pace was relentless, the filling of plant presses ever the urgent goal. Her lunch breaks, for instance, when she bothered to stop for lunch, were of the briefest. At all times she ate very little and she certainly never thought of stopping for anything so decadent as elevenses or mid-afternoon tea. The only diversion from botany she happily allowed herself was when some unusual mammal, bird, butterfly or other creature happened along. So, crossing a reach of open country, they paused to watch parties of roan antelopes, zebras and also her first hartebeests. Then a moment of real excitement:

> We drove right across the plain, in places very rough, big rocks and stones and also wet patches. Very hard going. Quite suddenly a lion sprang out of the grass in front of us, a male with a very fine mane. The first time I have ever seen a lion!

Eventually they left the Mweru Wantipa and moved down to Lake Tanganyika and the Sumbu Game Reserve where they joined a group fishing from a boat:

> The rods are very heavy and you let out a great deal of line . . . we began to catch Nile perch and yellow-bellies and I caught a large tiger fish and it was a hard job to get it in. The game reserve comes down to the edge of the lake. We saw some bush buck and a great many lesser black-backed and grey-headed gulls. We pulled ashore where cliffs came down to a sandy beach. While the boys made tea, Vesey and I went up to look for bats in small caves in the cliff. In one there were hundreds and Vesey caught five, one of which bit my finger while I was holding it. I collected some nice compositae and an *Indigofera*.

Seven months later, in April 1957, and without Vesey this time, Mary went back to the Mweru Wantipa in the rains but it was a difficult safari. The rivers were over their banks, some bridges were down and roads were flooded. At one place they came to a raging torrent where the bridge was intact but under water. Ali waded across and was worried but said he would try; and he managed to get the Land-Rover safely over. Then Mary waded after the Land-Rover, 'steadied by Mhilu as the current was very rapid'. It was only by sheer heroism that Ali managed to get the Land-Rover all the way across to Lake Mweru, getting bogged down in many places for hours and once for a whole day when he struggled from mid-morning until three hours after dark amid frequent downpours of torrential rain. The mosquitos were dreadful and driver ants added to the difficulties. When at last they reached Lake Mweru they found it was sixteen feet above normal level and rising all the time. Fifteen miles out in the lake was Kilwa Island, botanically unexplored, but when they got a boat there the island was too flooded for botanising. There were no birds either except whiskered terns, fish eagles and a few spur-winged geese. Despite all the travails of this Mweru Wantipa expedition, Mary managed to get many presses full of plants—she mentions proteas, crotelarias, utricularias, lobelias, acanthuses, sedges, grasses and water-lilies. But they had been harder won than on any previous trip.

*   *   *

Of all the places Mary got to in her Africa years, perhaps none was nearer her heart than the southernmost of the Southern Highlands of Tanzania which were very much wilder and with far rougher roads than today. The botanical wealth of these hills, plateaus and mountains around Mbeya, a region of highly fertile volcanic soils, had long been known; but in October, 1956, when Mary got there for the first time, she began to collect more thoroughly than anyone had done before. From Mbeya she and Vesey-Fitzgerald (on leave from his locust duties) headed south-east, beckoned by the Poroto Mountains, and found an idyllic camping site in 'a lovely spot with dense tropical forest rising on each side'. Mary was in a new world:

> Mhilu made tea and gave us bread and cheese and we went off to explore the forest of wild bananas, tree ferns and bamboos; it was all dripping wet. By the sides of the track were orange and yellow daisies, some climbing up the trees and hanging in curtains, some tall and pushing up among the ferns and bananas; on the ground great haemanthuses, a kind of lily with flowers like scarlet balls. Sunbirds flew round us, collecting nectar with their long, curved bills. We scrambled up a steep bank and sat on the edge of a wide valley. The whole mountain, which leads up to the crater lake, seems to consist of ridges and gorges. We sat still and colobus monkeys were quite close, swinging from branch to branch. They are lovely with their white collars. We heard birds but they were difficult to see. Presently a squirrel ran up a liana and on to a tree where a large pumpkin was hanging down. He nipped off the yellow flowers and ate the developing pumpkins. He was a rich brown with a black crest of hairs down his back and a brown bushy tail. It is difficult to describe this forest—huge trees, lianas, hanging moss, huge ferns, a mass of tangled, impenetrable vegetation, huge bamboos and climbing composite plants. The

129

sunlight filtering through and making brilliant patches of bright-green. We got back to camp at dusk and the temperature dropped about 20 degrees. Bed early to keep warm. The colobus monkeys made a great noise as they went to roost in the trees close to us.

Next morning Mary and Vesey were joined by David Orr, a keen naturalist and game department officer, and together they scrambled to over 7,000 feet in great heat through almost trackless undergrowth till they reached the edge of the Ngozi crater lake:

> It was an extraordinary sight—about 1,000 feet below us, almost sheer down was the lake, surrounded by the crater rim, rocks, precipices and dense forest clothing part of its sides. The lake was a misty blue; beyond again were mountain ranges . . . I collected a great many plants and ferns and a lovely epipactis.

Next day, while Vesey and David Orr tried to climb down into the crater, Mary, who never had a head for heights, botanised round camp with Ali, filling two presses, 'getting back to camp by 5 o'clock. A very cold night and heavy dew. I had a lot of plant notes to do but got so cold I gave it up and went to bed quite frozen.'

From Ngozi they made for the Elton (now Kitulo) Plateau, a high-level grassland above the tree-line, a scene of smoothly rolling hills that reminded Mary of the Montgomeryshire uplands around Plynlimon. But while the Plynlimon country is a botanically unrewarding grassland, that of the Elton Plateau was blessed with the botanical richness of the best alpine meadows. Although this first visit, being in the dry season, was too early for the spectacular flowering that would begin in about November, Mary made some good finds on the way up 'where giant lobelias push up their immensely long spikes by the side of the road'. She had a rewarding scramble down to the foot of a waterfall where there were 'clumps of a lovely fairy-like plant with lilac bells, an *Ardisiandra* [primrose family] which had been collected only once before'. In the rough grass up on the plateau

> the wand-flowers grow in great clumps, their lilac and pale-pink bells nodding in the wind; big bushes of *Helichrysum*, their silvery-grey foliage showing up their orange or yellow flowers; and tall orange and bright-red gladioli. These are dry season plants.

Their next objective was Rungwe, the 9,700-foot volcano that stands high in the southward view from Mbeya. 'I had set my heart on climbing Rungwe,' Mary writes. The problem was how to get there from the Elton Plateau but eventually they found there was a track a Land-Rover might take. At their base camp Vesey and David Orr spent that evening trapping rodents:

> We had two tables, one mine which I used to press plants and write notes; the other, belonging to Vesey, was our dining table. It was also used to skin the various rats, mice and squirrels collected. It was quite usual for Monday [Vesey's house-boy] to lay our meal at one end while a half-skinned rat occupied the other end!

Skinning was the task of Ananyia Mwangomo, a youngster who was a special protegé of Vesey's. As a child he had been crippled by polio, his leg left more or less useless. As Mary relates:

> Vesey got the doctor at Abercorn to operate on him. The boy was in hospital for months. The operation was successful and Ananyia is now getting about with his leg straight but still in plaster. He is always laughing, is a most cheerful soul and adores Bwana Vesey.

Next morning they made an early start:

> David Orr was a bit worried over me. He did not think a woman past three score years and ten could do the climb. We had an assortment of equipment. Vesey had a butterfly net. Ali carried my rucksack with a large press, bottles of spirit (to collect orchis), notebooks, pencils and a big vasculum. David and Tito carried rifles [a precaution against buffaloes]. I just carried myself. Monday brought up the rear with our food, but no water, as we expected to find plenty of good streams.

They walked up through a forest of tree ferns and wild bananas. Long fronds of a big stag's-horn moss trailed over the ground. Climbing begonias with pink and white flowers hung over the path. Orchids and ferns grew on the tree-trunks. It was dripping with moisture, hot and steamy.

> Two hours brought us into bamboo forest. In here it was almost twilight; the bamboos, sixty feet high, grew very close together. The fallen leaves made the path terribly slippery and I thought we would never get through those bamboos! At last there was daylight

131

ahead and we got on to open ground with big tree heaths in full pink flower and bushes of hypericum. We left the tree heaths and got on to stony ground with short grass and low bushes of proteas. A last steep pull and we reached the top on which was a small cairn of stones. We should have had a wonderful view but it was too misty because of the usual grass fires. We were thirsty but the streams were all down steep gullies and ungetatable. Then we started back. It was steep and slippery. I took one bad toss and fell headlong. Ali picked me up, none the worse except for a bruised toe. We all stopped at a stream and drank and drank. You have to be really thirsty to know the joy of mugs of heavenly cold water.

*　　*　　*

Another major venture of that third stay in Africa was a return visit to the Rukwa Plain in November 1956. Though the Rukwa was not botanically attractive Mary loved it for its mammals and its wealth of birds—cormorants, pelicans, herons, egrets, bitterns, storks, ibises, spoonbills, flamingos, ducks, geese, waders, birds of prey, vultures, cranes, bustards, gulls, terns, sandgrouse and many others. Quite remarkable was the gathering of Abdim's (or white-bellied) storks she encountered while in the Land-Rover. Breeding in North Africa, Abdim's storks fly south in October and November and those that Mary saw from the Land-Rover were probably tired migrants. They were standing 'in hundreds all along the road and on the road itself and would hardly get out of the way'. That a small finch, the red-billed quelia, was everywhere, was hardly surprising: six months earlier, at the end of the 1956 rains, Vesey had found a breeding colony on the Rukwa Plain. It was in tall *Sorghum* grass, the nests averaging five per square yard over an area of 83 acres, the estimated total of nests being two and a half million.

She had the luck one day to go for a walk in the woods with ornithological expert, John Beesley, then stationed in the Rukwa on locust service.

> He told me what the birds were:—sulphur-breasted bush-shrike, bou-bou shrike, bru-bru shrike, red-backed shrike, slaty bou-bou shrike, grey-headed bush-shrike, three-streaked tchagra shrike, emerald cuckoo, red-breasted cuckoo, African cuckoo . . .

The list goes on and on—sunbirds, warblers, doves, barbets, flycatchers, etc. and ends: 'I only wish I could remember them all but it will take ages.' From the depths of the Rukwa she climbed to the Ufipa plateau which separates the Rukwa rift from that of Lake Tanganyika. She found few plants because it was too early in the season in those high places. But she much enjoyed the spontaneous hospitality of the Roman Catholic mission at Chala; and the huge panoramas across the uplands to Lake Tanganyika and the Congo hills beyond.

Because Rungwe and the Porotos had been the most botanically exciting country Mary had yet encountered, it is no surprise that she was soon back there (January 1957) to see what plants the rains had produced. David Orr was again free to accompany her and on a safari of several weeks they explored the Chimala escarpment and the Elton plateau. This was a highly successful safari:

> As we got higher up on the Elton plateau the flowers were in bewildering profusion and they went on for miles and miles. A large rosy-red orchis and a red-hot poker grew together; anemones as large as tea-cups; sheets of a sweet-smelling, white-flowered member of the *Rubiaceae*; scarlet balsams grew with tall white orchids. There was a carpet of flowers of every size and hue. It was all quite different from when we were here in October when the dominant flowers were helichrysums . . . It took me ages to press the large quantity of plants I had collected and write up the notes; and finally I found myself asleep with my head on the presses, so I gave it up and went to bed.

Driving faced its usual problems. In October black volcanic dust had choked and blinded them on the way to Rungwe mountain. Now amid violent rainstorms their vehicle skidded or stuck in slippery red soils with Ali coping as magnificently as ever. Botany had to go on whatever the difficulties:

> We spent three more days collecting on the foot-hills of the Kipengere Mountains and I pressed an enormous quantity of specimens. The hills were grassy, with parallel outcrops of rock. The lovely *Thalictrum zernyi* grew among the rocks—it has beautiful pale-pink flowers. It would make a good plant to grow in an alpine house. The pockets among the rocks are thick with every kind of flower—tiny lilies, scillas, irises, asphodels, orchids and small ericaceous plants.

On 12 January they reached the top of nearby Mtorwi Mountain, up slopes of short grass thick with flowers which

133

included about half a mile of wandflowers (*Dierama cupiflorum*) whose pendant pink, purple or mauve flowers nodding in the breeze must have been wonderful.

> We followed a stream which presently came down in a waterfall from the rocks above. David went on, I undressed and had a cold shower under the waterfall. I had only a handkerchief to use as a towel.

Then they tackled the last steep and rocky climb to the summit:

> David and I went up different ways as we wanted to cover as much ground as possible. I got puffed as we reached the 10,000 feet level; anyhow, at every step there was a fresh plant to look at and collect. A thunderstorm growled on our right as we walked up a gentle incline to the top. Suddenly the mist came down and we were completely enveloped. It was bitterly cold and my hands were quite numb. We waited, hoping the mist might lift. There was a sudden rift in the mist and we had a magnificent view. The Kipengere Range formed a half-moon round us; on our right lay the Livingstone Mountains which rise on one side of Lake Nyasa; the ground below us fell away in steep slopes, the forest far below. It was a long weary track back. We got to camp just as dark fell. Mhilu met us with cups of hot tea.

*   *   *

While she lived at Kawimbe Mission, so close to the Tanganyika border, it was inevitable that the nearby Ufipa Highlands became a favourite collecting ground for Mary, especially after she had got to know Mrs Dam. That redoubtable lady, with her son, George, and his wife, had Malonje farm with over a thousand head of cattle about eight miles south-east of Sumbawanga, supplying meat to the district from Abercorn to Mpanda. Mary reports:

> The charming house is perched up, with a truly wonderful view— Chala Mountain, the Rukwa escarpment, Mbisi Forest and Rukwa Plain. Mrs Dam and her daughter-in-law gave me a huge lunch and then we took the ridge-back dogs, eight of them, and went up the mountain behind. They will kill a leopard and keep a lion at bay till she comes up and shoots it.

For several years, whenever she was in that area, Mary often called, sometimes stayed, at Malonje farm, as in March, 1957, when she set out to find the Chapota swamp between Sumbawanga and the south end of Lake Tanganyika. On that safari she spent about three weeks on those uplands with their roads so difficult in the rains, collecting a huge number of plants, among them a new composite that was named after her—*Bidens richardsiae*.

In May, 1957, knowing that the vegetation would have changed yet again, Mary made a third trip to the Poroto Mountains. The rains had not yet ended and the roads were worse than ever. They had to carry large planks and long rolls of wire-netting to get them over the deepest holes. The Land-Rover turned over on its side once and nearly did so many other times. They reached the edge of the Elton Plateau but could get no further. Mary was bitterly disappointed because she could see enough of the flora to realise what she was missing—new sedums, gladioli, orchids, sedges, heathers and 'a great many new helichrysums'. On Ali's insistence, they retreated down to the rain-forest zone where she collected for another week and saw her first Nyasa blue monkeys.

Back in Mbeya she heard that David Orr had to go to Lake Nyasa because of a problem about hippos damaging rice crops. For Mary this looked like a good chance of seeing a new bit of Africa but it ended in failure. The rains had been immense, there was huge flood damage to roads and when they got down to Lake Nyasa they found it was eight feet above normal level, villages had been flooded and people drowned. Heavy rainstorms were continuing and plant-collecting was out of the question. 'Sick of mud and water,' Mary called it a day. 'I am not often defeated,' she wrote, 'but really the weather was bad.' On the long journey back she felt unwell but a few days rest at Kawimbe revived her, especially when she heard from Kew that a new plant she had collected near Abercorn in 1955 had been named after her— *Tephrosia richardsiae*, a member of the *Leguminosae*.

Mary's nearly twelve months stay at Kawimbe ended on 24 June 1957, when she began her return to Wales, having said farewells all round Abercorn, uncertain if she would ever come back. She had loved being at Kawimbe. Quietly religious herself, she had felt at ease with mission life; and when not away on safari she had taken part in the life of Kawimbe church and the leper settlement, being especially helpful with the Girl Guides as she had been in Dolgellau for so many years. She had felt quite at home in November, 1956, when Lady Baden-Powell visited Kawimbe, and guides and scouts rallied there from miles around. Among them were about twenty—all lepers—from Kawimbe itself. She went home by air. But first Ali had to drive her in the Land-Rover the 600 miles to Dar es Salaam and there she received news of great sadness in a telegram from her son, Richard, saying that her beloved ten-year-old grand-daughter, Marguerite, had died.

Details are lacking about the next sixteen months which Mary spent in Wales (occasionally England) because the diary for the period is lost. But we know that life at Tynllidiart went on as in previous years. Her naturalist friends came and went, among them John Beesley on leave from Africa; and later on, Edgar Milne-Redhead from Kew and Peter Greenway from Nairobi Museum. Mary continued her work on the flora of Merioneth though now admitting that African plants had pretty well driven British plants out of her mind. On 13 August 1957 she was on the Berwyn range, walking from Milltir Gerrig to the top of Moel Sych to see cloudberry at its only Welsh locality.

In April, 1958, she went to Newborough in Anglesey with the British Ecological Society, the party including three eminent professors of botany—Paul Richards, W.H. Pearsall and D.A. Webb. On 23 April she was up at 2.00 a.m. to take her old friend, Frances Pitt, the well-known Bridgnorth naturalist, to see the dawn antics of the blackcock in conifer plantations near Dolgellau. In June she was at a meeting of the Nature Conservancy at the Rheidol gorge, Cardiganshire, discussing the creation of a National Nature Reserve there. 1958 was the year when she collected her last British plants, her final Merioneth specimen being lamb's lettuce from Hafod-y-calch near Corwen on 27 May. Her very last British plant came four days later. It was tree mallow collected on Ynys Gwylan Fawr, an islet off Aberdaron, Caernarfonshire, on 31 May, at a meeting of the field society she had founded five years before.

1958 was pivotal as the year she decided to settle in Africa. Getting back to Wales on 8 July 1957 she had written in her diary: 'So end my Africa days.' Can she really have believed they were over? Certainly not after she got a letter from Marian Gamwell in Abercorn reporting that their old friend, Mrs Draper, had had to quit her house, Ndundu, through illness, and that it was to be let. Mary did not hesitate. She wrote back asking Marian to arrange a lease on her behalf. So Tynllidiart was let as a holiday house, contact was made with Ali and Mhilu in Tanganyika, and Mary's life was finally committed to Africa. She returned there by sea because she was taking a new Land-Rover with her.

CHAPTER THIRTEEN

Her journey ended on 5 November, 1958:

> Dar es Salaam at last, two days late. Went to the New Africa Hotel where I found Ali and Mhilu, all smiles. Mhilu's wife and babies are to be picked up at Morogoro. Ali's wife is in hospital at Amani—a baby seems imminent.

Once more Ali drove them across Tanganyika to Abercorn where, for the time being, they again stayed at Kawimbe Mission, as Mary's new house was not yet ready for occupation. The next seven months, although plant-collecting went on with enthusiasm, were mainly a time for settling in at Ndundu. Five miles into the loneliness of the bush, half-way to Kawimbe, Ndundu was a small bungalow with a red roof of corrugated iron. It had a wide verandah, a sitting-room, two bedrooms, a dining-room, a bathroom and a kitchen. In front of it a large garden sloped to a stream that was buried in a ribbon of impenetrable evergreen forest of a type known as *mushitu* and was completely different from the deciduous, well-spaced trees of the *miombo* that surrounded the other three sides of the garden. The property also included a sizeable area of woodland. The water supply was a more or less perennial streamlet that came down through the trees past the house and across the garden. Thatch-roofed houses were built among trees behind the bungalow for Ali, Mhilu and their families.

Mary was lucky with the garden. Mrs Draper (by now she had died) had kept it beautifully and, being a New Zealander, had added colourful bottle-brush trees to the poinsettias, bougainvilleas and jacarandas so universal in African gardens. Tall, fragrant eucalyptuses formed a backcloth to the bungalow. The garden yielded oranges, lemons, grapefruits, pomegranates, avocados, mangoes and bananas. Flowers were everywhere, even extending outside the garden where tall white lilies had wandered out of their original bed to form stately groups under the trees. Mary was soon sending off to England for many more plants and in the next few years she established colourful beds of salvias, hippeastrums, gladioli, agapanthus, crinums, geraniums and zinnias against a background of roses, philadelphus, crotalarias, leptospermums, magnolias, *Catalpa bignonioides* and *Rhododendron simsii*. Beyond them grew huge raffia palms and clumps of giant bamboos. There was a place exclusively for aloes—a Mary Richards speciality. Tree orchids adorned most of the trees round the garden, their cultivation entailing nothing more than tying them to a branch with string, leaving the orchids to do the rest. Fuchsias grew just outside the verandah, their leaves much eaten by hawkmoth caterpillars.

The garden was often lively with birds, not those of villages or cultivations, but those of *miombo* and *mushitu* woodlands: white-rumped babbler, green turaco, Ross's turaco, boubou shrike, lavender waxbill, paradise, dusky and chin-spot flycatchers, little bee-eater and various sunbirds. Some were cheerful songsters—black-eyed bulbul, white-browed robin chat and emerald-spotted wood dove. Often in January the African thrush (*Turdus pelios*) sang all day, even through the afternoon heat. One year its nest was in a tree along the drive, in a fork about twenty-five feet above ground, the birds being quite unalarmed by people frequently passing below. An intriguing voice was that of Narina's trogon, a soft cooing which came from the dark recesses of the *mushitu* below the garden. But the bird itself was hardly ever seen. *Ndundu* is an interesting name: it is said to imitate one of the best-known bird voices of Africa—the deep booming, heard especially at dawn, of the ground hornbill.

*　　　*　　　*

200 miles south-east of Abercorn, Zambia rises steeply to the frontier with Malawi. It is a borderland of wild and beautiful hills stretching north and south and rising in the centre to the Nyika Plateau whose highest summit reaches 8,549 feet. Mary first got there in January, 1959, in the company of Vesey and a new botanical friend, Edward Robinson, a teacher in Southern Rhodesia. 'Very nice, has a large beard!' was her first comment on him. Milne-Redhead, writing from Kew, described him as 'an absolutely first-class collector and one of our most valued correspondents in Africa'. And Mary wrote: 'Edward Robinson is very good on sedges and I hope to learn a lot.' They soon got up into a world of mountain grassland with outcrops of rock. There were many marshes, streams, ravines, waterfalls and small,

scattered patches of evergreen forest. The views westwards over Northern Rhodesia were immense. From their vehicles they got glimpses of bush bucks, duikers, roan antelopes and zebras. (Nyika, already a game-reserve, was to become Malawi's first National Park in 1965.) Mary collected many specimens—scillas, lobelias, violets, orchids, balsams, thalictrums, combretums, proteas, sedums, red-hot pokers, lady's mantles, sundews, bladderworts and many others. But on the whole she was disappointed because it was evident that they were too early to see the flora at its best: 'There will not be much for another month or six weeks', she noted in her diary.

In the hope of doing better elsewhere, they retreated off that side of the Nyika and drove south to Rumphi at the end of the range, then north up the east side, above Lake Nyasa, with marvellous views of the Livingstone Mountains on the other side of the water. Near the lakeside town of Karonga they stayed at a rest-house where 'that evening the air was alive with tiny fire-flies'. By a tortuous mountain track they climbed into a forest zone rich in thunbergias and begonias:

> The path was steep and slippery. We came out on to a ridge of more open ground with remains of last year's giant lobelia flowers and a big senecio. Then we plunged into even denser forest where the light was quite dim. Immense trees towered above us . . . we walked a long way, the forest getting darker and darker. There were a lot of dracaenas, two kinds, one with finer leaves than the other.

Her final comment was: 'I hope to get here again next year.'

Mary had now been in Africa long enough to have seen many Europeans installed in great estates and fine houses but on the way back from the Nyika she was to find one that eclipsed them all. They were exploring the country along the Great North Road between Isoka and Mpika when

> we came to the turning to Shiwa Ngandu. The country is hilly and below us on the left was Lake Shiwa Ngandu with fine-looking *dambos*. It is a wonderful estate, hundreds of eucalyptus trees and a big timber yard. We stopped at the estate office and asked permission to use the rest-house. Then we met Sir Stewart Gore-Brown who insisted on coming up to the rest-house with us. He is a wonderful old gentleman, wears a monocle and is very early Victorian. We went up to Shiwa House to dine. It is an amazing house, rather like an Italian villa, on the hill overlooking the lake.

We went through a big hall, up a stair and into a huge drawing room full of nice furniture, pictures and china. One might have been in England. We had an excellent dinner with white wine and port. Mrs Harvey, Sir Stewart's daughter, was there. After dinner we looked at the chapel which is charming. They have services every Sunday, R.C. and Protestant. I thought the house slightly out of keeping with Africa! It was all in a very grand style!

After nearly a week at this Shangri-La whose wealth of plants and birds was mainly around the four-mile-long lake, Mary returned to Abercorn with a huge collection of specimens.

Another Mary appeared on the Abercorn scene on 12 February—Mary McCallum Webster whom Mary Richards had met in July, 1953, on the BSBI meeting at Forres, Morayshire. Invited to stay at Ndundu, Miss Webster had jumped at the chance of extending her knowledge of her favourite plants, the grasses. A species of grass she was particularly pleased to find was the rare one named after Mary Richards, *Richardsiella eruciformis*, described by Milne-Redhead as 'a new genus absolutely unlike anything known from Africa before'. In the next six weeks Mary took her guest all over the Abercorn district. Then off they went on safari with Vesey to the Mpui escarpment on the way to the Rukwa, camping the first night by Lake Kwela. There were many water plants to be collected, including pondweeds and bladderworts; and various birds to be watched—little bee-eaters, pin-tailed widow-birds, hobby, goliath heron, great white egret, crowned crane, white-backed duck, dabchick and, rare in that part of the world, great crested grebe.

Alas, Miss McCallum Webster's stay was not a success. Mary Richards found her heavy going, with no other interest in life except grasses. As she put it in a letter home:

> I have a woman botanist here. She came on February 12 and stays till April 26. She is not a very congenial companion and safari is a bit of a trial. However, I hope she is enjoying it all. The lovely country I think is a bit wasted on her! I shall not be sorry when April 26 arrives!

Probably this judgment was a bit hard on Miss Webster. Could it not be that the two Marys were simply unsuited to each other temperamentally?'

*   *   *

By getting back to Britain in May, 1959, for three months, Mary began a regime of annually avoiding much of the south-central African dry season when plant-collecting was least worthwhile. Her life from now on would resemble that of the swifts which, by their migrations, enjoy summer the year round. She reached London just in time for the Chelsea Flower Show on 26 May, a typically cool spring morning, but which to Mary, straight from Africa, was 'a bitter cold day'. Life in Wales she found had changed little except that her valued friend, Price Evans, had died a few weeks earlier—he who had taught her so much about Welsh mountain ecology. She resumed her collaboration with Peter Benoit on the flora of Merioneth, going first to Morfa Harlech where the marsh orchids were magnificent and where Peter showed her the hybrids between sea spurge and Portland spurge and between common cat's-ear and smooth cat's-ear. Three days later they got up into the wild rocks and screes at the head of Cwm Cywarch, Dinas Mawddwy:

> It is a lovely place, a narrow valley with high cliffs . . . we found a quantity of *Oxyria*, *Sax stellaris*, *Sax hypnoides*, a good deal of oak fern, beech fern, a small quantity of *Cystopteris fragilis* and parsley fern. Globe flowers and *Thalictrum minus* grew on the sides of the gorge.

Another valley new to her was Cwm Cynfal, near Ffestiniog, in whose meadows were masses of fragrant orchids, spotted orchids, both the butterfly orchids, kidney vetch and upright vetch (*Vicia orobus*). From there they went to Bala Lake and found much lesser meadow-rue by the waterside along with many sedges.

Mary went to Surrey in July to stay with her old friend, Florence Bristow. Then to Kew to discuss her next collecting programme. In London she saw a consultant about her hay-fever 'which has been bad in Africa and in England. He gave me dozens of pills.' She stayed with another old friend, Margo Masters, at Petersfield, Hampshire, and with her 'motored to Uppark (National Trust), a perfectly fascinating place. The Fetherstonhaughs still live there—one of them took us round—a most romantic place and story.' Then to Bath to stay with Sophie Blathwayt whose family had owned Dyrham Park near Chippenham for 250 years. 'We motored out to Dyrham which has been bought by the Office of Works and will go to the National Trust. The house is in a very bad state but they seem to be repairing it well.' From Bath on into the south-west to Paignton, Devon, where she found her cousin, Stephen Stokes, totally devoted to the welfare of Paignton Zoo to which Mary had lately sent some living plants from Africa.

She returned to Wales for several days of BSBI meetings centred on Bala, the first taking them to the calcareous ground that slopes up from the south side of the lake where among their finds were frog orchid, field gentian, mountain pansy, stone bramble and even chamomile, a first record for Merioneth. Two days later, in another lime-rich area, Craig y Benglog, four miles north-east of Dolgellau, their finds included mountain melick and narrow-leaved bittercress as well as common rockrose and wood spurge (both rare in Merioneth).

*   *   *

When Mary flew back to Africa on 22 August 1959, it was a happy home-coming:

> I found the house in beautiful order and they had put flowers in all the vases. The ceiling all redone and Ali had worked hard and cut lovely views of Lake Chila and Abercorn. Also the water is flowing hard. The garden has been watered—oranges and grapefruits are coming on and the kitchen garden full of peas, beans and lettuces.

She had been home about a fortnight when a most exciting event took place in the garden. It was a Sunday afternoon and a houseful of people had come to tea:

> We were all in the sitting room and Mhilu rushed in and said:— 'Simba!' [*Lion!*] We looked out of the window and there on the lawn was a large cheetah. I think he had come to drink. He looked at us and waved his tail, then walked away into the bushes. Mrs Anderson says there were two lions on Friday night on the Kalambo road.

It was the Kalambo Falls archaeological dig that preoccupied Mary's attention for the next week. Dr Clark, the director, had asked her to collect specimens of bark from local trees for comparison with the prehistoric bark he was unearthing in the various ancient living-floors he was investigating. Bark-collecting proved to be too hard for Mary but, as so often, Ali saved the day: 'Ali is excellent at getting the bark off. Got 16 trees—it takes a long time to get each square of bark out as most of the wood is very hard.' At the same time she supplied Dr Clark with a list of 82 trees and shrubs growing round the site of the dig. The specimens of foliage and flowers which she collected are now in the Department of Botany at Cambridge. The results of the dig were published in three volumes by the Cambridge University Press beginning in 1969.

Frequently entertained at Ndundu was one of the best-known Europeans and greatest characters in that part of Africa, Dr Hope Trant, an Irishwoman from Co Tipperary who for about forty years served as a doctor with missionary societies and other organisations, often working far away in the bush several days' walk from the nearest medical centre. Respected by whites and blacks alike, Hope Trant was humorous, good-natured and extremely devoted to duty. And to her tame monkeys, one called Audrey being her special favourite but which tended to snap at people. One account of her speaks of 'a large and jovial woman with short grey hair and oozing capability and kindness. Her house is an amazing muddle of books, lamps, oddments, sewing machines and kitbags and her room is absolutely full of monkeys and cats.'

When in later years Hope Trant wrote her autobiography she spoke of Mary Richards as

> one of the most energetic persons I have ever met. She was always up at six o'clock to work in her garden till breakfast, after which she often went off on a collecting expedition into swamps or up a mountain to return about tea-time with her collecting cases full of specimens which she sorted and put into presses in the evening. She had collected thousands of specimens for Kew Gardens during the eight years previous to my visit. However that night we did not talk botany; she took us to see a play put on by the Abercorn Amateur Dramatic Society.

About the time she acquired Ndundu, Mary got to know a new friend, Bill Morony, an Irishman from the west coast of County Mayo, who had retired from a long career in African agriculture and had settled in Abercorn. An all-round naturalist with a special interest in orchids, Bill Morony soon became a great help to Mary in her collecting and particularly in her herbarium work at the locust-control headquarters. For years to come he would spend Sundays at Ndundu whenever Mary was home, often helping her to sort out the latest additions to her growing collection of butterflies.

Although from 1959 onwards Bill Morony is increasingly mentioned in Mary's diary, he seldom went on safari with her. But he was with her on 27 September:

> Vesey and Morony came at 11 o'clock and we went to the Tanganyika border to look at some rocks for aloes, and possibly bats if we could find caves. Some very big rocks and we got some aloes. Found on the top of one of the rocks the nest of a speckled nightjar (*Caprimulgus tristigma*). The bird was sitting. It took me several minutes to spot her, she looked so exactly like a bit of wood.

Vesey and Bill Morony were again her companions when she set off for the Rukwa on 19 October. Crossing the plain, they saw the usual herds of topi, many bohor reed-bucks, a few elephants, hippos and wart-hogs and a great assembly of buffaloes. A new mammal for Mary was a serval cat they flushed out of the grass. They also passed over a vast gerbil warren that stretched for several miles—'the largest in the world, Vesey says'. Climbing into the escarpment woods they found many interesting plants— *Dolichos*, *Kaempferia*, *Thunbergia*, *Euphorbia*, *Amaryllis*, *Haemanthus* and others. Tsetse flies were 'quite awful and it is a sleeping sickness area!!' And they had to keep a look-out for elephants which had been shot at by poachers and had become dangerous.

When Vesey and Morony returned to Abercorn after a few days, Mary and Ali stayed on another month, exploring some wild country between Mpanda and Lake Tanganyika, a major ambition being to find a way to Kungwe Mountain which looks down on the lake from half-way up the eastern shore. Kungwe had been biologically unknown until earlier in that year of 1959 when an expedition from Oxford University had investigated mainly the fauna. Now Mary was keen to do the flora. But she and Ali had a very difficult safari. The heavy rains, the awful roads, the flies, the endless miles of bamboo forest, were all dismaying as they battled across the uplands to within fourteen miles of the lake. From there they had glorious views across the lake to the Congo mountains; and they saw Kungwe but it still looked a long way

Ali Omari, Mary Richards' first plant-collecting assistant. *Indigofera omariensis* was named in his honour.

Mhilu Abdalla, for 18 years Mary Richards' cook, handyman, fellow-camper and friend.

Mary Richards helping Tanzanian police with their inquiries on the Elton (Kitulo) Plateau, near Mbeya, December, 1963.

Approaching Mlanje Mountain in Nyasaland (now Malawi), June, 1962.
(*Photo by Mary Richards*)

The distinctive *Aloe mawii* of Mlanje Mountain, Malawi.
(*Photo by Mary Richards*)

One of Mary Richards' fellow botanists, Edward Robinson, amid rocks and aloes on Mlanje Mountain, Malawi.
(*Photo by Mary Richards*)

Mary Richards camped by these rapids on the upper Zambezi in Mwinilunga, Zambia.
(*Photo by Mary Richards*)

By Lake Ngami in Botswana was a tribe whose women were dressed in traditional Victorian clothing.
(*Photo by Mary Richards*)

Camping in the bush: Mhilu about to bake bread in a hole in the ground.

Rocky landscape (aloes in foreground) at Namakambili *c.* 40 miles east of Tunduru, south Tanzania.
(*Photo by Mary Richards*)

Mary Richards, Ali Omari and some tall aloes.
(*Anon*)

Tree spurges, a striking feature of many rocky hillsides and escarpments, here seen at Kambole near Abercorn.

Colobus monkeys are frequently
mentioned in Mary Richards' accounts
of botanising in montane forests.

(*Photo by J. Odier*)

The Elton (Kitulo) Plateau
near Mbeya, Tanzania,
immensely rich in wildflowers
in Mary Richards' day but
even then under threat by
farming and forestry.

Motoring difficulties.

(*Photo by D. Vesey-FitzGerald*)

Lurking danger. A sluggish, half-hidden puff adder on the Buhoro Flats near Mbeya.

Mary Richards found this tree lily (*Vellozia equisetoides*) not uncommon in rocky woodland around Mbala, Zambia. Eight or nine feet tall, its flowers were mostly very pale-blue.

Left to right: Bill Morony and Mary Richards (co-authors of the *Flora of Abercorn*); Penny Condry and Desmond Vesey-FitzGerald, 1964.

Mary Richards on the occasion of her honorary degree at Bangor, North Wales, July 1964.

Mary Richards, extreme right, with her family at Caerynwch on her 80th birthday, 3 August 1965.
(*Anon*)

The Great Ruaha River, Tanzania, where Mary Richards collected in 1965.
(*Photo by Mary Richards*)

Shapely rocks near Singida,
northern Tanzania.
(Photo by Mary Richards)

Kilimanjaro
from 30 miles
west at Momela,
Arusha National
Park, Tanzania.
*(Photo by
J. Beesley)*

Vesey-FitzGerald's
house at Momela,
Arusha. Mount
Meru in background.
(Photo by Ion Trant)

off. Eventually the road gave out altogether and Mary admitted defeat: 'I decided to go back and do Kungwe by the *Liemba* (the lake steamer).' But when, nine days later, she went down to the lake from Abercorn, the captain of the *Liemba* was unhelpful and would not undertake to put her ashore where he had landed the Oxford University expedition. And although for years to come Mary dreamed of getting to Kungwe, she never made it.

Often, over the years, Mary had gone west from Abercorn through the bush on the appallingly bad road to beyond Kambole Mission where from the escarpment rim she had looked at the vast panorama west across to the Mweru Wantipa and north to where Lake Tanganyika vanished into the hazy distance. She had longed to get down the escarpment to explore the botanically unknown woodlands and rocks above the Lufubu River which, through binoculars, she could see flowing into the lake amid wide swamps of papyrus. Early in December, 1959, with Ali and Mhilu, she managed to find a motorable track down the escarpment into woodland rich in flowers:

> There were quite a lot of the large *Eulophia* orchids, varying from pale to deep-purple mauve; a very lovely member of the *Asclepiadaceae*, tall with pink flowers, and another with creamy flowers all up the stem; a *Euphorbia* and a lot of *Cyperaceae*.

Down at the Lufubu's flood plain they came to many villages and intense cultivations. Here they passed a wayside monument commemorating that: 'Here in 1885 the *Good News* was built by the London Missionary Society.' The story of the *Good News*, the first ship to sail on Lake Tanganyika, is an epic of boat-building. The 14-ton ship was sent out from Britain to the mouth of the Zambezi in dozens of crates which were shipped up the Zambezi, then up its tributary, the Shiré, to the north end of Lake Nyasa. From there porters carried the crates to Lake Tanganyika along 200 miles of bush tracks through country torn all the way by slaving raids and war. As the total journey from the mouth of the Zambezi was about a thousand miles it is not surprising that some of the crates got lost or stolen and had to be replaced and that parts of the ship were still arriving at the mouth of the Lufubu two years after the first crates had arrived. The *Good News* sailed the lake on its missionary work for many years and later Mary was to see her as a half-submerged wreck in Kituta Bay near Mpulungu.

On 7 January 1960 Mary went off with Ali and Mhilu to revisit the Mweru Wantipa—a safari that was to be marred by accident. The rains were at their heaviest when they visited the Lumangwe Falls about half-way between Mporokoso and the Congo border.

> The falls are magnificent, they are in a wide semi-circle and the drop must be 300 feet. You stand on the edge of laterite rocks and look down at a jumble of rocks and vegetation. The spray is terrific. I was soaked in a few minutes and my hair was running with water. It would be difficult to climb down as the rocks are so slippery. I came back and had to change. Then it began to rain about 1.30. The river came down in flood and now, 5.15, the spray is so dense you can hardly see the falls.

In bright sunshine next morning she photographed a rainbow in the spray, then went plant-hunting in nearby swamps and on the many termite-mounds. Next day:

> A fine morning. We decided to go to the bottom of the falls and walked down a steep slope through woodland with large rocks. Collected an interesting white orchis—flat sessile leaves, the whole plant hairy. We came down to the river. Beyond was a steep, shady, rocky, wet bank and there seemed to be a lot of interesting plants. Ali and I scrambled up the rocks and wet, slippery mud. I had on my gumboots. Somehow I slipped and fell onto the rocks below. I was dazed, Ali picked me up, the side of my head was bleeding and my nose. And my side hurt. I managed to get back to camp on Ali's arm, bleeding violently. I was in an awful mess. I wrapped my head in a bath-towel and got out of my clothes and into a skirt and shirt. Ali put a fresh bandage on my head and stopped the bleeding. I then lay on my bed while the boys packed the car. They said I had better go to Kawambwa as it was nearer. When we got there, there was no doctor, so we went on to Mbereshi. My side was painful. The road was bad and I was very glad to get to Mbereshi. Dr John Parry put plaster and lint on my head and strapped my ribs.

As everywhere, Mary had friends in Mbereshi who looked after her and in a few days she was sufficiently recovered to resume a little gentle botanising here in the Luapula Valley. But it was hardly her sort of country: 'This is a densely populated part and we went through eight miles of continuous villages. The people are not healthy and there is much leprosy and blindness.'

Back in Abercorn her painful side was diagnosed as a broken rib and she was out of action for the next month, resting and watching the birds in the garden—sunbirds, streaky seed-eaters, fire-finches, mannikins, waxbills, robin-chats, wood doves and turacos.

Though her side still ached, Mary felt fit enough to resume collecting on 29 February. With Ali and Mhilu she went south just beyond Kasama where she stayed in a forestry rest-house. Everywhere the rains were heavy and the streams over their banks but, partly on foot, partly by canoe, she covered a lot of ground and filled many a press with plants. Probably her best day was at

the Malole Rocks, about five miles from Kasama. We found a quantity of things in the wet sand, then scrambled up the rocks. They are amazing—piled in masses and every size and shape, many covered with grey lichens and clumps of orchids, a lovely white one which turns yellow as it goes over, and a lovely *Bulbostylis* with long white flowers with mauve spots at base of lip. We climbed up the rocks and got onto a plateau of flat rocks and sand. At the far end of this plateau are some big overhanging rocks and in the sheltered surface of one are prehistoric drawings of animals. It is a most interesting place. The utricularias, yellow and blue, were out—in the wet sand between the rocks.

*　　*　　*

Mary flew back to Britain on 1 April 1960, for a stay of three months of which she spent only five weeks in Wales. She had her customary walk round Morfa Harlech with Peter Benoit where they saw the spring vetch (*Vicia lathyroides*) and the hybrid violet (*canina X riviniana*). They also discussed the publication of their list of Merioneth plants. With some of the family she went up Cader Idris from Cregennan. At a ceremony in Dolgellau on 6 May, she was happy to celebrate that her son, Richard, had been made High Sheriff of Merioneth, noting in her diary that one of the buglers for the occasion was 'a son of the man who bugled when Harry was High Sheriff in 1910'.

From Wales she went off for three weeks to see the art treasures of Italy with her daughter, Kate. In Florence she remembered that, in his younger days, her late husband had often stayed there with his mother, Louisa, who, years later, was to build Brithdir church:

Sunday, May 29: we went to early service at St Mark's English church. Harry and his family must often have worshipped here. Louisa Richards had a villa here and she afterwards married Charles Tooth who was chaplain here.

From Italy they drove north over the Brenner Pass to Innsbruck and then Oberammergau and the Passion Play. In London she wound up her stay in Britain with a visit to Kew Herbarium where she went over maps and plants. She also suggested to Kew that 'sometime a new plant found by us should be named after Ali Omari'.

CHAPTER FOURTEEN

Returning to Africa on 1 July 1960 Mary Richards, for the first time, took a friend with her. Kathleen Stevens was an old Africa hand, having spent most of her married life in northern Nigeria. She was an all-round naturalist and particularly good on African birds. In Abercorn the sedge expert, Edward Robinson, was just then paying another visit and Mary spent all morning with him on 10 July, going through the sedges in the locust-control herbarium. Meanwhile Kathleen Stevens was out-of-doors listing the birds and was interested to see how many species that were rare in Nigeria were common around Abercorn and vice versa. Down at Lake Tanganyika they met that strange character, Ionides, a former English public schoolboy who had been living for many years in south-west Tanganyika and from being a game-warden had become a professional snake-catcher. He had come to Mpulungu to collect the water cobras abundant in Lake Tanganyika. They watched him catch one:

> It was in the water, among large rocks. He has several long poles rather like the long clippers one uses to prune high branches of shrubs, but this clipper is lined with rubber and clasps the snake. With great care he clips a part of the snake, then another, and very carefully draws it out of the rocks and lands it on the quay. He caught five altogether. He is world-famous on snakes, also a mediaeval historian and very musical.

In a letter home she wrote:

> He is a charming man but very eccentric. He spends his life catching snakes for zoos all over the world and for the snake-parks who make anti-snake serum. He does get bitten but has never had a full bite.

To get Kathleen to a really good birding spot, Mary suggested a fortnight's camping at Lake Kwela which had become one of her favourite places. Beyond Kawimbe Mission they crossed the

149

border into Tanganyika, turned off at Mpui and reached the lake in the evening. It was in these wild surroundings that Mary celebrated her birthday: 'Wed, Aug 3. 75th Birthday—don't feel like 75!!' People hearing of her feats of endurance naturally assumed she enjoyed perfect health. In fact she did not. Quite often her diaries include remarks such as: 'I had plenty of work to do but didn't feel fit'; 'A temp. and in bed all day'; 'Am a bit off colour'; 'Bad indigestion all day'; 'I have not been very fit'; 'Felt rotten and went back to Ndundu'; 'A bit bronchial'. Tummy upsets increasingly afflicted her but she believed in ignoring bodily complaints as far as possible. All the same she had twice been in Abercorn hospital, first for blood-poisoning and later with appendicitis. And she had had an operation in St Thomas's hospital in London in June 1960. There was also a problem of incipient cataracts on her eyes; and if she did much mountaineering the varicose veins in her legs were painful. But no matter—as long as finding new plants and seeing new places continued to excite her, she would press joyfully on (though often predicting her early demise!).

Her diary for those few days by tree-surrounded Lake Kwela is full of the birds that Kathleen so enthusiastically named—bearded woodpecker, saddle-billed stork, crested coot, bateleur eagle, wire-tailed swallow, martial eagle, black-headed oriole, cloud cisticola, yellow-breasted longclaw, orange-breasted bush-shrike, white-faced duck, African pochard, grey-headed kingfisher . . . the list goes on.

From the lake they went on north-east to visit two relict patches of mountain rain-forest, the first at Nsangu, the second at Mbisi which Mary loved for its huge panorama across the Rukwa Plain. Along the fringes of these impenetrable forests she found thunbergias, peas, crassulas, tephrosias, crotalarias, indigoferas, scabious and a viviparous fern with young ferns growing from the top of the fronds. That evening, 8 August, 'a lovely big moon rose as we sat by the camp fire—not so cold tonight'.

From time to time Abercorn got a reminder that the wild was still not all that far away. There was not only the cheetah which had appeared in broad daylight on the lawn at Ndundu. A hippo turned up one day in Abercorn's own water, Lake Chila—it had presumably come up the streams from the Rukwa valley. A leopard was spotted in car headlights on the Kawimbe road just outside Mary's garden. A lioness and cubs had been seen passing by night along Abercorn's main street. And, following what was perhaps a primordial migration route, elephants occasionally passed through the town under cover of darkness, leaving huge footprints in people's gardens. Ndundu had such an elephantine visitation in September 1960. No one saw them but there were clear signs that they had tarried awhile in the thick cover of the *mushitu* below the garden.

It was now nearly ten years since Mary had first reached Abercorn. She had explored far and wide but had never felt any urge to go to any of the famous game parks. She was too much in love with the little-known corners of Africa and the idea of organised tourism had no appeal for her. So it was a surprise to everybody when she decided to visit the Luangwa Valley game camps. Her plan was to take two of her friends from Kawimbe Mission on a holiday that would not involve the primitive conditions of her style of camping. They set off on 3 October 1960, Ali driving them south for about 300 miles, staying the night in rest-houses. Mary was delighted with her first experience of a game park: 'a most thrilling place' was her initial comment. Here she saw her first wildebeest, her first greater kudu and her first rhino. There were elephants everywhere along with pukus, impalas, lions, hyenas, water bucks, zebras, giraffes, buffaloes, monkeys and crocodiles. The birds were magnificent: pelican, squacco heron, purple heron, green-backed heron, open-bill stork, African spoonbill, skimmer, hadeda ibis and numerous waders including terek sandpipers. When Kathleen and Mary stood on the high river bank with hundreds of brilliant carmine bee-eaters coming out of holes under their feet, Mary was reminded 'of the way the puffins fly out at Ynys Gwylan'. Among many other birds listed by Kathleen were trumpeter hornbill, water dikkop, purple-crested loerie, greater honey-guide, black-collared barbet, white-headed barbet, white-fronted bee-eater and large flocks of Lilian's lovebirds. Mary also noted 'a pair of puff-backed shrikes like balls of snow'. In the Luangwa Valley they enjoyed a change from the monotonous *miombo* woodland. Among the trees Mary lists are mopane, baobab, tamarind, sausage tree, strangler fig and *Acacia albida*. On the way back to Abercorn they saw an evening flight of termites, the winged females rising into the sky like flying ants and being taken in the air by a pennant-winged nightjar, a fiscal shrike and a bulbul.

*   *   *

Ever eager to see new country, Mary was quick to accept an invitation from Vesey to go to the Wembere Plain in Tanganyika about eighty miles north-east of Tabora. Vesey was going there on official business, the plain being one of the known breeding grounds of locusts. For Kathleen Stevens' sake it would be mainly a bird-watching safari, Vesey having promised birds in multitudes. They took the Sumbawanga road, then plunged down the zigzags into the Rukwa valley at Musé. In their camp next dawn they woke to the song of the morning warbler; and when they got to the edge of Lake Rukwa 'the birds were almost unbelievable, they were in such thousands'. Mary's diary lists flamingos, great white egrets, intermediate egrets, little egrets, glossy ibis, wattled crane, black-winged stilt, Egyptian goose, white-faced duck, Hottentot teal, African pochard and crested coot. There were also crowds of waders—marsh sandpipers, ruffs, little stints, Kittlitz's sand-plovers and Caspian plovers as well as a nesting colony of red-winged pratincoles.

They climbed out of the Rukwa rift north-east to Tabora and as they came near the Wembere Plain the country changed and became almost desert, for this is a low-rainfall region. No doubt the plain had once been rich in wild animals; for it is only sixty miles south of Serengeti. But now those which survived had to compete with ever increasing herds of cattle; and the whole place, according to Mary, was 'very much over-grazed'. Surviving wildlife included elephants and herds of the elegant little Thompson's gazelles. At one place they 'put up a cheetah who was asleep under a thorn bush. He moved away slowly, so we saw him well.' Up in a tree they spotted 'two bush babies asleep. They had big ears and long bushy tails . . . The plain stretches for many miles and in the hot sun there was a mirage which looked like a lake with trees on its edge.' Most noticeable birds on the dry plain were Kori bustards, secretary birds, Montagu's harriers, black-winged kites, two-banded coursers and various vultures, guinea-fowl and francolins. Among the savanna trees mentioned are various *Terminalia*, *Commifera*, baobabs and acacias, including patches of gall acacias whose conspicuous galls were crawling with the ants that lived inside them. Amongst trees and outcrops of huge rocks they saw a most colourful lizard—brown, lilac and azure.

The cattle herdsmen were also colourful:

> Several of them had the lobes of their ears enlarged and big rounds
> of wood fitted in. Others had the lobes stretched and cut and wore

long ear-rings and clips on top of the ear. Several were draped with long black clothes and all of them had necklaces and ivory and wire bracelets from wrist and elbow and also on the ankles.

Earlier Mary and Vesey had had trouble with tsetse flies. Now the problem was sweat-flies: 'There were some huge baobab trees and we had lunch under one. Vesey lit a fire of cow-dung to keep the sweat-flies off.' In the afternoon they reached Kitangiri, a lake some twenty miles long, lying below an escarpment. This was where Vesey had promised to show them birds and they were not disappointed: 'The birds on the shore were in thousands, principally white-faced duck, fulvous duck, red-billed duck and Hottentot teal. A line of flamingos behind. Numerous waders, pelicans, spur-wing geese, goliath heron . . .'—the list goes on. Eagles were nesting in the cliffs above the lake—the rare Verreaux's eagle, large and mostly black, and preying on the numerous hyraxes. About thirty miles beyond Lake Kitangiri is another, much bigger water, Eyasi, which Mary longed to get to. But Lake Kitangiri was to be their limit. When they tried to get round to the far end of it they found too much water in the long narrow channels that came out of the lake. 'Not seeing Lake Eyasi is a disappointment,' Mary wrote as they went back to Abercorn.

A month later (12 December 1960) she was off with Vesey yet again, this time back to the Mweru Wantipa. More and more she found she had to revisit old haunts in order to satisfy the Kew botanists' frequent requests for additional material—flowers, fruits, leaves, bark, etc.—of plants she had sent them previously. This was to be a safari of serious plant-collecting. Kathleen Stevens had now gone back to Wales and birds no longer filled Mary's diaries. But she did report one good bird in the Mweru Wantipa—the woolly-necked stork which is seldom seen in that area and was Mary's first. On 17 December they saw 37 in one group, far more than even Vesey had ever seen together. Though enormous rainstorms were almost everyday events on a safari at that season, this trip of December 1960 was one of the few that were washed out completely. As Mary reported:

Then on to Mporokoso and to the marsh near which we meant to camp; but thunder came up and an appalling deluge and it looked so bad we decided to make for home. Lucky we did, as we got into a belt of shocking weather—rain so violent it was almost impossible to see the road. This went on, storm after storm. The road was skiddy, so we had to go slow. Finally got to Senga Hill at dark.

*　　*　　*

In mid-January, 1961, Mary once again felt the call of Tanganyika's southernmost highlands. Reaching Mbeya on 16 January, she met John Procter for the first time though she had been in correspondence with him for the past four years. John was a government forestry officer and, like Vesey, an expert on plants, birds and mammals who was to go on many a safari with Mary during the next few years. Her first conversation with him, however, was not about nature but politics. Tanganyika had just become an independent state named Tanzania and, in John Procter's opinion, was 'going all right; but in a few years all Europeans will probably be replaced by Africans. Most of the white settlers are trying to sell their farms and all are very unsettled.'

From Mbeya, Mary and John Procter took the Tukuyu road southwards and made for Rungwe Mountain. On the way up, Mary noted: 'The whole place is quite altered—far more cultivation and much pyrethrum being grown.' It was inevitable. There are huge areas of Tanzania that offer little hope to agriculture; but up here on the plant-rich volcanic soils of Rungwe and the Elton Plateau the prospects were good for pyrethrum and other crops; for cattle, sheep and goats; and for plantations of fast-growing, exotic conifers like *Pinus patula* from Mexico. In the forested gorges on the flanks of Rungwe, Mary was anxious to refind a *Campanula* she had collected here before near a waterfall. Her diary reports: 'Dense forest and some bamboos. We found a great many ferns—fortunately with spores.' They battled through a wilderness of fallen trees and beds of stinging nettles:

> Ali went first and smashed a way. It was far rougher and denser than last time we were here. After about half an hour we saw the cliff and the waterfall. We went on getting ferns and there were aloes. We climbed up the left side of the waterfall. The Campanula was hardly in flower. It is much later this year.

But she managed to get some seed which Kew had asked for. They got ever more ferns and

154

a very sweet-smelling jasmine with trilobate leaves and large white flowers; a yellow umbellifer, a Carex, a large pink orchid, a good bramble, a large Chlorophytum—a handsome plant quite hopeless to dry well!—an Alchemilla, a Galium and two grasses. We sat and watched colobus monkeys with white collars and white tips to their tails. We had collected two vasculums packed full. There was a terrific thunderstorm and torrential rain. It only lasted about ¾ of an hour but everything was very wet and it was chilly. I went to bed, to keep warm, about 7.45!

Next day, October 21:

A lovely morning. Did not finish changing papers till 11 o'clock. We have eleven presses going and they do not dry quickly as it is so damp, late and early. Went down to the stream below the camp . . . Got back at 1.40 just as rain came on. It poured all afternoon while we pressed the plants. It cleared about 6 o'clock but it was damp and cold.

This weather went on and on. On 25 October Mary wrote:

> It began to rain and we hurried back to the car. It came down in torrents and we got soaked. It rained all the way back to camp and there we found it had rained even harder. For five hours it came down in torrents with thunder and lightning. Soon the whole place was flooded. The boys' tent leaked and they got very wet. Mhilu got the small primus stove lit and made some tea and I gave Ali an extra jersey and Mhilu my old coat. It got dark—Mhilu lit both Tilley lamps and the boys got into the back of the Land-Rover. It was a truly awful evening. Mhilu got me some corned beef and bread and butter and managed to get the fire going and made more tea. It rained on and on.

From Rungwe Mountain, John Procter having gone back to Mbeya, they ventured eastwards into what was new country for Mary. By yet another bad road they got through the highlands to the town of Njombe where Mhilu left them for a few days leave to see his family in Lushoto. Over the years Mary had become adept at taking advantage of the hospitality of the many mission stations of various churches scattered throughout central Africa, most numerous being those run by the Roman Catholic White Fathers. Without Mhilu to do the cooking, she managed very well next night by staying at the mission station at Milo high on a ridge above the eastern shore of Lake Nyasa, feeling perfectly at home when she found the place was run by a Welsh lady—Sister Pryce-Jones. From there she moved north to another mission at Madunda:

> The mission is right up against the foot of the Livingstone Mountains and is a huge place with a big church. One of the Fathers came out—they are Germans or German-Swiss and two Africans. I managed to speak some German and was given a very nice room and some excellent coffee.

Next day one of the White Fathers indicated a path up the hillside and provided Mary and Ali with a guide. So at last Mary set foot on the Livingstone Mountains she had so often seen from the mountains near Mbeya:

> It took ages to do the presses though I started before 6 a.m. We got off about 9.30, with a nice boy who carried a press. The cliffs towered above and I wondered how we should get up. We came to dense rain forest, the path steep and slippery. The forest got thicker, lovely ferns on rocks and tree trunks; and masses and masses of begonias with large orange flowers and big hairy leaves grew everywhere. And round a corner the whole sides of the path were a glorious mass of it, mingled with ferns. We at last came up to a ridge . . . there was a precipice below us and patches of forest. We got a lovely Commelina with three mauve petals and a bright-blue centre, a nice Eriosema, a sedge, and, under a big rock, a lovely Streptocarpus, pale-blue with deeper-blue centre. As we got back to the mission it began to pour with rain. Changed, and started on the plants—17 presses—and it took me all afternoon and evening to do the notes and pressing, Ali helping. Had an excellent supper, cooking German. I found I got on quite well in German. The Fathers are most cheerful and laugh and joke and certainly feed well! This is a lovely place, tucked under the mountains with glorious views.

*   *   *

As soon as she got back to Abercorn, Mary had to make a quick decision. Vesey met her with the news that he and his son Michael would be off in three days time for a very long excursion that

156

would take them to Nyasaland (Malawi), Mozambique, Southern Rhodesia (Zimbabwe) and then into Bechuanaland (Botswana); and Mary was invited to go with them. At first she declined. Such a trip would be too soon after her so recent safari; and, besides, she had commitments. In the end she found the temptation too much for her. When could she hope ever to get to Bechuanaland if not now? With frantic haste she got ready for the most ambitious safari she had so far undertaken.

They set off east on 15 February 1961, to Tunduma, then south to Fort Hill and Chisenga until in three days, stopping to collect all along the way, they arrived under the Nyika Plateau where Mary had last collected two years before with Edward Robinson. Never able to resist the lure of the Nyika (it has been described as 'a naturalists' paradise, one of the most beautiful places in southern Africa'), they turned left up into the hills, collecting indigoferas, balsams, commelinas, lilies, umbellifers, grasses, a deep-purple *Moraea* and, as usual, an exciting range of aloes and orchids—for by now aloes and orchids, along with bladderworts (*Utricularias*), were firmly established as being among Mary's specialities. When Vesey spotted molehills he dug deep in the hope of finding the golden mole that lives in the mountain forests of East Africa. But his luck was out; as it was next morning also when he got bitten by a scorpion. From the Nyika they got down to Lake Nyasa at Nkata Bay, seeing on the way a raiding party of Matabele ants crossing the road, intent, Vesey explained, on attacking a nest of termites, the only food they eat. At a nearby fishery research station they learnt about the remarkable number of fish that are found in Lake Nyasa and nowhere else in the world, just as Lake Tanganyika likewise has a wonderful population of endemic species. The fish were fascinating to watch in the clear water—'There were dozens, all small, many bright colours, iridescent blue, yellow, pale-blue and spotted.'

They continued southwards along the road that goes parallel with Lake Nyasa to Dezda: 'Endless bush and no flowers, a great deal of maize cultivation and many villages.' As they got near Dedza the scenery and wildflowers improved, the country became hilly and a skyline of rocky peaks built up as they followed the Mozambique border and reached the Shiré River, crossing it on a ferry. They camped that night at Zomba where Vesey called on his friend, Swynnerton, of the Agriculture Department. Next day they collected along the Shiré River where it flows through the Mpatwamanga Gorge:

We came out onto huge rocks; and the river, tumbling down the rapids, was a wonderful sight. But it must have upset Livingstone who was trying to get by boat to Lake Nyasa, as it meant considerable portage. It is the most lovely river and a glorious spot. We found heaps of interesting plants and shrubs—an Entada with big seed-pods, several Tephrosia, an Asclepias—in fact a vasculum full.

From there they got to Tete where Mary saw the Zambezi for the first time. At Tete:

We bought two large, straw-covered flagons of Portuguese red wine. Tete is one of the oldest Portuguese settlements—they have been here since the 16th century. We stopped by a tributary of the Zambezi. There was a very lovely orange Crotalaria.

And a colony of black-headed weavers were nesting in the riverside bushes. That night they camped on dry sand amid thickets of *Commiphora* trees and acacias near some huge baobabs.

From Tete in Mozambique, with no stops for collecting, they drove to Salisbury (Harare) in Southern Rhodesia (Zimbabwe), where they were hospitably received by several of Vesey's botanical friends who showed them round the fine herbarium there and took them to two spectacular aloe gardens. They also had a seventy mile trip to Mpakwe Mountain, a choice botanical site with several endemic species. Next day they left Salisbury on the Bulawayo road but soon ran into persistent heavy rain. They had planned to camp just short of Bulawayo but, in weather like that, camping was unthinkable. As they passed through Bulawayo the streets were running like rivers. By now it was dark and they were forced to spend a miserable night sleeping in their vehicles on the side of the road to Plumtree on the Bechuanaland (Botswana) border. It was still pouring next morning as they passed through the customs and into Bechuanaland:

The road to Francistown is very bad. It rained in showers. We stopped once and I collected some nice plants. Then got on to within half a mile of Francistown, turned left off the road, opposite a small hill, and found a nice place to camp. The rain held off for a short time and we got the tents up. The flowers are most exciting. We had a large lunch, then I collected and it took Ali and me all the remainder of the afternoon to press and name, as I hadn't done Sunday's lot. Still raining at night.

So they came to the famous region where the Okavango River which, like the Zambezi, is born in the rainy highlands of Angola, flows south-east to lose itself in the sands of the northern edge of the Kalahari semi-desert, spreading into a delta amid 6,500 square miles of shallow swamps—a flood plain rich in antelopes, buffaloes, zebras, giraffes, hippos and lions along with huge numbers of birds. West from Francistown they passed through many miles of mopane-acacia savanna scattered with low bushes of *Grewia* and *Combretum*, collecting many plants on the way until they crossed the Nata River which flows southwards into the Makarikari, an often swampy salt-pan covering a huge area. Driving deep into this saline land, they reached a shallow lake: 'It stretched for miles and I could see sand-dunes in the far distance. Across an arm of the lake were a big lot of flamingos feeding in the mud.' Other birds mentioned are chestnut-backed finch-lark, clapper lark, chestnut-banded plover, black-breasted snake-eagle, black-bellied bustard and vast flocks of waders, mostly ruffs. Six ostriches, the first she had ever seen in the wild, ran away at great speed. The only mammals of note were hartebeests. The plants were rewarding:

> We went across the causeway which crosses an arm of the Makarikari and on the other side stopped and collected Cleone diandra, a lovely plant with orange petals with a rich-purple mark at base and very linear leaves. With it was an Asclepias; and a semi-prostrate Abutilon with large, lemon-yellow flowers with rich, red-brown centre. After this we went on for some miles over an awful road—sandy, with huge ruts and holes, the country very bare and sandy, with low, scattered bushes and a few acacias. We climbed a slight bank and are camping under a tree looking onto the Pan—a vast and lovely view. A wonderful sunset.

They drove slowly west out of the Makarikari along a deeply rutted, sandy road and camped six miles short of Maun, their gateway to Okavango. This was a region from which wild animals were retreating before the advance of cattle-rearing, an advance only possible because of an endless battle against tsetse. When they inquired at Maun about how best to get into the Okavango Swamp they were advised to follow the roads made by the tsetse-fly controllers.

For several days they collected in sandy grassland under mopane trees, working their way round the south to the western side of Okavango. One day they had lunch under a baobab whose girth they measured at 66 feet. Though much of the going was over deep, dry sand, their vehicles got bogged down here and there in black, oozy mud. Animals were scarce, though they heard lions grunting and hyenas howling by night. They reached Tsau, a small trading centre, camping with difficulty because of heavy rain. Then they were off again along the tsetse trails, moving from dry grassland to park-like savanna, then to wet ground, collecting as they went. At a river choked with vegetation, Mary ventured on to a quaking mat of water plants: 'I fell in up to my waist but struggled on and got some *cyperaceae* and a few grasses for Vesey but it was very treacherous going.' The birds were good. They saw martial eagles, chanting goshawks, carmine bee-eaters and more ostriches. Crowned plovers and blacksmith plovers were noisy everywhere. And some of the birds were reminders of Europe—red-backed shrikes, Montagu's harriers, white storks, rollers and swallows. They came to a tsetse camp called Nokageng, half-way round Okavango from Maun and there they turned back. It was now, for the first time in her life, that Mary got seriously lost in the bush. When she woke on 22 March, her hay-fever was 'rather tiresome'. So when Vesey went off to look for locusts she spent a quiet morning with Ali, drying papers and changing presses. After lunch she wandered off looking for plants around camp. Nothing is easier than losing oneself in woodland that endlessly repeats itself.

> About 3.45 I decided to turn for camp but after a bit I found I had no idea where I was. I knew by the sun where the plain should be, so made in that direction and walked a very long way till I came to the plain, then had no idea in which direction camp was.

Eventually she met up with six men who took her on a long walk to one village, then to another, finally reaching camp at 6.45 p.m. Vesey, she found, was out looking for her in the opposite direction.

Returning round the south side of Okavango they chose a different track but it was no better than the one they had used before. It was hard to follow in the long grass and one of the Land-Rovers fell into a deep aardvark's hole which caused a long delay. But it was not a profitless day because, as well as finding some plants, Mary saw a new mammal: as they watched a colony of ground squirrels they spotted amongst them a mongoose-like animal which Vesey identified as a meerkat. Their goal, on this southern edge of Okavango, was the lake called Ngami. But Ngami is a shallow water that may dry up for years on end; and 1961 was one of those years. Not only was the lake dry, the trees were also dying. 'A weird-looking place,' was Mary's verdict, 'and in the dry season must look like a dead land.' But the local tribe greatly interested her:

> They wear—the women only—the same early Victorian clothes they were first dressed in by the German Lutherans in S.W. Africa. They revolted and the Germans tried to exterminate them and they fled here to Lake Ngami. They are fine, tall women and wear full skirts trailing the ground, shawls, and a kind of rush-cap head-dress.

In the store at Sehitwe village was a Bushman 'and I persuaded him to let me photograph him. He was short, very pale-skinned—pale coffee-colour.'

Withdrawing from Ngami along a road that was under water for long stretches, they got onto higher ground and camped in a woodland of *Acacia* and *Terminalia* trees. A thunderstorm raged all round but all they got was a shower. Next morning, Vesey having gone off to Maun to get petrol, Mary took the vasculum and went off alone to collect, Ali laughing and saying to her as she left: 'Don't get lost!' Yet that is just what she managed to do, for the second time in her life, and only three days after the first. This time, after wandering about for several hours, she managed to find her way back to camp unaided but very hot and thirsty. The only new bird that day was the stone curlew of southern Africa, the Cape dikkop, a 'thick-knee' Mary called it, using the name familiar in the days of her youth.

From the Makarikari Pan they made their way north-east towards the Rhodesian border at Panda Matenga on a much-flooded road through scrub and woodland, taking their time as there were many plants to collect. Though there was plenty of elephant dung they saw no elephants. What they did see were, for Mary, two new antelopes—Sharp's steinbok and southern oryx, or gemsbok. They left Bechuanaland at Panda Matenga, got on to a tarmac road and soon reached Livingstone where Mary got her first view of the Victoria Falls, first in sunlight, then even more beautifully by moonlight. Next day they were off on the 300 mile drive to Lusaka, then north to Abercorn by way of Kapiri Mposhi,

Serenje and Kasama, collecting in several places, including the Lunsemfwa River, some rocky hills near Serenje, Lake Lusiwasi, the Lwitikila River and finally the Chambeshi River, south of Kasama. So, after a safari of two months, Mary got back to Ndundu on 8 April, 1961, to find the house in good order, Mhilu having been left at home to look after things.

After two long journeys, one so close after the other, even Mary Richards felt a need to slow down for a while if only to cope with a huge pile of plants to be parcelled off to Kew, a task which took many days. With Vesey and Bill Morony she opened a bottle of champagne to celebrate that she had now sent Kew 15,000 specimens. She had a couple of strenuous walks on successive days, first up Sunzu Mountain, then up Kito Mountain, trips that left her with aching varicose veins. But soon she was off again with Vesey and Ali up the Kalambo River as far as the Sansia Falls: 'The river was in full flood and the falls a fine sight. I got a tiny, pale-blue *Utricularia* growing in crevices in the rocks.' That day Vesey, ever on the look-out for snakes, had a curious little experience that must have delighted him. Finding a bird's nest in a bush, he felt in it to see if there were any eggs. But what was curled up in that nest was a little twig snake which bit one of Vesey's fingers as it glided out. Luckily, for this is a poisonous snake, the bite did not penetrate the skin. After that excursion Mary spent a fortnight helping to run a girl-guides' camp at Abercorn. In June, John Procter came from Mbeya and was enormously helpful over the identification of the many species of *Brachystegia* trees.

CHAPTER FIFTEEN

It was now over a year since Mary had seen any of her family—her longest continuous spell in Africa so far. She flew back to England on 23 July and celebrated her 76th birthday (3 August 1961) by walking up the Beacon Hill at Haresfield, Gloucestershire, with her grandson, Mark. Meanwhile came disturbing news from Northern Rhodesia. Political unrest had been brewing for several years as the famous 'wind of change' blew ever more gale-like through Africa. Now came news of riots near Abercorn and of bridges destroyed near Kasama.

This time Mary was three months in the UK, dividing her time between Coed in Wales, Haresfield Court in Gloucestershire and Doddington Place in Kent, the homes of her three children. At Coed she found that Richard and Pam would be moving back to Caerynwch, no longer a hotel, as soon as it was ready; but at present it was being extensively repaired. She had a day out with Peter Benoit in a boat on Tal-y-llyn lake, looking for a hybrid water-lily; and as they ate their lunch by the inlet stream Mary got her first look at their joint *Contribution to a Flora of Merioneth* which Peter had completed in her absence in Africa. Her diary comment was: 'Peter has done it well and written a first-rate preface.' They ended the day with a quick look at Tynllidiart, her old cottage: 'No one there. Garden very neglected though the shrubs look well. Bog garden and rock garden a wilderness. Sad, but inevitable.' Very likely she came out with one of her favourite expressions for such occasions: '*Tout passe, tout lasse, tout casse.*'

After two days of gales and driving rain, she went with the family and bathed in the sea at Friog, though the water was still rough. On 23 September she was out with her Merioneth field society at Mochras. Twenty-five members came and it was a happy reunion. On the shore they saw redshanks, lapwings, a spotted redshank and a large flock of golden plovers. In the dunes they found that the rare angular Solomon's seal was spreading. She said farewell to Wales on 26 September: 'Very very sad on leaving Wales. Stopped at the top of the Pass for a last goodbye to Cader.'

163

She went first to Gloucestershire and Haresfield Court where she presented her grand-daughter, Juliette, with a copy of Bentham and Hooker's *British Flora*:

> She is quite keen—hope we may have another botanist in the family. Dined with the Peter Scotts. He has just come back from a wildlife conference at Arusha and was very interesting—also told us about his trip to the Galapagos Islands and showed us his notebooks, such lovely drawings—a most thrilling evening.

She ended her UK visit in Kent, staying with Jonnet and Jack at Doddington and seeing many old friends. She also consulted a doctor about turns of giddiness she had been experiencing. After a blood test he pronounced her fit, saying the giddiness was a result of the fall she had at the Mweru Wantipa waterfall the previous December. So, relieved of anxiety, she said goodbye to everyone and to a Kentish landscape painted with autumn colours and flew back to Africa on 1 November 1961.

* * *

Kathleen Stevens soon joined her at Abercorn and off they went on their travels. First they had a few days at the Mweru Wantipa, getting plants that Kew had asked for. On that trip 'a wood full of red-hot pokers' was a memorable sight. Next they went off with Vesey and his son, Michael, to Mbeya in Tanzania where they joined up with John Procter, the plan being to collect in some mountains near Iringa. It was a safari doomed to failure. With difficulty they negotiated dreadful roads across the Buhoro Flats above the headwaters of the Great Ruaha River. Then the mountainous part of the trip turned into a near disaster because of their vehicles getting endlessly stuck in swamps or suffering from engine trouble and punctures. But they did manage one good day when on 15 October they walked to the top of Image Mountain near Iringa: 'The forest, very wet and steamy, was full of good plants and some huge trees.' At the end of the whole safari Mary put as brave a face on it as she could:

> Finally got to Mbeya at dusk. Stayed at John's house. Finished the evening with Tchaikovsky's 5th Symphony, Bach's Brandenberg Concerto and an excellent dinner. It has been a very unfortunate safari—so much has gone wrong, but we all enjoyed it.

Whether she would have been so cheerful without the Tchaikovsky, the Bach and the excellent dinner is a matter for speculation.

She did not know it then but in fact that difficult journey across the Buhoro Flats in December, 1961, had in it an element of triumph. While Vesey and Ali were struggling with a Land-Rover and trailer stuck deep in mud, Mary and Kathleen had gone off collecting:

> We came to more open woodland with spaces of grassland. Here grew thousands of a lovely aloe in flower—rather sparsely flowered, single heads and narrow, unmarked leaves. We stopped and collected and overhead flew hobbies (at least 70-100) hawking flying ants.

That vermilion-coloured aloe eventually proved to be new to science and was named *Aloe richardsiae* by the aloe expert, G.W. Reynolds. In *The Journal of South African Botany* for April, 1964, Reynolds was to write:

> Our very distinctive new species is named after Mrs H.M. Richards who is one of the most outstanding collectors there has ever been in Tropical Africa. She started collecting in 1951 (at an age when most men had already retired), and in the following 12 years has collected over 1,800 gatherings, many from places hitherto unknown botanically, mostly in the backwoods of Northern Rhodesia and Tanganyika.

Mary and Kathleen, having spent Christmas Day, 1961, with Hope and Marian Gamwell at Chilongolwelo, were soon off again, this time to the North Rukwa Plain because Kathleen just had to see the animals and the birds again. Also in the party were Vesey, Michael and Edward Robinson. Down on the Rukwa Plain they found all the animals they had hoped for; and on the escarpment, at Lake Katavi, all the birds. Amongst the rocks high above the Rukwa, they celebrated New Year's Eve with a huge camp fire, a bottle of champagne and the singing of Auld Lang Syne. In the first three days of 1962, despite heavy rainstorms and getting lost in mountain mists, Mary collected a great many plants. The only mishap was when Edward Robinson was driven from his bed at 4.30 a.m. by an invasion of driver ants. In her diary Mary summed up their homecoming:

We got to the customs post. The Lumi River bridge was nearly washed away but we just got over. The old Sumbawanga road is very bad. Got in at 6 o'clock. It's been a good safari but very wet.

After Kathleen Stevens had gone back to Wales in mid-March, Abercorn had such rains as Mary had never before experienced. Day after day her garden was strafed by unbelievably heavy downpours and the drive up to the house was turned into a ravine. Lake Tanganyika was three feet above normal level and down in the Rukwa those rains were to change the scene on a big scale. When Mary had first seen North Rukwa in 1954 it was a far-extending plain with local swamps and pools. But in the last two or three years it had been getting ever wetter and forming a central lake. By 1962 that lake had spread hugely and now people spoke not of North Rukwa Plain but of North Rukwa Lake, a water sixty miles long and sixteen across, a lake with no outlet but with swollen streams flowing into it from escarpments east and west. It was a lake with a long future and Mary would never again see Rukwa as a great plain. Meanwhile the rains continued at Abercorn and on 3 April Mary noted despairingly: 'All botanical work held up by bad weather and impassable roads.' The downpours and cloudbursts did not ease off until well into May, by which time Mary was planning an ambitious safari with Edward Robinson.

They set off, with Ali and Mhilu, on 1 June 1962, for Nyasaland and in particular Mlanje (or Mulanje), the spectacular block of mountains which, encircled by precipices, rise in isolation to 10,000 feet and cover nearly 200 square miles of country. Mlanje had long been known for its magnificent cedars (not related to the northern hemisphere cedars) called *Widdringtonia whytii*. Found wild only on Mlanje and neighbouring uplands, this cedar can attain a huge size but had been much exploited in the past and had also suffered greatly from bush fires. Probably its forests once covered Mlanje extensively but by the time Mary Richards got there they had long been reduced to small relict patches in ravines and sheltered hollows. Not that these cedars were what had attracted her to Mlanje. Like many others she had been thrilled by Laurens Van der Post's book, *Journey into the Interior*, in which Mlanje was described in the most vivid terms.

As there was no road up Mlanje they had to hire nineteen porters to carry all their gear, including beds and bedding, up the formidable first 4,000 feet:

The path got steeper and we went through wet woodland and then along a wide path on the mountainside. The views were wonderful—the great precipices and the plain below and in the distance Zomba Mountain. Then through more woodland. I had already collected a lot of plants and we stopped at 1.45 and had bananas and bread and butter. Finally we got on to open mountainside—again wonderful views—and had a long climb to the top of the ridge. I must say it is one of the hardest climbs I have done and my legs ached. On the top of the ridge we looked across at Main Peak but there was cloud. We went up and down past gullies and streams and finally came to the Lichenya hut on the edge of the forest with Mlanje cedars and planted conifers.

The rugged terrain all round reminded her of 'the slopes of Cader Idris by Llyn Cau—precipices and flat rocks, worn and scratched but not by glacial action.' Mary was delighted to discover that the most spectacular plant on Mlanje was an aloe: reaching a ridge at 7,000 feet they found that

the whole mountainside was covered with Aloe mawii, a wonderful sight, hundreds of them, with their great hanging or rather bent-over spikes of carmine-orange flowers. The helichrysums are coming out and are a glorious sight—orange and yellow. We walked along the top of the ridge till we could see Chiperone Mountain in Portuguese East Africa—this is where the bad weather comes from.

Next day, 7 June, the weather being good, they got to the top of Cilemba, one of the lesser peaks (7,741 feet):

The view at the top was wonderful—the huge precipices below us and the wide plain. There are many proteas, but not out. A small shrubby pea, *Aeschynomene*, which is all over Mlanje, has a delicious scent. Ali and I started down and got a *Dierama*. I should like to be up here in December, the plants must be most interesting.'

Edward got up early next morning to tackle Main Peak (9,843 feet) but this was not for Mary: 'Edward walks far faster than I do now and also the mountain is very precipitous.' In the event Edward did not make it either. He missed the path and got lost amongst a chaos of huge boulders deep in vegetation. But he did find magnificent aloes, seven or eight feet tall with orange-red flowers; and also saw the tree-lily *Vellosia splendens*, covered with its very aromatic, white flowers. 11 June was also a day to remember for rocks and aloes:

> Through the glasses we could see aloes above us. The ground got steep and the rocks larger—a tumble of rocks with streams underground and huge holes and crevices. We came on our first aloe, height about 3-4 feet, with lovely carmine flowers. Above the masses of rock we saw bigger ones. On we scrambled, Ali hauling me up the worst places.

On the same hillside they found huge tree heathers and tree ferns along with small ferns, orchids, utricularias and lobelias.

For a last look at Mlanje they went round to the south side, making their way through miles of tea plantations up to a camp site on the bank of the Great Ruo River where it emerges from

> a narrow gorge with high mountain peaks each side. The gorge is very wet, they have 180 inches of rain in a year. The forest is magnificent—enormous trees—*Brachystegia spiciformis* and many strangler trees. There is a lovely mauve convolvulus climbing over the shrubs.

They got three miles up through the gorge-side forest, following a path to a hydro-electric reservoir. All the way, plants, especially labiates, were many. They could hear plenty of birds in the dense vegetation but saw very few. As it was mid-winter it was very cold at night ('I am in my tent with a Tilley lamp trying to keep warm!') and they were relieved to get out of the gorge after a couple of days and accept the hospitality of the tea-planters on whose land they were camping. Travelling back to Abercorn, Mary was well pleased with the haul of plants she and Ali had made. Yet on the whole, had Mlanje quite come up to her expectations? One remark of hers about Van der Post's book may be significant: '*Journey into the Interior* is very exaggerated.'

*　　　*　　　*

On 28 July, 1962, Mary flew back to Britain for a couple of months and, as always, went first to stay with Jonnet and Jack in Kent. From there she went into London to meet up with old friends like Freda Davies and Margo Masters and she spent a useful few hours on her 77th birthday at the herbarium of the

Natural History Museum talking to Dr Edmund Launert who had used some of her specimens in his recent monograph on the begonias. He urged her to go and collect in Mwinilunga, the high-placed region near the source of the Zambezi in the north-western part of Northern Rhodesia. From London as usual she went to Kate's in Gloucestershire where she found 'the family well, quite absorbed in ponies!' While there she made contact with a fellow Africa botanist, Lord Methuen of Corsham in Wiltshire:

> Motored to Corsham, lunch with Lord Methuen. He has been collecting at Mtali, Southern Rhodesia and got a lot of crinums and epiphytic orchids. We had a most interesting afternoon. He has been successful in bringing things home and getting things from seed. The large crinums he sent by sea in tea chests. Epiphytes by air. I have promised to send him orchids, crinums and liliaceous bulbs. Also saw his glorious pictures, a lovely Fra Filippo Lippi among them.

Returning to Kent she went on with the social round, gave a talk on Africa to a British Legion group and much enjoyed visits to the gardens at Wisley and Windsor Great Park. She had long sessions at Kew where she was given a list of plants they wanted. And, like the Natural History Museum, Kew thought Mwinilunga would be a rewarding place to go. They also suggested the Mtwara region on the coast of Tanzania. Then she drove across to Wales, arriving in time for tea at Caerynwch where she was delighted to see all the many alterations that had been made to the house, now that it had ceased to be a hotel: 'It is wonderful to be home again—twenty years since I left and neary thirty since the house was in order.' She visited several of her old botanical haunts and was pleased to find the long-leaved sundew (*Drosera intermedia*) 'still in considerable quantities' in a bog by one of the Cregennan Lakes. In Cardiganshire she was shown forked spleenwort growing in masses on lead-mine ruins. On 2 September she went to a BSBI meeting at Bangor where she was the guest of Professor Paul Richards and his wife. Among the lectures, she especially enjoyed hearing R.H. Roberts on marsh orchids. Next day they were shown a colony of marsh gentians in Anglesey and also grass of Parnassus which Mary had previously seen only in Shetland.

*   *   *

Mary flew back to Africa on 9 October, 1962, and was met at Abercorn by Bill Morony and Marian Gamwell. By 1 November, she was off with Ali and Mhilu to the wilds of Mwinilunga as Kew had requested. Edgar Milne-Redhead had collected extensively in Mwinilunga in the mid 1930s but there was still plenty to be done in that remote corner of Northern Rhodesia (Zambia) which in both its flora and its fauna has some affinities with the rain-forests of the Congo, distant though they are. Mwinilunga is over 500 miles from Abercorn as the crow flies; but as the road went, via Ndola and Kitwe, it was vastly more. From Kitwe they pressed on north-west to Solwezi where they caught up with two Canadian botanists, Walter Lewis and Sam White, whom Mary had met in Abercorn. At Solwezi she was made welcome by the local forest officer, Wilf Holmes, and his wife, Dora. Wilf Holmes, an expert on orchids, was able to give Mary valuable advice about the best places to make for. For three weeks they explored the Mwinilunga district, even crossing into Angola and collecting there for a day until Mary remembered that Angola was not covered by the *Flora Zambesiaca*! They also made a brief sortie north into Katanga in the Congo. But most of the time they did not stray far, camping in delightful woodland by some rapids on the Zambezi River. It was a strange countryside: vast areas of flattish rocks reaching between the trees and around marshes and open grasslands with plenty of variety in the flora. The usual sudden downpours gave them many a soaking; but it was also very hot, enabling them to dry out quickly between the storms. Many genera of plants are mentioned in the daily record. Orchids were everywhere and at one place were 'a wonderful sight—hundreds of a white *Habenaria* with long spurs, quantities of a lovely vermilion orchid and some of a bluish-purple orchid.' The same day they saw a stream covered by a mixture of blue and yellow water-lilies. In rocky places, aloes were a feature:

> Left the Land-Rover on the side of the road and went up the rocks—flat granite with huge boulders. Masses and masses of aloes—two kinds, one with brownish, much-marked leaves, and a larger aloe with much greyer leaves and faint markings.

When they got back to Solwezi, Wilf Holmes was able to name nearly all the orchids that were new to Mary—a good end to a very succesful safari. In her diary of 25 November, Dora Holmes noted: 'Wilf and Mrs Richards orchidised. Her energy and memory are really amazing and we enjoyed her visit.' They got back to Abercorn on 29 November, after just a month away, Ali having driven something like 2,000 miles.

In a letter in December, 1962, Mary mentions a mysterious bird called a pitta, a brilliant, multicoloured, thrush-sized bird of secretive habits feeding on the ground in dense woodland. Living in a world of shadows, it would hardly be known to anyone were it not a nocturnal migrant which, often around Christmas in Zambia, comes to grief by crashing into lighted windows. Abercorn was a well-known place for such pitta accidents and Mary's letter mentions that 'we are having a pitta invasion'.

In December, 1962, and again in January, 1963, Mary went on two short visits to the Mbeya-Iringa district. In December the main object was to get more specimens of the new aloe she and Kathleen Stevens had found twelve months before and which were needed by Dr Reynolds in South Africa. With John Procter she soon found the aloe in great quantity but the season was six weeks later than in the previous December and flowering had only just begun. From there they continued east to Iringa and a marvellous wilderness which, a year later, became the Ruaha National Park. Among the animals they saw were hippos, elephants, zebra, crocodiles, greater kudu (a speciality of the area), impala, dikdik and a small, graceful antelope new to Mary, an oribi. She went back to Mbeya on Friday, 25 January, for a long weekend, collecting with John Procter in the evergreen rain-forest on Rungwe Mountain. Mary got plants galore but, as always when she was with John Procter, the emphasis was on trees: 'I hope I learned a lot of trees and shrubs. John is most inspiring.'

Mary's last long journey of the 1962-3 collecting season was, as Kew had suggested, to Mtwara on the far-away coast of Tanzania. She left Abercorn on 25 February, 1963, with Ali and Mhilu, their route being via Mbeya, Njombe, Songea, Tunduru, Masasi and Newala. As ever, Mary and Ali collected plants all along the way. But the road was bad:

> Deep valleys, road twisting and turning, surface cut up and wet and skiddy. I was scared and got out and walked the worst places, collecting a number of plants. I was very glad when we finally got down and the road was dry.

Beyond Tunduru they 'came to fascinating country with huge, round, humpy hills with precipitous sides. Stopped in a narrow gorge between two of these hills for lunch and collected.'

On 5 September they reached Mtwara where they had an introduction, arranged by Kew, to Dr R.L. Markham who proved most helpful. He and his family lived close to the sea near the extensive harbour which, Mary notes in her diary, 'was to have been a large port for the ground-nuts scheme'. Alas, the Mtwara district turned out to be botanically disappointing. Mary explored the nearby north bank of the Ruvuma River, the adjacent parts of the coast and several off-shore islands but found little of interest, the only excitement being when Dr Markham's dhow got stranded on a sandbank by the receding tide and they did not make land until 1.15 a.m. Happily it was a windstill, moonlit night.

Mary did not enjoy the hot and steamy coastal climate. She developed 'a vile cold' which quickly went to her chest and, worse still, having lost her hat at sea, she got her face, especially around the mouth, badly sunburnt. The plants continued to disappoint: though she prospected inland from Mtwara for thirty miles, 'there was nothing of interest'. Next day, to combat her cold, she swam in the sea and saw wonderfully coloured corals and coral fish. Then she lazed on the shore and watched red-backed shrikes and lilac-breasted rollers on the telegraph wires. The following day was better botanically. Just outside Mtwara she did well in a coastal marsh, collected her first mangrove specimens and noted that 'the shrubs and trees are most interesting. I got two *Loranthaceae*. My cold is still tiresome and my sunburn very sore.'

When they finally left Mtwara on 16 February they were soon in trouble with broken springs on the very rough road to Masasi. Then just over half-way from Masasi to Tundura:

> We found a stream and a flat place to camp, just short of a gorge where the road goes between huge rocks, and we were just going to turn the car in when an African stopped us and said no one stopped there at night as lions come there to drink. He told us to go on through the gorge and camp beyond.

So they discovered the best collecting spot of the whole trip, a weird landscape of wild, precipitous hills that had impressed them on their way to the coast a fortnight before. They camped near a tall rock called Namakambili and a charming young boy from a nearby village offered his services as guide. Named Ali, he was immediately called Ali Toto (Ali Junior) to distinguish him from the other Ali. When they found an outstandingly beautiful blue water-lily in a sluggish stream it was Ali Toto who collected it for them. On the rocks they got many other plants—gladioli, sedges, peas and unknown trees. A mystery plant was an aloe that looked exactly like the very distinctive *Aloe mawii* which Mary had thought peculiar to Mlanje Mountain. For several days they botanised in this strange, semi-wilderness land of huge rocks rising out of woodland, Ali Toto always with them. Here and there impenetrable jungles of long grass defeated them; and every evening flies in huge numbers crawled over them and their food.

They returned via Tunduru and Songea where Mary observed how few Europeans were left now that Tanzania had achieved independence. She had been dreading the road over the mountains between Songea and Njombe but in the event, 'We were lucky. After two days dry, the escarpment was quite good; but it's a very rough, steep road.' And so back to Abercorn on 28 March, 1963, after an odyssey of over 1,500 miles.

April and May she spent quietly. There was a cheerful evening on 17 April at the Lake View Hotel, when she dined with Bill Morony, Vesey, Freda Davies and Marian and Hope Gamwell to celebrate the collecting of her 18,000th plant. Now in charge of the Red Cross in Abercorn, she had meetings to attend and a Red Cross market and dance to organise. And she had a good day's birdwatching at the Uningi Pans, seeing crested coots, a lesser lily-trotter, African pochards, white-backed ducks, egrets of three sizes, African marsh harrier, glossy ibis, hammerkop, dabchicks, palm-nut vulture and squacco heron. A few days later, after putting Ndundu house and garden in order, she flew to London, arriving 18 May 1963.

CHAPTER SIXTEEN

This time Mary was in the UK for ten weeks only, which was fortunate because the summer of 1963 was not up to much. She faced the cold and the rain as well as she could as she travelled round the south of England seeing many relatives and a few old friends including Florence Bristow and Sophie Blathwayt, both of whom she had known for 63 years since their school days in Belgium. As usual she had several days at Kew Herbarium, met various botanists and noted their requirements. She even tried to get some travelling expenses out of the Director, Sir George Taylor, 'but he was not very co-operative!' (She did get some expenses eventually.) Sir George was always most polite and sometimes very complimentary, as when, for instance, he had written in 1961:

> I feel that this may be an appropriate occasion both to congratulate you on the outstandingly high quality and interest of the collections that you have made for us during the past several years . . . I think it is safe to say that your collections are among the largest and scientifically most important that have ever been made in tropical Africa.

Such comments no doubt went down well with Mary Richards who by now was probably beginning to see herself as following in the footsteps of great men like Ludlow and Sherriff who had also collected for Sir George.

She went to Wales, staying at Caerynwch where she enjoyed a big party

> of all the tenants, their wives and children and anyone who had been at Caerynwch in Harry's and my day. 70 people. A huge tea in the dining-room, then songs in English and Welsh. John Price, Fron Oleu, spoke and said some poetry.

She also had a happy day among the orchids of Morfa Harlech. Tynllidiart garden she found to be still in a state of neglect, but she cheered herself up by finding many marsh and spotted orchids in the nearby fields and two specimens of small white orchid in the lane. On 3 August, 1963, she spent her 78th birthday with Kate at Haresfield, Gloucestershire. Then on 22 August she flew back to Ndola where she found Ali and Mhilu waiting for her at her hotel, having driven the 500 miles from Abercorn in the Land-Rover.

At Ndundu she found that 'bush bucks have played havoc with the garden, eating hollyhocks, carnations and amaryllis. We are a game reserve!' Amongst other wildlife in the garden were paradise flycatchers nesting in a gum tree behind the house; black and yellow caterpillars devouring her crotalarias; and a death's-head hawkmoth which was a new record for the garden. Toads (*Bufo regularis*) croaked loudly all night. Five miles away at Abercorn, Mary had a good afternoon's birdwatching from Vesey's boat on Lake Chila, seeing little stints, curlew sandpipers, greenshanks, rufous-breasted herons, cape wagtails and hobbies. A black-winged kite hovered overhead like a kestrel.

Ever fascinated by the Rukwa Valley, Mary was off there again with Vesey in mid-October, 1963, one of the attractions this time being an albino giraffe that had been reported. It was by a great stroke of luck that they chanced upon this striking, pure-white animal on their first day. They stayed in the locust-control houses now sadly deserted because locust-spotting was now done mainly from the air. The flooding had dispersed many of the game animals but had attracted huge numbers of birds, among them migrant flocks of lesser kestrels which Mary had not met with before. A striking plant was *Ipomoea aquatica* growing in half-dried mud on long, creeping stems, its flowers large and mauve. Eastwards they reached the Rungwa River whose banks were scattered with *Hyphaene* palms and magnificent acacias and fig-trees along with bushes of a small blue *Vernonia* covered with white butterflies.

During their month on the plain, or what was left of it, they saw two herds of buffaloes totalling about a thousand and an estimated five hundred zebras. But there was little sign of the thousands of topi of a few years before. As Mary said, it was 'all very sad—I can't see the plain returning to normal for years'. By now they had moved south to the narrow waist between the two Rukwa lakes. Here they inspected the massed burrows of porcupines and wild dogs and saw an eight-foot mamba disappear into one of them. On the plain they sighted a freakishly marked zebra with spots instead of stripes. Waterside birds were in great numbers—flamingos, herons of all kinds, ducks, geese, spoonbills, waders, ibises, egrets, pelicans, cranes, eagles, harriers, secretary birds, kites, vultures—'the most I have seen in one place', Mary wrote. A marvel in the lakeside trees was the nest of a pair of white-crowned shrikes. Tightly bound with silvery spiders' webs, it was skilfully woven on to a pliant acacia twig, evidently to place it out of reach of tree-climbing snakes (the Latin name of this shrike is *anguitimens*—'snake-fearing').

On the way back from the Rukwa, having climbed the escarpment hairpins with much boiling of radiators, they spent the night on the edge of the Mbisi Forest, camping where they could see and hear red colobus monkeys. 'Vesey took us up to the high point where you see the Rukwa. We could see the places we had been to. The whole place is a vast lake.' And far away, through binoculars, a small white blob at the north end of the lake was, Vesey explained, a large nesting colony of pelicans over which he had recently flown in the course of searching for locusts.

Mary's next safari, a fortnight later, took her to a new part of the Rukwa Valley. Picking up John Procter at Mbeya, she went north up the escarpment and over to Chunya in the Lupa goldfield, and so got to South Lake Rukwa for the first time. They stayed at the Outspan Hotel which offered simple accommodation for visitors bringing their own food. When built in the 1930s, the hotel had been well away from the lake but now the water was almost to its doors and still rising. A fringe of dead trees, including a huge old baobab, stood out in the lake, marking where the shore had been. South Rukwa Lake, Mary discovered, was completely different from North Rukwa Lake. The north lake was margined by plains, swamps and flooded woodlands; but this south lake was close under the steep, tree-covered cliffs of the escarpment.

With John Procter's help, she collected flowers, fruits and foliage of various acacias and other trees. Along the lakeside were plenty of hippos but no crocodiles. Yet a description of the place, written 27 years before by Kate Bartam and Janet Trant, had said:

> the beach was absolutely covered with crocodiles, so thickly they were lying on top of one another and as we came near they all clambered into the water—a tidal wave of crocodiles—some of them must have been quite eighteen feet long.

But by the time Mary Richards got there in 1963, all those crocodiles had been turned into ladies' handbags and other

176

commodities. On their last night a majestic thunderstorm raged for hours, bringing high winds that caused waves to break up the hotel lawn, leaving the front steps piled up with water lettuce (*Pistia stratiotes*). The storm was a clear warning of what must happen to the Outspan Hotel if the lake went on rising. And not long afterwards it was abandoned to the waves. Perhaps not for centuries had water levels been so high, killing ancient baobabs.

Mary got back to Abercorn in mid-December just in time to receive a consignment of garden plants from Hilliers of Winchester. On New Year's Day, 1964, she was on Lake Tanganyika in the trimaran *Triton* with Vesey and others, collecting plants along the lakeside. They also went birdwatching by motor-boat up the Lufubu River which flows into the south-west corner of the lake. For the first two miles the wide river was edged by twelve-foot walls of papyrus whose great mop-heads closed in their world completely. Beyond the papyrus zone they got another eight miles upstream, almost to where, Vesey said, rapids would have blocked further progress. It was a day full of pied and malachite kingfishers, white-fronted bee-eaters, ospreys, crested and bateleur eagles, herons and darters, and large flocks of bright-yellow weavers and dazzling blue glossy starlings. On 18 February Mary celebrated her 19,000th specimen at the Lake View Hotel with her three oldest Abercorn friends, Freda Davies and Marian and Hope Gamwell. She drank to Freda's health for first suggesting she should come to Africa; to Marian's for inviting her; and to Hope's for launching her on collecting African plants.

*   *   *

Mary flew to London on 13 March, 1964, staying as usual with Jack and Jonnet in Kent. She was driven to Wales by Jonnet; went to the Grand National at Aintree but did not back a winner; returned to London in April to see an optician about a cataract on her right eye; went to an exhibition of ultra-modern pictures at the Tate Gallery: 'They are extraordinary and to me completely incomprehensible. Then up to see the Turners—lovely and such a relief.' She got her bad knee examined and was given an injection for it. She had two days at Kew, talking to E. Milne-Redhead, P. Taylor, J.P.M. Brenan, J. Gillett, W.D. Clayton, C. Jeffrey, R.M. Polhill and Mary Grierson. She was pleased to see some of her aloes flourishing there and was delighted to learn that Ali Omari was to have an *Indigofera* named after him. From Kew she was taken by car through the Sussex countryside into Hampshire, ending up at Selborne. She loved Gilbert White's old church and his memorial window depicting birds.

While in Kent she received terrible news from Vesey in Abercorn: Ali Omari had been found dead by his bicycle on the roadside near Vesey's house. He had died of a stroke. Mary's diary comment was brief: 'It is a terrible shock. He was a faithful servant and a dear friend. I can never replace him.' And she never did. Ali had collected and pressed plants with her for eight years. But he was far more than just a plant-collector. He was the hero of countless miles of accident-free driving on awful roads and across trackless plains and mountains, often in appalling weather; of endless rescues of their vehicles from floods and swamps; of fording streams on makeshift bridges; of an uncountable number of running repairs to failing engines, broken springs and bursting tyres; of finding camp sites and setting up tents, sometimes in the dark or in torrential rain—all accomplished with calm efficiency. He was a very rare character and he made a huge contribution to Mary's success from 1956 to 1964. She had only one thought with which to console herself a little—Ali had been very happy, a few days before he died, to be told by Vesey about the plant named after him—*Indigofera omariana*.

She drove to Wales from Kent on 9 July. It was rhododendron time. 'The rhodos on the hillside at Dinas Mawddwy are a glorious sight—ponticums—all shades of mauve.' Next day she botanised on Tir Stent with Kathleen Stevens, revelling in globeflowers, butterworts and orchids. Mary Grierson came up from Kew and they had a good day at Morfa Harlech: 'The *Orchis purpurella* were enormous—magnificent spikes of flowers and huge leaves—and numerous hybrids with *O. ericetorum* and *praetermissa*.' Three other lady botanists—Ursula Duncan, Miss Leather and Miss Beattie—came one day and in very hush-hush circumstances were shown Killarney fern behind a Merioneth waterfall.

18 July 1964, was a red-letter day on which Mary was made an honorary M.Sc. by the University of Wales at Bangor, a ceremony for which she had to wear a gown of 'gold and green shot-silk and a mortar-board which did not fit very well'. (It had to be stuffed with a copy of *The Times* because her head was so small.) She was presented for her degree by Emeritus Professor of Botany, Lily Newton. All the family were there; and Edgar Milne-

178

Redhead and Peter Taylor came up from Kew. So, after 64 years, she got the botany degree to which she had aspired when trying to enter Birmingham University in 1900. Maybe she also remembered what a long way she had come from being the little girl who once picked flowers along the Lichfield lanes with Fraulein Wahl.

*   *   *

Returning to Africa on 24 July, she was met at Abercorn airfield by Bill Morony and Vesey. At Ndundu the garden was full of flowers and her pets too were flourishing—Mwarka, her ridge-back dog; Desmond, her giant rat (named after Vesey); and her several tortoises. She spent her 79th birthday packing to go to the Rukwa yet again. John Beesley happened to be in Abercorn just then and she had a day's birdwatching with him at Kalambo Falls, seeing a Verreaux's eagle which they looked down on as it flew out over the gorge mobbed by two augur buzzards and a peregrine. Also in the cliffs were mottled swifts, rock martins and red-winged starlings. Mary now had a new driver to replace Ali. This was Sam who came from a village near Abercorn and had been one of Vesey's drivers in the locust service. Sam's first safari with Mary proved to be a testing one: they went down into the North Rukwa Valley but after only three days had to call it off because the ever rising lake had advanced yet another mile towards the foot of the western escarpment, flooding the road in too many places.

Mary came back to Abercorn and depressing news. Like so many other settlers, the Gamwell sisters were selling up and leaving Africa. Their departure was understandable. For long years they had enjoyed their Arcadia under the escarpment—their splendid farm, their lovely English garden and their army of employees. But now they were getting too old to cope. Above all, the country was about to achieve independence, bringing an end to the long years of white dominance. It was too big a change for dyed-in-the-wool colonialists like the Gamwells. They stood for a way of life surrounded by uniformed servants who served them tea on impeccable silverware. They had had a wonderful run in old colonial Africa and now it was time for them to go. Their farewell party took place at the Lake View Hotel on 25 August and an era came to an end, leaving Mary wondering what would happen next, especially when Vesey announced that he too would soon be on the move because he was leaving the locust-control service, having been offered a post as a scientific officer in the Tanzania game department based in Arusha.

So now Vesey was off to Arusha to find out what the job would entail; and as he would be visiting famous game parks, he invited Mary to go too. They set off on 29 August for Mbeya and Iringa then north to Dodoma, reaching Arusha after a journey of 700 miles. They took two vehicles, Sam driving Mary's Land-Rover, Mary collecting plants wherever they stopped for lunch or camping.

At Arusha, Vesey went to see the man who had offered him the post, John Owen, head of the game department. Then Mary and Vesey drove into the nearby uplands that are dominated by Mount Meru on whose slopes is the Arusha National Park where Vesey would be living in a house not yet completed. On African standards this was a small park of 50 square miles with comparatively few visitors but with a huge variety of habitats. Its lowest levels are at 5,000 feet and from there the ground rises through mountain forests to the 3,000 feet cliffs that lie under the summit. Mount Meru is a dormant volcano, having erupted within the last hundred years. But its most sensational eruption is of very long ago when an almighty explosion blew many thousands of feet off the summit, creating a vast caldera. Ten miles away and several thousand feet below, is a special feature of this upland park, the Ngurdoto Crater, which is, in fact, a miniature caldera containing a tree-scattered, partly marshy plain a mile across and complelely encircled by a high, forest-clothed escarpment. The world first heard of Ngurdoto Crater in 1958 when Princess Margaret of Britain looked down on its herds of buffaloes, elephants, giraffes and water bucks from the escarpment a thousand feet above. Two years later the Ngurdoto National Park was created. Then in 1967, when the area was much enlarged by the addition of Mount Meru, the name was changed to Arusha National Park.

On their first visit Vesey and Mary had time for only a brief look at Ngurdoto Crater and the cluster of soda-rich Momela Lakes near one of which Vesey's new house was being built. Next day they were off to the next park, Lake Manyara, where waterside birds were abundant and there were groups of impala and giraffes. At one place grazing elephants blocked the road and showed no sign of moving, and Mary was very amused when the game-scout riding in their Land-Rover 'got out, blew a small whistle and waved to the elephants who walked off'. Manyara was famous for lions that climb trees to escape the flies and it was no surprise when the scout 'pointed out three lions resting up trees, two in one, one in another. They were spread out on a large branch, their paws and tails hanging down. We got almost under the tree and they took no notice at all.'

From Manyara they went to the world-famous Ngorongoro Crater with all its mammals and birds. The plain was covered with wildebeest and zebras and a hyena ran in front of them along the track for about half a mile. Sam said: 'No need for a guide when we have a hyena to lead us!' They camped in an official site at Seronera, the Serengeti headquarters, where they were told to keep lamps burning outside their tents because of lions. 'Went to bed early,' reports Mary's diary, 'lions were heard near our camp and hyenas scavenged among our saucepans and carried one off. I slept soundly and heard nothing.'

They moved north into Kenya, crossing the vast Mara reserve, and then on to Nairobi where Mary discussed her plants with Peter Greenway and Jan Gillett at the Coryndon Museum. A day trip from Nairobi took them to Hell's Gate where high precipices soared above a deep, narrow valley with interesting plants including a stinging nettle fifteen feet high and a striking mauve form of *Hibiscus cannabinus*. And there was a wealth of aloes on the cliffs. Yet it was not a good day: 'Dr Greenway was quite thrilling over plants but not too easy to take in as I was feeling rather unwell, with a nasty pain.' Next day she was no better but insisted on going the seventy or so miles over the Ngong Hills and down into the heat of the soda-lake at Magadi, an arid region where she collected a desert rose (*Adenium obesum*) which had masses of vividly pink, tubular flowers. Birds were many— thousands of flamingos, along with pelicans, spoonbills and a local race of the chestnut-banded sand-plover, whose range is restricted to lakes Magadi, Natron, Manyara and nearby waters. But Mary could not really enjoy Magadi. The day was 'very, very hot and I was sick going home'. She rested several days in Nairobi, her trouble having been diagnosed as 'the beginnings of a gastric ulcer'. Then came the long trek back home via Arusha, Dodoma, Iringa and Mbeya where she summed up dolefully:

> This has not been a very pleasant safari. I suppose my last with Vesey who leaves November 1st and I expect will seldom be in Abercorn . . . We have had some really good safaris together but all nice things end.

The day after she got home she went to Chilongolwelo where the Gamwells were completing their packing:

> It is very, very sad to see the house all dismantled. I have been so happy there, and 1951, when I first went there was the beginning of a new life. I love the place and Marian and Hope. It's just heartbreaking to see it all and know that in a week they will be gone. Now Vesey will be going in a month and then it will be lonely.

It was as well that she was distracted from these miseries by the arrival of daughter Jonnet and her husband on a month's holiday. And as with many of Mary's visitors they were taken on safari to Lake Tanganyika, the Rukwa and Kambole. Between trips, on Friday 23 October, 1964, they attended an independence celebration at Abercorn:

> We got seats in a small stand. There was an excellent band and African dancing and singing. At twelve midnight the Union Jack was lowered, lights were turned out and then went on and the Zambia flag was substituted. We sang 'God Save the Queen', then the Zambia National Anthem. The ceremony was well carried out except that some persons tried to destroy the Union Jack but it was rescued by two Englishmen. Drink was forbidden, so there was no rowdyism and there was not a very large crowd. Finished up with fireworks.

With Jonnet and Jack gone home to England, Mary settled down to work on her flora of Abercorn and to her gardening. There was a flurry of excitement on 13 November when she woke to find that two lions had woken Sam and Mhilu by roaring just behind the house. Two prides of lions were reported close to Abercorn where thirty cattle had been killed on one of the farms. In the second week of November she got to a district that was always inaccessible in the latter part of the rainy season—the Chambeshi Flats near Kasama, about 110 miles south of Abercorn. Late in finding a camp site on the first night, Mary had to press her plants by lamplight and did so under the gaze of two African schoolmasters from a nearby village: 'I explained our work as they wanted to know what good it was.' Some days the visitors were female—'the usual rather tiresome invasion of village women who sit in a row and I can't talk to them nor they to me.' Another visitor was a leopard that hung about so close to the camp after dark that they had to keep a fire and a lamp burning all night. On the whole this was a botanically rewarding week that included one gruelling day when Mary, Sam and a guide walked for twelve hours over very difficult terrain which included

> about two miles of mud and in places deep water up to my thighs. I was very stiff and tired. Sam gave me a hand and finally we got on to firm ground. Then it got dark but at 6.30 we reached the car. I was truly thankful.

Though tired she was evidently very fit and fully recovered from the alleged gastric ulcer the doctor in Nairobi had diagnosed three months back.

1965 began well with a successful safari to the upper reaches of the Lufubu River, some forty miles south-west of Abercorn, a region of woods, swamps and termite mounds where Mary collected many grasses, sedges and orchids. But the outstanding moment of the whole week was provided by crinums seen through the trees:

> We came to an opening where we could see for miles across the swamp. I looked through my field-glasses at what I thought were masses of orchids far away, too far to make out exactly what they were. So we made for the plain, soon in water over our ankles, and saw that what we had seen were thousands of large crinum lilies, pink with a band of reddish-pink on each petal. They stretched as far as we could see. I have never seen such a wonderful sight. We dug up three bulbs for Kew and Lord Methuen.

Along the Yembele River they came to a few splendid forest trees known locally as Mupeta (*Canarium schweinfurthii*): 'They were magnificent trees about 60ft high with lovely dark-green pinnate leaves. Altogether we saw nine trees. White says only six in his *Forest Flora of Northern Rhodesia*.'

In February, Mary, Bill Morony and Sam had a few day's collecting at Kalambo Falls. By now Sam was much more than a driver. To some extent the mantle of Ali Omari had fallen on his shoulders and he was fully involved in the collecting, drying and pressing of plants. At Kalambo Mary comments: 'Sam has a good knowledge of the names of trees, etc. in the Lungu language and I am learning a lot.'

Since coming to Africa in 1951 Mary had been on many a far journey but one of the longest began on 18 March, 1965, when she set off along the Tunduma road with Sam and Mhilu. They were to be away two months, Vesey having invited her to do another round of his new bailiwick at Arusha, Serengeti and Lake Manyara. She did some good collecting along the road, especially north of Chunya in and around the Rungwa Game Reserve. Then near Itigi, camping by the roadside, she found Vesey who had come to meet her, much to her delight: 'It is very nice to be on safari with Vesey again.' Interesting plants abounded all around, among them a spectacular member of the *Convolvulus* family: 'It was growing to about eight feet up trees and over some lower bushes. The flowers were a glorious rose-pink with broad white bands on each petal.' They passed through a strange open landscape where gigantic rocks were balanced improbably on others. The weather was stormy and at times violent and Mary's tent collapsed on top of her during a night of torrential rain. As they journeyed on they found an aardwolf dead on the road, a rare animal Mary had never seen before. From Arusha they drove up to Momela where Vesey's new house was almost completed. Mount Meru towered over them in the north; and thirty miles east they could make out the hazy outlines of snow-capped Kilimanjaro.

One of the highlights of this safari was a walk part-way up Mount Meru from Momela at 5,000 feet as far as the caldera rim at 8,000 feet. They passed through a zone of grassland and sage scrub up into a forest of vast and ancient trees—pencil cedars (*Juniperus procera*) and yellow-woods (*Podocarpus gracilior*) which were surviving up there because their remoteness had saved them from exploitation. The canopy of these great trees reached to about 120 feet above ground; beards of mosses, lichens, ferns and orchids waved along their boughs and lianas hung everywhere. Yet she felt she might have been on the Welsh hills when she saw lady's-mantles, wood sorrels, sanicles, violets, plantains and filmy-ferns, all obviously close cousins of those around Dolgellau:

> The floor of the forest was carpeted with *Selaginella* and there were scattered plants of a lovely *Kniphofia*, a brilliant orange and scarlet. We came to a large *Podocarpus* and about thirty feet up was a glorious hanging mass of a white *Aerangus* orchid quite beyond reach. But the game-scouts were determined to get me some of the orchid and had a great time throwing sticks and in no

time got me several sprays of flower—pure white, with a pale, orange-yellow spur several inches long. In a slight clearing was a very bright-pink *Indigofera*. We crossed a stream which came down in a lovely waterfall into a deep rocky gorge hung with ferns. Beside the stream was a flat grassy place carpeted by a tiny blue *Lobelia* about half-an-inch high. After leaving this lovely glade we came to the most wonderful part of the forest—great *Podocarpus* trees hanging with lichens, mosses and ferns. Just beyond were a lot of colobus monkeys with long white tails and manes. From now onwards the path became really steep, rough and slippery

Finally, they got up to the rim of the caldera in a zone dominated by a forest of bamboos and *Hagenia* trees. And in the centre of the great basin of the caldera they saw a volcano within a volcano—the splendid, sharp-pointed ash-cone that peaks up to 3,000 feet from the caldera floor. Beyond it the walls of the caldera rose to about 7,000 feet. Above those vast precipices the slopes continued up through an alpine zone to Meru's summit at almost 15,000 feet, making it the fifth highest mountain in Africa.

By now it was 4 o'clock, so we started down and as we got to the bottom of the first steep slope there were elephants on our left and a herd of buffaloes rushed down through the forest. Finally we got down to the river, waded across and found our Land-Rover. A really wonderful walk.

For over a fortnight they explored the rest of the park, collecting plants all the time, around the little lakes and in the olive woods. One of the lakes was

a mass of blue water-lilies whose scent came up to us in waves. The lake has forest all round and is a perfect gem. Among the lilies were white-backed ducks, jacanas, great white egret, intermediate egret, a few cormorants and a yellow *Utricularia*. Sam took off his boots and went and collected some—also leeches which fastened on to his legs. We sat in the sun and looked at the lake. Then walked along and I collected a tiny *Lemna* and a rather large *Azolla*.

Most of the rest of this safari Mary spent at Serengeti where one memorable day, close to Lake Victoria, they drove through about five miles of closely packed migrating wildebeest.

*   *   *

When she flew back to the UK in June,1965, Mary did the usual round of friends in and around London, reaching Wales and Caerynwch on 8 July. With the Merioneth field society she had a day on Puffin Island which she had never managed to get to before. They climbed to the top of the island, struggling up through its unique forest of elderberry bushes, and saw guillemots, razorbills, kittiwakes, shags and cormorants. There were very few puffins but thousands of herring gulls. This was to be her last landing on a Welsh island. Back in London she made her routine visit to Kew, then went to check up on Freda Davies and the Gamwell sisters now living in London. Their news was not good: Marian was in St George's hospital, having been knocked down and badly injured on a pedestrian crossing in Sloane Street. Freda was also unwell; and Hope, greatly missing Africa, was 'a bit bored and difficult. I am worried about them all.' Then back to Wales, by train this time, to celebrate her eightieth birthday at Caerynwch on 3 August. On the fifth, with her grandsons, Andrew and Mark, she did the Precipice Walk on the Nannau estate but, as she put it in her diary, it was not the happiest of afternoons: 'Nannau is sold—a tragedy—the whole estate derelict, the paths and tracks all overgrown and quite difficult to find.'

*   *   *

She flew back to Africa on 18 August, 1965, getting down straight away to working on the Abercorn plant-list with Bill Morony. She was also busy in the garden where for several days there was a flock of up to thirty plum-coloured starlings along with a crowned hornbill and a brown-hooded kingfisher. On 22 August she went to a meeting at which Zambia's Minister of Education opened an Outward Bound School at what had been the Lake View Hotel and then:

> I had a wonderful two days last week. I went with the Outward Bound instructors to the Issi Falls. Vesey and I had tried to get up there from Lake Tanganyika but it is almost impossible. With the Outward Bound we took the Land-Rover about 20 miles along the Kambole road and had a three hours walk. I got a cousin of Sam's to help carry our kit. We took a blanket and a tent each and enough food for two days. Sam cut grass and I slept on it, rolled up in a blanket. I slept well—glorious night, no lamps, so we supped by the light of a camp fire. The falls are quite magnificent—far better

186

than Kalambo Falls—a huge red sandstone gorge and you look down on the lake 3,000 feet below. Also a lovely river to bathe in.

For her first safari of the season she crossed into Tanzania to the Lake Katavi Game Reserve, arriving there on 13 October 1965. With Sam and several game-scouts she had an exciting few days among the many buffaloes, giraffes, topi, elephants and hippos. Birds were numerous—spoonbills, helmeted guinea-fowl, yellow-throated sand-grouse, Caspian plovers, pratincoles and a honey-guide which, by its rattling cries, led them to a bees' nest in a hole in a tree. They got into mud up to their knees and Mary thought of Leslie Brown who nearly lost his life by getting stuck in the burning-hot soda-crust of the half-dried bed of Lake Natron where he was trying to reach a breeding colony of lesser flamingos. From the Katavi Reserve they made their way down into the Rukwa Valley but were depressed to find the locust-control houses at Musé all deserted and that there was no longer any petrol nor drinking water available. The road up the escarpment had been practically washed away but 'Sam really drove splendidly' and got the Land-Rover up despite a broken spring. On the top of the escarpment Mary was reminded of Hope Gamwell by finding a small patch of *Gamwellia flava* which Hope had first found on the heights above Chilongolwelo. About eight miles south-east of Sumbawanga, Mary came to Malonje where she found Mrs Dam very gloomy about the future. The farm was no longer paying and the local people were 'terribly poor; in fact they seem to be going back to pre-Livingstone days'. Mrs Dam also warned Mary that the Ufipa highlands, where Mary had done so much of her collecting, were becoming a dangerous region where strangers were liable to be molested. But all was peaceful that night where Mary camped at the foot of nearby Mamya Mountain: 'The young man who brought us here was very helpful and got us some wood . . . the whole village came to look at us and brought eggs. A new moon, a lovely night, bed early.' Next day on the mountain was perfect. 'In places the hillside was a mass of yellow *Compositae*, *Dolichos* and two kinds of bright-blue *Pentas*. We got four small euphorbias and one large aloe.' They followed the edge of sheer cliffs to the summit with its magnificent panoramas of the Rukwa Valley.

It was a good day for walking, a nice breeze and some sun. We came down the steep hillside, collecting a nice *Scilla* and several other plants. At the bottom of a small gorge was a huge *Eulophia*

187

orchid. Sam went down and collected some. The plant was over six feet high with huge pink flowers and long leaves.

*   *   *

At Abercorn in November, Mary was delighted to see Vesey (he still had his house there) and to be invited to spend Christmas with him at Momela. Another item of good news came when John Owen, head of the Tanzania game department, turned up at Abercorn on holiday and suggested that she should go and collect in the Ruaha National Park. To be one of the first to botanise in that slice of wilderness was an opportunity not to be missed and she agreed to collect there after Christmas. Meanwhile she was getting letters from the family suggesting she ought to leave Africa because of the crisis caused by Rhodesia's Unilateral Declaration of Independence. Mary's comment was: 'The English papers are alarmist. Here all is normal.' So on 3 December off she went with Sam and Mhilu on the long journey to Arusha which they reached in four days. She collected around Momela for a fortnight, then she and Vesey were off to Lake Manyara to meet Iain Douglas-Hamilton, a young Oxford zoology graduate who, at John Owen's suggestion, had come to study Manyara's large elephant population. Ten years later he was to write his classic book: *Among the Elephants*. By Lake Manyara they came upon large numbers of buffaloes, impalas and elephants and saw rufous-tailed weavers at their large, untidy, hanging nests.

Back at Momela on the eve of Christmas, 1965, they watched elephants

till it was so dark we could just distinguish the gleam of their tusks. The top of Kilimanjaro came out of the cloud, white with snow. A very still evening. The hippos below us gave an occasional splash. A skein of sacred ibis flew over. Cormorants came to roost in an acacia below us. On the further shore some egrets were roosting in another acacia. Faint small bursts of song from small birds going to bed. Then silence and one star came out beyond a yellow sunset and deep, dark clouds.

Two days after Christmas they walked up to Mount Meru's great caldera, their camping gear carried in large paniers by six donkeys. So Mary spent her first night on this mountain that was destined to dominate much of the rest of her life. From the caldera rim they looked back at the Momela lakes; and when they looked up at Meru they saw 'a beautiful lammergeyer with wedge-shaped tail soaring among the clouds'. Then, risking the danger of rhinos, they went down into the *Podocarpus* forest in the caldera, finding many unknown plants.

On 6 January, 1966, she was off with Sam and Mhilu to begin collecting in the Ruaha; but it did not take her long to realise what an awesome commitment she had let herself in for in that very new and very wild National Park. For as well as a lack of roads—something she was well used to—there were other difficulties. Elephants, for instance. They were not only abundant but also dangerous because they had been much harassed by hunters. So they had to be given the right of the road at all times, which meant long, frustrating delays while waiting for them to move on. But the elephants had their uses: they made paths through the thickets; and in one place they had knocked down two species of *Commiphora* trees, so enabling Mary to obtain their fruits. Worse than elephants was the weather. It was extremely hot and so dry that few flowers were showing. 'It is a maddening place,' wrote Mary, 'and tsetse flies are in clouds.' Fortunately, although they often bit her, they left no after effects. The Ruaha vegetation was of a type she was not at all used to: 'The trees and shrubs are quite different from anything we have met before. I wish Peter Greenway could come here for a day!' When Sam went down with malaria she had to do all the pressing on her own: 'I worked all day . . . I was very weary. This morning a large herd of buffaloes came down the hill just where we were collecting yesterday. They say they are very wild and charge cars and people.' After six weeks of heat, drought, hostile animals, flies and hay-fever, she was quite glad to leave the Ruaha and make her way home to Abercorn which she reached on 23 February, having collected fewer specimens than she had hoped.

If Mary now settled down to a quiet spell, it was mainly because, at that time of political and economic uncertainty, petrol was severely rationed. So she got on with the flora of Abercorn, spending long days in the herbarium. She did a lot of gardening, collected plants locally and kept an eye on the birds, noting the great flocks of black kites and white-bellied storks passing over daily in early March. Her first visitor from the UK in 1966 was a butterfly expert, her old friend Frank Best of Llangollen. He stayed nine days and had a marvellous time chasing butterflies with Mary in choice spots like Kalambo Falls, Lunzua Falls and Sunzu Mountain.

CHAPTER SEVENTEEN

In May, 1966, Mary handed over the running of Abercorn's Red Cross to a committee of Africans, now that it was the Zambian, not the British, Red Cross. She then flew to Europe for a holiday in Sicily with her daughter, Kate, and for a week they enjoyed the historical and architectural delights of Palermo and other centres. Then to London, staying with Jonnet in Kent. She grieved to find one of her oldest friends, Florence Bristow, very ill. She went to see Vesey's wife, Octavia, at Ringwood, Hampshire. Then to Wales and Caerynwch. On 30 June, Vesey, on leave from Africa, arrived at Caerynwch with son, Michael, and daughter, Maureen. With Kathleen Stevens they enjoyed the plants and birds of Morfa Harlech. Next day they botanised along the upper Dyfi valley with Peter Benoit, a good find being the calcicole grass, mountain melick. But its finding involved a testing scramble up a scree which brought Mary a recurrence of her old knee trouble.

In July she went back to London to see her friends at Kew where she 'spent the morning looking at maps and undoing the last twelve parcels of plants I sent and getting some of the Ruaha ones named by Verdcourt, Peter Taylor and Polhill'. On 19 July she flew to Jersey in the Channel Isles where the Gamwells and Freda Davies had now settled in 'a nice house and garden overlooking the sea' at St Aubin's Bay. She found Marian much recovered from her accident but Freda very lame. Back in London she had an injection in her bad knee before returning to Wales for her 81st birthday party held at Bont-ddu Hall Hotel. But the whole district was in a state of shock following an accident on the Mawddach estuary where fifteen people had been drowned when their boat crashed into Penmaenpool bridge. She ended her stay in Britain with a visit to Longleat's famous lions which she thought looked 'in splendid health'; and by being interviewed on BBC radio about her life in Africa.

*   *   *

Getting back to Abercorn at the end of August, Mary was pleased to get a letter from the head of the International Red Locust

Control, Mr Du Plessis, thanking her for her work at their herbarium and granting her an honorarium of £100. There was an interesting incident at Ndundu that October when she and Sam decided to fight their way into the dense *mushitu* below the garden:

> When we came to the big fig trees there was a rush of wings and large flying creatures, about the size of a jackdaw, pale tawny-red, crashed through the branches—there must have been over one hundred. They were epauletted fruit-bats and they were feeding on the figs.

She had never seen so many before. That same month a bird-song was persistent in the garden—the voice of the emerald cuckoo, one of the best-known sounds of the African bush though the bird itself is seldom seen because it lives a secretive life in the tree-tops. It is something of a brain-fever bird, its four notes, usually translated as 'Hello Georgie', going on all day long.

For Christmas, 1966, Mary was again invited to Momela by Vesey. With the help of Abercorn friends she got hold of enough petrol and went off along her now familiar route via Mbeya, Iringa and Dodoma, collecting on the way; and on 16 November she reached the Lake Manyara National Park where she had arranged to meet Vesey and his daughter, Maureen. Along the lakeside and in the escarpment woods were the usual exciting numbers of elephants, buffaloes, impalas and others along with a multitude of birds. Mary also went through the plants preserved in the park's herbarium, collected by Peter Greenway of the Coryndon Museum. Her comment was: 'He, I consider, dries his plants far too much—they are brown and brittle—he dries them over a lamp. I prefer drying mine slowly and changing the papers each day.'

From Lake Manyara she went to Arusha and up to the heights of Momela where she had her usual room in Vesey's house (with elephants almost looking through her bedroom window at night) and was able to spend the whole of December collecting plants or watching wildlife, including night herons which were new to her. At Momela she was saddened to hear from Marian Gamwell that Freda Davies had died of a heart attack in Jersey. As Vesey was away much of that time, busy with his duties at Lake Manyara and Serengeti, she and Sam explored the park on their own or with a game-scout, everywhere being careful not to come face to

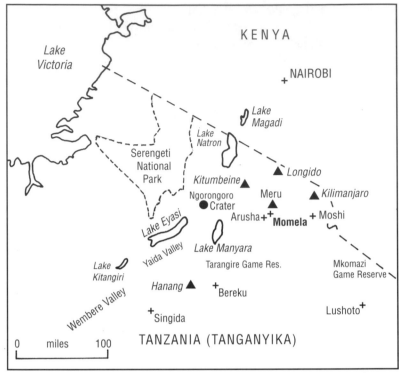

Northern Tanzania where Mary Richards, based at Momela, did much plant-collecting in her later years.

face with buffaloes or rhinos along the narrow animal-made paths winding up through the trees. Among the birds they watched in Meru's cliffs were breeding colonies of white-fronted bee-eaters; and horus swifts identified for her by John Beesley, formerly of the locust service, now the Arusha National Park warden.

The year ended on a dismal note. Mary had a tummy upset that went on for over a week and by Christmas her back was also giving her trouble. But on 1 January, 1967, she felt able to fling these afflictions aside and go off with others on a day-trip east into new country—the western slopes of Kilimanjaro. They followed a river through high-level forests, collecting many plants among which, surprisingly, 'in the forest road the English shepherd's purse was growing'. We are left to speculate how it got there. Mammals seen on that brief visit to Kilimanjaro's slopes included colobus monkeys and a red forest duiker.

A week later she was venturing even further east, beyond

Kilimanjaro to the Mkomazi Game Reserve, an area of 1,350 square miles in north-east Tanzania adjoining the southern boundary of Kenya's huge Tsavo National Park—a land of open plain, thornbush and scattered rocky hills. Mary went there at the suggestion of John Procter, then stationed at Lushoto on forestry duties. In three days at Mkomazi, she found a dry-country vegetation that was largely new to her and she collected a lot of strange shrubs, the most astonishing being *Adenia venenata*, a member of the passion fruit family: 'We saw one huge plant spreading its branches in all directions. They call it the barbed wire plant—the huge terrestrial tuber looked like a rock and we calculated it must be twenty feet round and four feet high.' An unwelcome find was an alien, the South American prickly pear in great masses: 'We got the small fine thorns in our hands and trouser legs, very painful.' Mkomazi was a rewarding place but as it had been 'very, very hot' and the mosquitos tiresome, it was with relief that she got up to the cooler heights above Lushoto where John Procter was living. She had a good day at Lake Manka, some 30 miles from Lushoto towards Moshi; and as John Procter was with her she learned a lot about the local commiphoras and acacias. The lake had largely dried up but in the surrounding scrub they got a long list of birds, including blue-cheeked bee-eater, slate-coloured boubou-shrike, white-bellied go-away bird, Von der Decken's hornbill, blue-cheeked mousebird and two winter visitors from Eurasia—red-backed and red-tailed shrikes. Next day they were off to Tanga on the coast. So for the second time Mary found herself botanising at the edge of the Indian Ocean among coconut palms and mangrove swamps. But not for long—she had been away for nearly three months and it was time to take the long road back to Abercorn which they reached on 27 January, 1967, after a round trip that Mary estimated at 4,000 miles.

Mary said goodbye to two old friends early in 1967. In February, Dr Hope Trant moved south to live at Kasama; and in March came the news that Edward Robinson, with whom she had had so many good days in the field, would be going back to live in England in September—'a great loss to African botany', Mary noted. Meanwhile she worked hard on the Abercorn plant-list and for the first time we hear her voicing that universal moan of field botanists about so many plant-name changes. They were causing her and Bill Morony 'a lot of extra work'.

Mid-April brought an unfortunate incident when Mary and Sam set off along the Kambole road to collect in the Inyendwe valley. They took a wrong turning and got onto a very rough track where Mary, mindful of her bad back, urged Sam to drive carefully. Instead 'he went too fast and we crashed into a bad hole'. Mary was thrown forward and sideways and again sprained her back. She struggled for a couple of days but her back got no better and eventually she gave up:

> I found the walk back painful and held Sam's rather unwilling arm. I sat still all afternoon. I am afraid I can't do much. Rain started about 9 p.m., and it rained all night. My back is painful and no better, so the only thing is to go home. Very disappointing. We had to take the tents down wet, Sam in a tiresome mood.

*   *   *

That year, 1967, she began her annual summer visit to the UK on 12 June, starting in Kent as always and seeing as many friends and relations as possible. She much enjoyed being shown round Canterbury Cathedral by one of the officials; and at a music festival at Wye College she heard Bach's *St John's Passion*: 'It was a wonderful performance. I was very much moved. The last chorale was magnificent.' The social round went on to include a huge wedding party on 8 July at Lord Cobham's Hagley Hall in Worcestershire. Then she flew to Jersey where she found Marian and Hope Gamwell surviving fairly well. For a couple of days they showed her some of the sights of Jersey, including a mediaeval castle on Gros Nez, a headland with views along a wild and rocky coast and a distant peep at Sark. Looking for wildflowers, they came upon a broom which was new to Mary, 'a curious broom which spreads flat over rocks and ground.' Common dodder was a conspicuous parasite sprawling over gorse and heather. She learnt about the island's rarer plants from a flora lent to her by Jersey's leading botanist, Frances Le Sueur, who for many years was well known for her hospitality and help to visiting naturalists.

Mary was in Wales for her 82nd birthday, staying at Caerynwch with Pam and Richard. Also as usual she had days in the field with botanical friends. Near Machynlleth she was shown a rare tree—the wild service; and she had a good day among the wildflowers in the sand-dunes at Ynys-las. Back in London she had physiotherapy for her knee and her back; then went to Kew and was shown the splendid new herbarium.

*   *   *

She flew back to Africa on 7 September and was met by Sam at Ndola where she collected a new Land-Rover. They got to Abercorn two days later and now for the first time Mary calls it Mbala, its name since independence. Ndundu she found in good order and she soon settled into her old regime—dividing her days between gardening and working on her plants at the locust-service herbarium which now had an official keeper, a very capable African named Modesty Simane. Mary was pleased to find that Modesty 'had worked hard getting the cupboards in order and labelled'. Meanwhile there were two wildlife incidents of interest: Sam saw two leopards on the road near Ndundu; and elephants passed by at night: they were not seen but their fresh dung was sufficient evidence. Mary continued to explore locally, finding streams and gorges' 'and patches of relict forest she had not known about before. On 23 October Sam took her to see a large *dambo* that was quite new to her. In a long walk in intense heat she got some interesting plants including two bladderworts, one yellow, one blue. A big yellow *Eulophia* orchid was flowering abundantly and the white flowers of a *Thunbergia* dominated the swamp. She noted with satisfaction: 'My back is better. It is the longest walk I've done. I was a bit stiff, we did about eleven miles.' On that walk she also had the company of two new friends, both expert botanists, Graham Williamson from Lusaka and Brian Simon of Salisbury, Rhodesia. After sixteen years of collecting Mary had become widely known and every botanist visiting the Abercorn district beat a pathway to her door, as Thoreau would have put it (Mary had recently read a life of Thoreau). And as Graham Williamson and Brian Simon expressed a special interest in orchids, aloes and grasses, they were more than welcome. Two months later Brian and Graham were back at Abercorn to spend Christmas at Ndundu, Graham this time bringing his family to camp in the garden. For several days they explored the local marshes and rocky places with much success. Mary noted that she had 'never seen the orchids in such good flower and such very large plants'. On the way home 'a big *Acacia albida* was a wonderful sight—orchids in masses on all the branches'. Nine years later Williamson produced his classic *Orchids of South-Central Africa*. In it he paid tribute to Mary's hospitality and achievements:

> Mrs Mary Richards arrived in Mbala (Abercorn) in 1951 at the age of 66 and methodically collected the orchid-rich areas of northern Zambia and southern Tanzania. The total number of

her gatherings exceeds 20,000, a monumental achievement. *Habenaria richardsiae* is named in her honour.

Yet though life was calm enough on the surface, clouds were gathering. It was depressing to learn that many of the old locust-service staff were leaving; and then came the news that one of Mary's remaining Abercorn friends, Ann Parton, was condemned to be deported from Zambia as an undesirable alien, having in some way fallen foul of the new regime. She was arrested early one morning and kept in custody at the airfield until the plane took off. Mary happened to be there, seeing off some friends. No one was supposed to speak to Ann but, says Mary in her diary: 'I went and shook hands and said goodbye. No one else dared. It's all a scandal.' No doubt this act of defiance was duly noted by the town's new officials. Perhaps it was no coincidence that four days later Ndundu's woodland was set on fire in two places. Everything was tinder dry and the fire was put out only with the greatest difficulty.

Ever under the spell of the wild uplands of the Nyika Plateau, Mary spent most of November, 1967, with Sam and Mhilu in Malawi. But it was not pleasant on the way to find their camp inspected by the Zambian police 'to see what I was doing. They were very civil but it does give one rather a shock to realise that one cannot turn into woodland and camp peacefully and undisturbed as one used to.' At first even the beautiful Nyika was disappointing. Everywhere was extremely dry and few plants were yet in flower. Then they got down into a damper valley where

the banks were a mass of flowers. The large purple *Vernonia*, various yellow *Compositae*, purple *Moraea*, yellow and white *Umbelliferae*, the lovely mauve dwarf *Polygala* and white and pale-mauve asters. For about 600 yards the bank was covered with pale-green aloes. We walked to the top of the ridge and got a beautiful dwarf *Abutilon* with large, rose-coloured flowers. It was quite a long tramp but with lovely views of green, rocky hills and valleys.

When they moved on two days later the scene changed from rocks and relict forests to

great, rolling, grassy hills with deep valleys. We looked into a valley on our left and there were fifty eland, some zebras, then reed-buck, roan, a few bush-buck and duikers. It is a vast place and the animals are very scattered. I collected a lot of plants, some I did not know, and the wandflower (*Dierama*) was everywhere, in places the hillside pink with it. Edward, our game-scout, who had been rather doubtful about plant-collecting, waxed most enthusiastic and helped.

Among the few birds she mentions are 'a Stanley's bustard walking sedately through the grass' and 'three lovely wattled cranes feeding on the hillside'.

They got back to Abercorn on 29 November and at Ndundu all was well except that the fuchsias had been shredded by hawkmoth caterpillars. There followed a quiet couple of months during which Mary carried on working at the herbarium with Bill Morony and Modesty. Then 1968 began smoothly enough until Friday, 19 January, when Sam suddenly informed Mary that he was quitting her service and that she would have to get another driver for her next safari, due to begin the following Tuesday. Since independence relations between white employers and black employees had become extremely delicate and Sam brought in one of the new local labour officials to represent him. To quote Mary's side of the argument:

Sam talked in an excited way for half an hour, told the labour officer I was unkind to him on safari and unsympathetic when he was very ill. I was very much annoyed as it is completely untrue. I gave him notice to leave on March 1st. I shall be sorry to lose him, he is a first-rate collector and does the preparing and pressing of plants beautifully. But he is neurotic and sometimes very moody and does not get on very well with the other men.

Next day she and Sam were out collecting as if nothing had happened: 'Sam came and did excellent specimens. I think he regrets his stupidity.'

But the break had been made and the problem of finding a driver for the forthcoming safari was solved by the fortuitous arrival that weekend of Ion Trant, a well-known farmer from Welshpool in Wales who had come to visit his aunt, Dr Hope Trant. He volunteered to do the driving and off they went on 24 January, bound for Mbeya and Arusha. After a night at Mbeya and another at the Rungwa Game Reserve, they had a good day near Itigi:

197

A lovely hot day. We decided to camp in the Itigi Thicket and found a delightful track into the Thicket. On each side were bushes of *Baphia* in full flower, a marvellous sight like a long avenue. The buds and calyx were reddish-brown, the scent almost overpowering. I collected a *Euphorbia* with very stinging hairs on the leaves. A lovely starry night.

They reached Arusha and then Momela where Mary was much pleased to see that 'a really amazing road' had now been made by Vesey up the lower slopes of Mount Meru 'far past our old camp site up into the juniper and *Podocarpus* forest and ends about half a mile from the crater rim in an open space on the lava flow where they will put up a rest-house.' With Ion Trant and Vesey she had a day scrambling up a gorge on the flanks of the huge ash-cone that rose from the floor of the caldera. She collected many ferns and flowering plants: among them *Helichrysum*, *Lobelia*, *Stoebe*, *Viola*, *Astragalus*, *Anemone*, *Gladiolus*, *Dierama*, *Senecio*, *Satureia* and *Trifolium*.

She took Ion Trant to see Lake Manyara and photograph its wealth of wildlife (he was well-known for his films on British television). He was anxious to photograph the tree-dwelling lions and was lucky: two acacias had two lions in each, lying asleep along the branches and he had to whistle to get them to lift their heads. On the lakeside he was much impressed by the great flocks of marsh sandpipers and white-winged black terns. They returned to Momela and after a few days Ion had to go home to Wales. Mary stayed on for another month, being joined from time to time by visiting naturalists curious to see this unique mountain park. One of them was Stewart Irvine, a butterfly expert, with whom she went up into the Meru forests with John Beesley and John Procter. Irvine demonstrated how to set up butterfly traps baited with fermented bananas. Almost at once the butterflies came to it, especially the genus *Charaxes*. They saw also the local race of the Kilimanjaro swallowtail, found only in these Meru forests between 7,000 and 9,000 feet. In lovely weather on 25 February, Mary went east towards Kilimanjaro with John Beesley and had a good collecting day. Three good birds of prey were crowned eagle, mountain buzzard and pygmy falcon.

She got much closer to Kilimanjaro two weeks later with Peter Greenway who came down from Nairobi. Starting from the Marangu Hotel, they headed up to the Bismarck Hut with porters, first in Land-Rovers then, when the road became impassable, on foot. The Bismark Hut was not a success: 'The whole place was filthy, outside and in. There were beds and mattresses but these were wet. Had some very indifferent supper and went to bed. Did not undress, rolled myself in the one dry rug and slept solid all night.' Next day they climbed from 8,800 to 10,300 feet where they were on moorland above the forest. Up there she noted that the tree heather (*Erica arborea*) which in the forest was 'a huge tree, ugly and lanky and covered with lichen', grew in the form of bushes in a scrub of *Helianthemum* and *Stoebe*. She collected *Protea kilimandscharica* and two umbellifers but the rest of the flora did not impress her: 'I must say I was very disappointed with the flowering plants—very little out and I don't think at any time it is a rich flora like the Porotos, Kippengeres or Livingstones which, of course, are not so high.' The weather did nothing to help: 'We decided to walk down to the car, it poured the whole way and we got soaked.'

Mary's return journey to Abercorn (Mbala) was fairly uneventful for the first three days. Her driver was Samuel (as distinct from Sam), who worked for the Arusha National Park, and she was relieved to find how well he handled the Land-Rover on the rough and skiddy roads across Tanzania. But the journey turned into a nightmare once they were into Zambia. Because of enormously heavy rains the roads all over the district were awash and bridges had been swept away. It took them four days and hundreds of extra miles to get from Tunduma to Mbala (normally a four-hour journey): 'I cannot speak too highly of Samuel, he drove superbly and was always cheerful' was Mary's verdict. Samuel then went back to Arusha by bus.

Real trouble began on 11 April 1968. Her dismissed driver, Sam, demanded extra money from her and again invoked the help of local officials. They summoned Mary to a meeting which ended in her being roughly handled physically, leaving her very much shaken for days. The following weekend was Easter and she helped to decorate the church with flowers from her garden. On Good Friday she went with two young men, visiting American botanists, to Kalambo Falls. By Saturday she was already half-resolved to quit Zambia and to ask Vesey if she could move to Momela. By Monday, after a sleepless night, she had definitely decided to leave, feeling 'utterly miserable'.

This was not a decision reached without help. Her friends were unanimous that the local officials would inevitably go on making things worse for her. And many others of the white community were also going. So she relinquished her tenancy of Ndundu and with much help from friends, especially Karl and Margo Kuhne, she packed her belongings in five big cases for shipment to the UK. One of her last walks was up the hill behind the house for a farewell view of the Nkali Dambo, one of her first collecting places with Hope Gamwell in December 1951. She also had a final walk along the edge of Mbala's little Lake Chila:

> Owing to rain everything is wonderfully green. It was a lovely afternoon, the blue waters of the lake sparkling in the sun. The blue *Smithia* bushes were in flower and yellow *Kotschya*. Round the far end the *Hyparrhenia* grass was eight feet high and quite difficult to force one's way through. Karl and Margo Kuhne met me in the car as a deluge came down which became more and more violent all evening and into the night.

One of her last farewells was to her dog, Mwarka, which she was happy to have placed in good hands.

CHAPTER EIGHTEEN

By the time she left Zambia for the UK on 8 June 1968, Mary had decided she must come back on a visit in October, her anxiety being that if she did not return to oversee it, her flora of Abercorn would never be published. Meanwhile the stresses of recent weeks had taken their toll. She was exhausted and by the time she reached Jack and Jonnet in Kent she was seriously ill with bronchitis from which it took her a month to recover. By 1 July she was out and about again and had a delightful evening at Glyndbourne hearing the Tchaikovsky opera, *Eugene Onegin*. But two days later she certainly was nowhere near fit enough to cope with the strenuous walks organised in Snowdonia for the summer meeting of the British Ecological Society. Yet go she did and much enjoyed meeting old friends including Professor and Mrs Paul Richards and Norman Woodhead. While the others went scrambling up to the Devil's Kitchen and the top of Glyder Fawr, Mary pottered about in Cwm Idwal bemoaning her 'tiresome bronchitis'.

She stayed as usual with Pam and Richard at Caerynwch, had a couple of good days botanising, and had lunch at Maes Mawr, Welshpool, with Ion Trant who had driven her across Tanzania in January. A remarkable coincidence that came to light was that Ion's wife, Janet, had been an old Rukwa hand. In 1936-7 she and her friend, Kate Ricardo, had, as young graduates in Natural Science at Cambridge, taken part in a survey of the fish of South Rukwa Lake. An account of their adventures there, and also while investigating the fish of Lake Nyasa, Lake Bangweulu and the small lake at Shiwa Ngandu, is well told in a privately published account, *Letters from the Swamps*, edited by Ion Trant. Even in those early days Dr Hope Trant had been active in Northern Rhodesia, then being stationed at Mwenzo Mission, Tunduma. It was there that Janet, then Miss Owen, first met her, never imagining that she herself was destined in due course to change her name to Trant. That process began a few years later when she and Ion Trant were both involved in agricultural studies at Aberystwyth.

Mary spent her 83rd birthday with Marian and Hope Gamwell in Jersey, then went to Paignton to see cousin Stephen Stokes and visit the zoo where she especially enjoyed the tropical houses. From Paignton she went by train to Sherborne in Dorset to see an old friend of Kawimbe Mission days, Gladys Strickland. They visited the famous abbey church and went 'into the museum where there was a lovely collection of old botany books'. On to London and her usual discussions with her Kew friends about future collecting. She was delighted to hear from Vesey that from now on she could base herself at Momela and that he would fetch her from Mbala where she had to go first to pick up her camp kit, collecting things, books, etc, which she had left in the herbarium. In late August she had two good days visiting gardens, first Wisley; then the Saville Gardens where the roses were still flowering well and *Lilium auratum* was at its best. She spent much of September with Kate at Haresfield Court, Gloucestershire, then returned to Wales because, having lost her African home, she was now negotiating to get back her beloved Tynllidiart cottage. She had a day at the National Library of Wales, Aberystwyth, seeing an exhibition of some of the famous Hengwrt manuscripts which she remembered at Hengwrt, a house near Dolgellau, many years before.

*   *   *

As planned, Mary returned to Mbala at the end of October 1968. She went straight to the herbarium, sorted out her kit and went over the plants which Modesty had collected in her absence. By next day, vasculum in hand, she was collecting at one of the local marshes and it was just like old times. She visited Ndundu and wished she hadn't: 'The whole garden is dried up. Orange and grapefruit trees dying and the whole place a shambles. I shall never go there again.' On 5 November, a Land-Rover arrived to take her to Arusha. Sent by Vesey, it was driven by Samuel and also brought Mhilu. She spent a happy weekend with old friends, Eric and Viva Balson, at Mbeya; but next day was disgusted to discover that her favourite camp-site near Itigi had been ruined: 'We planned to camp in our usual place in the Itigi Thicket. The Thicket has been entirely cut down and burnt.' They camped there all the same: 'Mhilu put up my tent and bed, I rolled myself in blankets and had no supper. I felt rotten and very tired and was violently sick. I took two aspirins and slept till 5.15 a.m. and woke up better but I am still not too good after the chill on my kidneys.' That evening she was very glad to reach Momela.

It took her a week to get over her kidney trouble and go off on a safari to a game reserve she had not previously visited—Tarangire, an area of over 500 square miles of dry acacia thornbush close to Lake Manyara. Mhilu and Samuel were with her, Samuel being now her official driver. In the reserve they saw many animals—kongoni, waterbuck, zebra, large herds of impala and a species new to her, the fringe-eared oryx. They camped by a river whose water was too alkaline to drink and where hyenas howled through the hours of darkness. Though it was mostly an arid environment there were swampy areas where Mary filled two presses with plants by lunch-time. After lunch there was a mishap she had never experienced before:

> Started to label plants and suddenly there was a whirlwind and torrential rain. The front part of the tent was blown down and everything on my table whirled away—plants, papers, lenses, two bottles of spirit, one being broken. There was a horrible mess of papers and plants, all wet and muddy

Sadly, after only three days in this exciting reserve, Mary again went down with kidney trouble and had to go back to Arusha where she saw a doctor and rested for a fortnight with John Owen and his wife.

On 9 December she returned to Momela and next day was chasing butterflies above Ngurdoto Crater. 'I am really well again,' she reported. One of her best days was 18 December when Samuel drove her round to the north side of Mount Meru to the Longido area near the Kenya border and the Amboseli Masai Game Reserve. They went as far as the foot of Longido Mountain (8,625 feet) and Mary's comment was: 'I plan to camp here after Xmas. The mountain looks very interesting but a bit steep!' She was much impressed by the huge Masai Plain covered in part by *Acacia tortilis* savanna and scattered for miles with huge blocks of lava and volcanic ash. They came to 'a big clump of large *Euphorbia* trees. I have not seen one like it before. John Beesley does not know its name, nor does Peter Greenway.' On the way home 'there was a magnificent sunset and Kilimanjaro's snow-covered head came out, draped with rose-coloured clouds'. The road back, in the dark, 'was absolutely awful—huge rocks and stones; we went very slowly and got a bad shaking'.

. Mary spent Christmas 1968 at Momela and then began packing for the trip she had been planning to Longido Mountain. She set off on 29 December with Samuel, Mhilu and enough food for a fortnight. The trip went well from the start. They were hardly on their way when Mary 'stopped to collect fascinating mauve and orange asters, blue *Pentas*, quantities of orange *Compositae* and a lovely white *Heliotropium*'. That day and next she filled many presses as well as seeing a new animal typical of arid scrub, the gerenuk, whose long, slender neck enables it to reach up and browse on trees, often standing on its hind legs. 1969 began well. Mary 'woke to a lovely, sunny New Year's Day'. The only trouble was a strong, unpleasant wind which blew her drying papers everywhere. It was a very hot day that ended in a beautiful night of full moon. Next day, not yet seeing a way up Longido Mountain because of its mantle of dense scrub, they kept to the rough tracks across the plain below where 'John Beesley says be careful, as he thinks there are a lot of rhinos. We went twelve miles along the track, the first part bush with some open spaces. We collected a good many specimens.' Going into Longido village next day to get water they were soon surrounded by

> Masai men, tall, with large necklaces and huge ear-rings, their ears in some cases inches long. Some had shaven heads and some had long hair plastered with grease and red ochre. They came all round the car and shook hands. The women, also in blankets, had large circular flat collars round their necks embroidered with beads, and long varied bead earrings.

As the area was a game reserve they were able to call on the services of a game-scout to help them find a way up Longido Mountain and on 8 January they managed to struggle up the first thousand feet. They started up a very steep, rocky path where a white geranium was flowering in masses. Then 'the path, after about an hour's climb, got very steep and I felt I should get up it all right but find it difficult to get down. In my 84th year I am not as active as I was.' So while the others climbed higher, she sat on a rock admiring, amongst other things, the brilliant colours of a variable sunbird that stood on a branch quite close. On the whole she was pleased to find she was coping so well and that she had quite recovered her balance which was bad after she was ill. After a very satisfactory fortnight in this dry land Mary went back to Momela feeling very fit and full of ideas for further safaris.

A good month's collecting followed, mainly on day-trips from Momela with Samuel, in the country around Arusha. She was intrigued one day to hear that an American, reputedly the richest woman in the world, was coming to Momela to camp for one night. She required tea and dinner and had to have proper beds. Mary's diary reads:

> Had a great spring clean of the house which wanted it badly. Vesey went off to meet Mrs May and her companion, and John Beesley and I saw to tents and beds. In the end she and her companion and John Owen did not arrive till 6 o'clock. Both of them were charming but had very strong American accents. An excellent dinner done by Mhilu.

Two days later along came another V.I.P.—Malcolm Macdonald, one-time British High Commissioner for Kenya. He was taken up into the Meru forest with Mary and others but a thunderstorm and torrents of rain cut the trip short and they got back to tea very wet.

In early February, 1969, Vesey, Mary, Samuel, Mhilu and park rangers had three interesting days on the Shira Plateau, a part of the Kilimanjaro massif. The rocks were volcanic and Mary thought them 'rather like our pillow lava on Cader'. Grey-leaved helichrysums were everywhere, some with white, others with yellow flowers. Mary also mentions crucifers, composites and 'a magnificent thistle, a *Carduus*, with pink flowers. It is a fascinating bit of country, the flat plateau and peaks all round, dominated by snow-capped Kibo.'

A memorable visitor to Momela was the American writer-naturalist, Peter Matthiessen who has left us a lively cameo of Vesey and Mary in his book, *The Tree where Man was Born* (1972):

> Vesey, who is the ecologist for Tanzania's national parks, had been kind enough to invite me to Momela, at the foot of Mount Meru, to learn some 'bush botany' from himself and his dear friend, Mary Richards, a beautiful Welsh lady of eighty-three who, like Vesey himself, had transferred her botanical field work into Tanzania when the political situation in Northern Rhodesia, now Zambia, became a nuisance. But Vesey and Mary were much too busy to bemoan the passing of the grand old days, for he was completing his work on African grasses, while she was negotiating the purchase of a new Land-Rover for a botanical safari into the

remote plains beyond Kilimanjaro. Vesey and Mary are pioneer African botanists, self-taught . . . In the evening, over a stiff drink, they compare notes, recalling old times in Abercorn, and old friends like Ionides, called 'Iodine', and J.A. Hunter, the hunter and game warden, and Wilfred Thesiger, the desert traveller, and Peter Greenway, the eminent botanist at the Coryndon (for their generation, Nairobi's National Museum, which acquired its new name at the time of Independence, will always be the Coryndon, just as this land will always be Tanganyika).

Collecting went on apace all through March—at Manyara, Tarangire, Meru Caldera and on Mount Kitumbeine (9,378 feet) in Masai country about 30 miles north-west of Arusha. Mary found Kitumbeine disappointing botanically and very hard going:

> It was the roughest country possible, rocks and boulders and loose stones, in places thick with acacia bush, mostly *Acacia mellifera* whose thorns catch one firmly; in places long dry grass and you can't see the rocks. We climbed up and up and it got very dry. I decided it was not worth it . . . we did get quite a lot of plants on our way down.

A fortnight later, describing a trip up to the Meru caldera, she says: 'I got many of the usual plants for Germany'—an interesting statement since this is the first mention of sending plants there. A few days later she sends off ten boxes of plants to Kew including one of live specimens. In a bird-count on Big Momela Lake she and Samuel (a good bird man) recorded 50 red-billed ducks, 400 African pochard, 370 Maccoa ducks, 207 Cape wigeon, hundreds of dabchicks, 190 black-winged stilts, 39 Egyptian geese, two Hottentot teal, one pintail, many avocets and flamingos, a hobby and an osprey.

At the end of March, Samuel drove her and Mhilu across Tanzania to Mbala which she found had suffered 'an extra-ordinary change'—most of the shops had closed and food shortages were worse than ever: 'The whole place looks asleep.' Mercifully she found the Kuhnes 'very well and very welcoming'. Then Samuel and Mhilu returned to Arusha, both having agreed to work for Mary when she got back there in September. For the next two months (April-May 1969), Mary stayed with the Kuhnes and worked harder than ever on the Abercorn plant-list, feeling that its completion must be now or never. She worked day after day in the herbarium with occasional time off for collecting with her delightfully named helpers, Modesty and Ambrosia, both locust-service Africans. In the herbarium on 8 April she wrote:

> Bill Morony came to discuss the possibility of editing and producing the Abercorn checklist of plants. After such a lot of work it seems a pity not to do something with it. When we started about eight years ago there were people here who were interested and also outside people who came. Now everyone is leaving and no one comes to Mbala.

Three weeks later she sounds pretty close to despair: 'Herbarium all day—there is an overwhelming amount of work to do.' Botany apart, the event of the month was the departure from Zambia of Dr Hope Trant who was given a farewell party attended by Europeans and Africans before she went into retirement in an old people's home in East London, South Africa. She had put in 44 years of devoted medical service.

On 27 May Mary sent off 21 parcels of plants to Kew and six to Germany. Then with Modesty and Ambrosia she battled through thick undergrowth on the slopes of Sunzu Mountain, getting many specimens—'a hard but successful day'. It was almost the last time she would collect in the Mbala district. Next day she wrote a short preface for the plant-list and committed its production to Bill Morony and Karl Kuhne. It was titled: *Check List of the Flora of Mbala (Abercorn) and District* by Mrs. M.A.E. Richards, M.B.E., R.R.C., M.Sc. and W.V. Morony, Esq., Mbala, 1969. There was a very limited edition of cyclostyled copies consisting of 294 quarto pages with a folded map. It was a splendid piece of work produced in the end against all the odds and owing much to the devoted labours, in its later stages, of Modesty Simane and one of Mbala's few remaining British residents, Pixie Mclochlan, who did much of the typing. But it was Bill Morony who, egged on for years by Mary, was the backbone of the editorial side of it. Without her the plant-records would never have been made. Without him they would never have been put together. On 4 June she wrote: 'My last day. I hate leaving Mbala. I have always loved it, though under present circumstances it is not too pleasant.'

*   *   *

Three days later she was back in Kent at Doddington Place and after a month she dressed in her best to go to Buckingham Palace to receive the MBE awarded for her botanical work. She went to see an optician about getting stronger lenses and saw a doctor about a hearing aid. Back in Wales on 3 August, her 84th birthday was a lovely day. Friends took her to the upper Dyfi valley through Llanymawddwy and up to the pass of Bwlch-y-groes where she noted how tarmac had improved what she had always known as a very bad road. They picnicked at the top of the pass with its fine view north to the shapely peaks of Arennig, then on to Y Parc near Bala where she was given a birthday tea and supper by her old Merioneth field society friends, Harold and Gertrude Armfield. Next day, with friends in north Cardiganshire, she took part in a successful hunt for those strange-looking creatures, the caterpillars of the puss moth. On the same sallows they found caterpillars of the eyed hawkmoth and on nearby rose-bay willowherb, both types of larva, the black and the green, of the elephant hawkmoth. On 21 August she made her now annual visit to check on the Gamwell sisters in Jersey. Then came the routine few days at Kew where, with Roger Polhill, she mapped the places she had been to in the Longido area and on Mount Meru. She also had discussions with Peter Taylor, Edgar Milne-Redhead, Bernard Verdcourt and T.G. Tutin. Then on 27 September she left London for Nairobi where she saw Jan Gillet and Peter Greenway at the Coryndon Museum.

*   *   *

Mary did not go straight back to Tanzania. Instead she did something she had long had in mind—she accepted an invitation to visit Ethiopia as the guest of her friends, Ian and Ann Robertson, Ian being in the Desert Locust Control there. They lived at Asmara in Eritrea and for three weeks took Mary on a sight-seeing tour of the local mountains and inevitably she collected plants, especially aloes she had never seen before. Then back to Nairobi where she was met by John Beesley, Mhilu and Samuel in her new Land-Rover. From the road to Arusha on 30 October, they noted that Meru's summit had received a fresh fall of snow.

In mid-November, a friend from England, Diana Massey, came to stay with Mary. Together they collected at Lake Manyara and at Tarangire but were mainly intent on game-viewing. Tarangire was

A fine pencil cedar (*Juniperus procera*) in the montane forest on Mount Meru, Arusha, Tanzania.

Stream in a gorge on Mount Meru, Arusha, Tanzania.
(*Photo by Mary Richards*)

Giraffes at Momela, Arusha National Park, Tanzania.
(*Photo by Ion Trant*)

Animal-rich woodland by Lake Manyara, Tanzania.

Elephants at Lake Manyara, Tanzania, were the subject of a classic study by Iain Douglas-Hamilton.
(*Photo by Ion Trant*)

Lions at Lake Manyara National Park, famous for their tree-climbing habits.
(*Photo by Ion Trant*)

Ol Doinyo Lengai, an active volcano between Serengeti and Arusha, Tanzania. Mary Richards collected on the plain below.
(*Photo by J. Beesley*)

Mother-of-pearl butterfly, widespread in Africa.

Mary Richards botanising on the Shropshire Union Canal, 1970.
(*Photo by Richard Richards*)

Samuel Arasulula, Mary Richards'
assistant after she left Zambia for
Tanzania.

(*Photo by Mary Richards*)

Mary Richards and Vesey-Fitzgerald
looking at *Gloriosa* lilies in the
Arusha National Park.

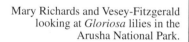

Plant-presses
drying in the sun,
Longido camp,
Arusha.

(*Photo by J. Beesley*)

An aloe named in honour of Mary Richards—
Aloe richardsiae—which she found 'growing in
many thousands' fifty miles west of Sao Hill,
Tanzania, in December 1961.

(Photo by Mary Richards)

Costus probably *spectabilis* near
Sao Hill, Tanzania.

(Anon)

Thunbergia elliotii
near Arusha.

A climber, *Strophanthus welwitschii*, near Kawimbe, Zambia.

Mary Richards and a giant tree lily (*Xerophyta splendens*).
(*Anon*)

A colourful composite (*Erythrocephalum zambesianum*).

Left to right: Peter Benoit and Mary Richards (co-authors of the *Flora of Merioneth*); Penny Condry and Kathleen Stevens.

Roadside sedges (*Cyperus hemisphaericus*) near Mbeya, Tanzania. (*Photo by Mary Richards*)

Orchids (*Platycoryne buchananiana*) Kawimbe, Zambia. (*Photo by C. Earle Smith*)

An orchid (*Eulophia thomsoni*), Mbisi Forest, Tanzania.

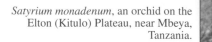

Satyrium monadenum, an orchid on the Elton (Kitulo) Plateau, near Mbeya, Tanzania.

Tynllidiart, Mary Richards' last garden. Cader Idris beyond.

(Photo by Mary Richards)

Two bog orchids amongst grass on Tir Stent, 10 August 1975, Mary Richards' last day in the field.

especially rewarding when they were taken to a section of the park that was new to Mary:

> After crossing the flood plain, we came to delightful country—woodland and grassland—and saw a beautiful herd of oryx, a herd of wildebeest and some hartebeest. Then we came to a gorge with the river below us; here were three lesser kudu females, one young one and a beautiful male. Went down into woodland and saw a rhino with a young one about a year old.

Their next safari took them north. Mary was anxious to explore the northern flanks of Longido Mountain but the trip was disappointing. As on her previous visit to the mountain, almost everything was hopelessly droughted:

> The only thing in flower is a really lovely *Ipomoea* which grows in all this desolation in huge bushes of pale-pink flowers with a deeper centre.

There were a few birds of interest, including the big magpie shrike and the long-tailed fiscal shrike. Though far into the semi-wilds of Masailand, Mary was thinking of Wales: her diary for 20 December notes that her grandson Andrew's 21st birthday dinner-dance was being held at Caerynwch that night.

In January, 1970, Mary ventured, with Samuel and Mhilu, into new country—the Yaida Valley, some 130 miles west of Lake Manyara. It proved to be extremely rough ground—a mixture of woodland, tall grassland, rocks, gorges and escarpments as well as a vast area of swamp. The valley was inhabited by the Mangati, a cattle-raising people very different from the Masai; and by other tribes, some really primitive. Along with the cattle-rearing the Yaida Valley was also a game-reserve. Mammals and birds were many and plant-collecting went well despite huge rainstorms that turned the roads into rivers. There was one major disappointment: Mary longed to get to Eyasi, the big lake north of the Yaida Valley, a lake she had failed to reach from the Wembere Valley back in 1960. Yet, though she hired a guide, all he did was to get them lost and she reluctantly decided to turn back, so ending 'a most interesting eighteen days'.

In February they were off again into new country, this time to the north of Lake Manyara towards the active volcano, Ol Doinyo Lengai. From the main road they drove north to the Masai village of Engaruka. Despite thunderstorms it was extremely hot and dry, plants were few but Mary had never seen so many butterflies. One night there was

> a terrific thunderstorm, as bad a one as I have ever seen in Africa. With it was a gale of wind. Our tents didn't collapse, the reason being that Mhilu, clad only in a mackintosh, hammered in all tent pegs. But my tent and the store tent leaked badly.

Next day they met a party of men illegally hunting leopards, probably for the lucrative leopard-skin markets in London and New York. But when Mary challenged them they were very evasive.

Ol Doinyo Lengai is a textbook volcanic cone, sharply pointed, steep-sided and grooved by lava flows. It beckons from afar to those in the south near Lake Manyara and to those in the north at Lake Natron. When Mary got there in 1970 she noted in her journal that although it had not erupted for four years, the remains of burnt forest were still visible. Higher up they could see only arid lavas devoid of plant life but they looked round them across a beautiful land of rolling grassy plains and high mountains. They saw no animals on the mountain but on the plain were hundreds of wildebeest, a lot of eland, zebras, Thomson's gazelles and many ostriches. And that day and the next, Mary collected plants but then came frustration. Just as in the Yaida Valley she had failed to reach Lake Eyasi, now she was foiled from pushing on north to Lake Natron:

> Samuel finds our steering is loose—also the bushes are wearing out—so reluctantly we have given up Lake Natron and will go back to Momela on Monday.

As they found their way back to camp that afternoon they saw hundreds of yellow-billed storks scattered across the plain. But small birds she was now finding difficult because of her failing sight. Her final note on that safari referred to the well-known habit of butterflies assembling to drink communally: 'On a small patch of wet soil were 3 or 4 dozen papilios gorging themselves on what I think must have been some animal's urine.'

Just as when they lived at Abercorn, Mary and Vesey had always chosen the Rukwa Valley as the place to take visitors to see wildlife, at Momela the obvious place to go was Serengeti. So in March, 1970, when Vesey's neice, Geraldine, arrived, off they went to Serengeti together with Brian Hawkes, a wildlife photographer from Kent. They saw nearly all the wondrous assembly of animals except that wild dogs eluded them. They observed the spectacular mating display of the male Kori bustard in which, to quote Praed and Grant, 'he appears to turn himself inside out and becomes almost white all over'. They also watched another of Africa's wildlife entertainments—a crowd of mixed vultures squabbling over a kill. The final and most unforgettable scene came when they got down into the Ngorongoro Crater and saw about a quarter of a million lesser flamingos massed at the edge of the alkaline lake, making the whole shore pink in the light of the rising sun.

In the second half of March, Mary went north from Momela, ever drawn by Longido Mountain. This was an ambitious safari in that, having collected around Longido, she aimed to go on a further fifty miles to Lake Natron which she had failed to reach from Mount Ol Doinyo Lengai a month earlier. The trip began well with a day of good collecting followed by a starlit night. But next day was a battle:

> The grass very long and we got covered with ticks . . . The mountain was covered with dense vegetation in places so thick it was an impenetrable wall. We followed elephant tracks but found no plants. Back in camp just before 4 o'clock. Tea and a very welcome bath. It looks like rain this evening.

How right she was! Next morning, Good Friday: 'Deluges of rain last night. My tent leaked and we woke to water all round us.' Heavy rain continued on and off; she managed some collecting between the storms but by Easter Monday conditions had become so difficult that even she admitted defeat. A rueful entry in her journal said: 'We had meant to go to Lake Natron today!' Driving home through the rain, they saw a large bird-of-prey carrying a snake which it dropped on the road. It was a puff adder.

A fortnight later (16 April 1970) she flew back to England which, after Africa's warmth, she found 'still plunged in winter'. But the daffodils at Doddington were lovely and in the nearby woods the anemones were 'a wonderful sight starring the ground with their tiny white blossoms'. Two brimstone butterflies and a comma also delighted her. Three weeks later Kent had become really springlike. The thermometer reached 70°F, cuckoos were calling, primroses were showing, beech and birch were covered with young green leaves and the whole county seemed white with cherry-blossom. 'I had forgotten how lovely the celandines are with their open faces of bright-yellow,' Mary wrote. On 9 May, she went to Kew for the BSBI annual meeting: 'It is years since I was at a BSBI general meeting. I knew hardly anyone.' This was to be her last BSBI meeting, outdoors or in. A few days later she was out with Brian Hawkes, one of Jonnet's neighbours who had been at Arusha National Park two months before. He took Mary to see early spider orchids and other choice Kent flowers and when his van got stuck in a muddy lane she couldn't resist writing 'shades of Africa!' in her diary that night.

On 3 June she went to Wales. Since, having left Ndundu, she had no home, she was anxious to reoccupy Tynllidiart but it was not immediately available. Although the garden, she found, was in as great a mess as ever, she was relieved to find that many azaleas and rhododendrons had so triumphed over the weeds that some even needed to be cut down. A new experience for her was a trip along the Shropshire Union Canal in 'a narrow-boat painted in gay colours—blue and red', belonging to Richard and Pam. For three beautiful days they cruised through the Cheshire plain between 'fields golden with buttercups, the sides of the canal thick with cow parsley, water docks, comfrey, mimulus and field daisies. Stretches of water with lovely views of rural England.' Next day, beyond Nantwich, they came to 'a lovely reach through woodland—fine trees—huge ash, beech and oak'. The boat's log for the occasion reads: 'Mary, as expected, did quite a lot of botany but was somewhat restricted due to resting a broken toe.' (This refers to an accident she had had recently in Africa.)

Back in Wales she won botanical glory in Cwm Cywarch on 19 June when, with Kathleen Stevens and other friends, she toiled up a formidable scree in search of alpines and what does she find but that elusive flower which had always been her Merioneth speciality, the small white orchid, a first record for Cwm Cywarch—not a bad achievement for someone nearly 85 years old, with very poor sight and suffering from a painful foot.

Following what had become an annual ritual, Mary spent a few days with Marian and Hope Gamwell in Jersey where she was pleased to see they still had the native red squirrel and none of the American greys. A wildflower that delighted her was the rare purple broomrape growing as a parasite on yarrow. From Jersey she went to Paignton to see cousin Stephen and while there visited a garden at Dartmouth belonging to Viscount Chaplin. It was full of plants from all over the world including some very delicate ones. Back in Kent she celebrated her 85th birthday by having a flutter on the horses at Folkstone races but as she says nothing about winning anything, it looks as if we must fear the worst. Anyway she enjoyed 'a long hot day' and some champagne was drunk.

*　　　*　　　*

Three days later (6 August 1970) she flew back to Nairobi where she was met at the airport by Vesey and Peter Greenway. And in a few weeks she was off with Samuel and Mhilu on a very long journey. Kew had asked her to go back to the Mpanda area of Tanzania which was so little known botanically and so rewarding. Uppermost in her mind was a species of *Indigofera* which she had found there long before and sent to Jan Gillett at Kew. He had written back in some excitement:

> You will be interested to learn that you have collected what is perhaps the strangest plant to reach Kew in the last decade—your *Indigofera* collected on 28/10/1959 in the Mlala Hills with peltate leaves like those of a water-lily. Such leaves have hitherto been quite unknown in the whole of the *Leguminosae*, so you may imagine what a sensation your plant caused when it was unpacked here. I am describing it as *Indigofera peltata*.

As flies the crow, Mpanda is about 450 miles WSW of Arusha but hugely more the way the roads wind their way there. They went via Mbeya, crossing into Zambia to reach Mbala and then back into Tanzania via Sumbawanga to Mpanda and the Mlala Hills. Those hills proved difficult, clothed as they were with trackless bush; and there was no one who could guide them. The days were very hot and dry, tsetse flies were awful but far worse was the wholesale logging that was going on, devastating the countryside for miles around. And huge areas were blackened by fire. Happily there were swamps and streamsides rich in plants, and collecting went on briskly even if hope began to fade of finding the much desired *Indigofera*.

It was on this safari that Mary had the most uncomfortable night of all her camping years. Yet it started so well. There they were, in a lovely moonlit camp amid roadside trees and they had

213

had such a good day's collecting that they were still putting plants into the presses until dark when 'Mhilu cooked us a good supper of corned beef rissoles and chocolate pudding.' They went to bed early but then occurred the disaster she had feared ever since the Gamwells had warned her against it at Chilongolwelo when she first got to Africa in 1951:

> At 12.30 we were woken by thousands of *siafu*—biting ants, all over the camp, in the store and men's tents and in my bed. They got into my hair and I must have had well over 50, very painful, as well as all over my body. Mhilu got the insect spray and sprayed my head and all over all of us. I got a good many of the ants off my scalp but they had bitten deep into the roots of my hair. Finally we got rid of most of them and climbed into the Land-Rover but were thinly clad, I in my pyjamas, Samuel pyjama trousers and a shirt, and Mhilu shirt and blanket. Samuel got in the back of the Land-Rover and Mhilu managed to get my mackintosh and a blanket and they lent me a pillow. We passed a very uncomfortable night. I dozed at last and woke at dawn. Mhilu had gone back to his tent and I went to mine. The *siafu* had gone and I slept till 8 a.m. I washed the remains of *siafu* and spray out of my hair. My head is still sore.

Very hot, stifling days succeeded each other, collecting went remorselessly on but there was still no sign of the *Indigofera*. Samuel, Mary acknowledged in her journal, had by now become a real expert: 'He is a good and keen collector and does practically all the specimens with exactitude.' So from now on she gives him the credit for this by naming him as the collector in the daily records—'Samuel Arasulula'. She now felt they must give up the quest for *Indigofera peltata*, having spent over three weeks in the search—surely the longest time she ever devoted to looking for any one plant. When she happened to meet two Russian geologists who were prospecting for minerals around Mpanda she found that one of them was interested in plants and he undertook to keep an eye open for the elusive *Indigofera*. They returned to Mbala where Mary had a final day's collecting with Modesty. Then came the long trek back to Iringa where the long safari was by no means over. They now turned into the Ruaha National Park and met up with Peter Greenway and for the next nearly four weeks went collecting with him. It was too dry for many wildflowers but trees and shrubs were blooming here and there and Samuel did stalwart work climbing up to get leaves, flowers and fruits. It was the hottest time of year, with the thermometer often at 100°F in the shade.

Mary got back to Momela on 14 November after a disastrous journey home when the Land-Rover broke down, forcing her to finish the last 150 miles to Arusha by bus. But she cheered up a few days later when to her amazement, she got a letter from Mr Prizov, the Russian geologist she had met near Mpanda. He had found *Indigofera peltata* in a different locality from where she had once collected it. His letter enclosed two leaves and two flowers which she immediately passed on to Kew. The rest of November and December, Mary spent in and near Momela, exploring the Mount Meru gorges, many of which were still botanically unknown. Christmas Day, 1970, she spent with Vesey and Peter Greenway up in the Meru caldera where, amongst other things, she collected one of her beloved orchids, 'a very beautiful *Disa*'.

It was about this time that a well-known English journalist came to Momela. In an article in *The Observer Review* for 31 January, 1971, Katharine Whitehorn discussed the ecological problems of managing national parks. She also mentioned Mary and Vesey:

> The most astounding creature I saw in the Arusha National Park was a botanist. She was wearing a battered bush hat on wild white hair and had a knife stuck in her safari belt. She was carrying a plastic bag full of obscene-looking roots and was entirely covered with mud. Later, after a bath, Mary Richards turned into an elegant elderly lady, but scarcely less surprising: until she was 65 she had been a straightforward upper-class English wife and mother. Then her husband died and she said: 'Now I'll go and be a botanist in Africa.' She spends her time careering around the continent in a Land-Rover or clinging to crags reaching for remote plants; she is 85 and shows no sign of flagging. Beside her, the gnarled Desmond Vesey-FitzGerald seems quite junior; he is a retired entomologist turned ecologist who can get up at 5.30 on a chilly morning in a thin shirt and not even notice the ice forming on his shorts.

After the strenuous safaris of late 1970, Mary was content not to go far afield in the first four months of 1971, apart from a week's camping in Masailand around Longido in February where she did quite a lot of collecting. One day on Mount Meru was spectacular. Mary was thoroughly accustomed to thunderstorms overhead but on 15 March, in sunshine above the clouds, she looked down on a great storm raging over Momela. On another day, in a magnificent gorge outside the park Mary sought for the flowers of the wild banana (*Ensete ventricosa*). It was hard going over rocky terrain:

> a real scramble, Samuel gave me a hand over the worst places. We walked up the gorge for about three hours, collecting ferns and shrubs, the wild bananas were very fine—when they flower and seed, the leaves and plant die. It was very steep and slippery, not a nice place and the path faded out. Finally, pulled up by Samuel, I got to the top, very out of breath and a bit scared. On the ridge we had a very fine view of Meru. Stupidly I did not bring my altimeter.

As the park got better known, the number of visitors gradually increased. One whom Mary especially welcomed was Philip Wareing, Professor of Botany at Aberystwyth. And Vesey had been particularly looking forward to a visit by Sir Julian Huxley, then aged 84. Alas, the great man, when they took him and Lady Huxley to the Ngurdoto Crater, was having one of his bad days ('very shaky' was how Mary described him). By now Mary was packing to go to England but just before leaving she was amused to report in her diary how she took part in an unusual session of mist-netting with John Beesley who was keen to ring migrant birds. The exercise was not a great success. First an elephant chased them off by coming down a hill at them 'lifting his trunk and screaming'. Then, just as they had managed to get three willow warblers into the net, six more elephants came down the hill, fortunately just missing the net. 'Quite an exciting bird-ringing,' wrote Mary that evening.

CHAPTER NINETEEN

Back in Kent on 26 April, 1971, she found everyone upset by the decision, later quashed, to create London's third airport at Foulness. She went birding at Dungeness, saw very little and lamented that there were no longer any Kentish plovers nor thick-knees breeding there. Her eyes were now giving her serious trouble with cataracts on both. She went to Jersey to stay with the Gamwells and on 25 May she was at Chelsea Flower Show making a list of plants she would like to have at Tynllidiart which she had now managed to reoccupy. She got back there in June and her first visitor was Vesey, on leave from Africa. With help she tackled the garden with enthusiasm, battling against a jungle of brambles. She ended her stay in Wales with a restful few days on the canal with Richard and Pam and returned to Kent where she had her 86th birthday.

＊　　　＊　　　＊

A few days later she flew back to Nairobi and had a couple of days in the herbarium there before going on to Momela. The rest of August and much of September went in collecting both locally and at Lake Manyara and Tarangire which were now firmly established as favourite places to visit—the fauna and flora were always wonderful and she was now so well known to the wardens that she was ever welcome and well looked after. Then, as if national parks and game reserves were not wilderness enough, she was off on 25 September on a major safari right across Tanzania and into Zambia, reaching Mbala on the 29th. At the locust-control herbarium she was pleased to find Modesty in good form and that he had 'collected quite a lot of new plants'. Bill Morony she did not find—he had broken a femur, was in hospital in Ndola and she was destined never to see him again. From Mbala her plan had been to get to her old haunts in the Mpanda area but she was advised that very bad anthrax was raging there, that buffaloes, hippos, rhinos and elephants had died and that it would be unwise to go there. So what about the Mweru Wantipa, always so rewarding botanically? No, that was out also because no petrol was to be had there. She now turned her thoughts to the Serenje area, 320 miles south of Mbala which, as she knew from previous trips to Ndola, was a good district for plants. To her delight the Roman Catholic bishop, who was in Mbala, readily gave her permission to camp in the grounds of the White Fathers' mission at Serenje.

But before leaving Mbala she decided that the time had come to start winding up her African experience. Characteristically, though now in her 87th year, it was not through reasons of age that she reached this decision but simply because of the ever increasing frustrations caused by political events. Since independence, officialdom was becoming ever more tiresome. Frontiers were more difficult to cross, police were everywhere, camping was increasingly restricted and stores and petrol less and less available. On 5 October she wrote: 'Have quite definitely decided to leave Africa for good next year. I shall be very sorry to leave but feel it is time I went now that I have Tynllidiart to go to.'

Meanwhile there was no question of slackening the pace of her collecting. For a month, with Samuel and Mhilu, she collected with vigour around Serenje. It was a lovely time of year with the *miombo* trees in their fresh leaf colours. The rains had now started and heavy storms were bringing their usual problems of flooded tents and getting the botanical papers dried. On days without sun they had to light fires by which to dry the papers. Mary suffered three bouts of stomach upsets and a bad throat—all probably due to the doubtful quality of the drinking water. The return journey to Mbala produced an unfortunate incident. Camping in the dark one evening they discovered, just before going to bed, that they had inadvertently pitched their tents near a large African burial ground:

> Mhilu was very upset and quite hysterical . . . I found in the morning that he had not slept all night and had kept Samuel awake. It is a good camp site and we could do a lot of good collecting in a short time, but it was impossible to stay there as Mhilu was in such a state—and it is possible the inhabitants would not have liked us in their woodland graveyard!

Two days later they were back in Mbala where Mary said farewell to Karl and Margo Kuhne who were also quitting the place. Then, just twenty years after her first arrival there, she left Mbala for the last time. Getting back to Momela on 5 December she pronounced the trip 'a great success'.

Christmas Day, 1971, was a happy occasion:

> Got up at 5.45 and went to mass at Arusha Church at 8 o'clock. A pouring wet morning. Back to breakfast at 10 a.m. After lunch we went up to the Meru Crater and had a thunderstorm. Uta and John Beesley came to dinner and we had a very good evening—chicken instead of turkey which is unobtainable, then plum pudding and mince pies and crackers brought by Zoë Goodwin from Nairobi.

But the year ended sadly: just after Christmas, Mary got a most unexpected letter from Kew saying they wanted no more specimens from her and that henceforth her plants should be sent to local herbaria. She was hurt: 'A bit of a shock after twenty years collecting for them; and a rather abrupt letter.' In the first two months of 1972 she collected on or near the slopes of Mount Meru and had a week under canvas at Longido. She enjoyed it all but by now had to accept that, because of her failing sight, it was really Samuel who was the collector and that her function was nearly restricted to the preparation of specimens and labelling them with their names and localities.

She flew to London on 5 March, 1972, and before long she was buying a whole new lot of camping equipment because, though her next visit to Africa would be her last, she had big plans for it. Her collecting career was not going to end with a whimper. She had an operation for cataract on one of her eyes on 25 April; she had her customary few days in Jersey with Marian and Hope Gamwell; then her other eye was operated on. She had her 87th birthday with Kate at Haresfield and next day she went to Wales and rejoiced 'to get back to Tynllidiart'. Despite considerable expense the garden was still in poor shape with bracken and brambles springing up everywhere. But she worked hard in it and also, as she had years before, found time to welcome old friends, among them John and Uta Beesley, on leave from Africa.

*   *   *

She flew back to Nairobi at the end of September and quickly settled down to life at Momela. John Beesley was no longer there, having moved to a post in Botswana, and his place as warden had been taken by Myles Turner. That October brought a tragedy at Momela. In Mary's words:

A terrible accident has occurred today. A patrol of rangers caught some poachers who had speared a rhino. The poachers made off but the rhino charged and killed one of the rangers. The rest went up trees. Vesey-FitzGerald came in a truck. The rhino charged and got its horn wedged in the truck and was finally killed. The man leaves a wife and three young children.

The first week of November, Mary spent in the Tarangire reserve with Vesey but it ended badly: 'Woke up feeling rather giddy. I am seeing badly and had a fall. Vesey persuaded me to go back to Momela.' She was all right in a few days but then her long-awaited new spectacles arrived from London and proved to be little better than the ones she had already. On Christmas Day, 1972, there is unusual despair in her daily chronicle:

Went up Meru for a picnic organised by the Turners. They all went down to a waterfall but I didn't go as I can't see and am only a nuisance. All right when Samuel is there to give me a hand. I am going on safari next week. I think I can manage with Samuel's help and he will do the collecting. Have definitely decided to go back to England in March, settle at Tynllidiart and not come back to Africa where, owing to my sight, I can do practically no botanical work and I am anxious to get Tynllidiart garden going well again.

Her spirits soon recovered and she spent three productive weeks in January and February, 1973, in what was to be her last great collecting area. This was Bereku ('a wonderful place for plants' she called it) on the Arusha to Dodoma road between Babati and Kondoa. Apart from being floristically rich, the Bereku area had another great appeal at a time when, Mary complained, there was no longer the freedom to camp where you liked. At Bereku, however, she was made very welcome by the local people. She and Samuel collected widely around Bereku until on Sunday, 4 February (a day of rest, like every Sunday throughout her collecting years), she wound up the safari: 'My hay-fever was bad in the night. I didn't get up till late and spent most of the day in the tent and in the shade of the baobab tree.' Two days later: 'Packed up and left by 10.30—a very hot day. It has been a very successful camp.'

Back at Momela life went on smoothly apart from minor troubles with wildlife both outdoors and in. As everywhere she lived Mary grew aloes in pots outside the house but 'elephants and buffaloes are round the house every night' and they had eaten some of the aloes. Indoors the problem was the spotted genet, a carnivore about the size of a domestic cat. A family of genets had found their way into the roof of the house and were so noisy at night that 'Vesey has had to sleep downstairs!' Eventually Vesey live-trapped the genets and released them far away; but it did not take them long to find their way back to his roof.

*   *   *

When she flew to London at the end of March, 1973, she hastened to her optician who assured her that, with new glasses, she would see well. Then she headed for Wales, anxious to see how Tynllidiart was faring. It was a relief to find the cottage in good order but the garden was 'still in a bad state'. Soon she was buying new plants—shrubs, heathers, pansies, polyanthus, snapdragons, lavenders and rosemary. Day after day she weeded and planted and by 8 July she could write:

> The garden is now partly in order. The rock garden we shall leave till next year. We shall do the bog garden last. I am thankful I am so fit and can do a really hard day's gardening.

There was still a big problem with brambles and she had to engage professional help to deal with it.

Visitors came, one after another: her old school-friend, Sophie Blathwayt; Edward Robinson, the expert on African sedges; then Vesey-FitzGerald, on leave from Tanzania. On 3 August, her 88th birthday, she had dinner at Caerynwch where one of the guests was her old friend, Frank Best, with whom she had gone butterfly-chasing around Abercorn in 1966. On 17 September, there is a significant entry in her diary:

> Philip Leedal came this evening to stay. He is a White Father and lives in the Mbeya district of Tanzania. He is a geologist and a botanist and is writing a flora of the Mbeya district.

Philip Leedal stayed a week at Tynllidiart and made many friends in the Dolgellau area, Mary's final comment on him being: 'We all liked Philip very much.' It was presumably through mutual friends at Kew that Father Leedal first made contact with Mary

Richards. What is certain is that Mary was able to give him plenty of information about the flora of the Mbeya area. In the next few years he was to write extensively about the botany of the Southern Highlands of Tanzania.

On 8 October, she was depressed to hear from her optician that nothing else could be done for her eyes. She went to Jersey to visit the Gamwells (it would be the last time she would see them); then to Paignton to see cousin Stephen Stokes; then back to Kent for the wedding of her grandson, Andrew, in Doddington church, after which she flew to Nairobi where she was met by Peter Greenway. Friends took her on into Tanzania where a fresh fall of snow was visible on the peak of Mount Meru. But it was not snow but flamingos that occupied her attention over the next few days. Flamingos in multitudes were not typical of Momela's nine small lakes. Yet now:

> There are between 7,000 and 8,000 of them. They have a place where they are making nests. You can watch them scooping the mud up with their beaks into mounds. They have not laid any eggs and Vesey does not think they will. There is a good hide put up to watch them.

At the end of November she was off to Tarangire with Vesey and then on to Serengeti. But that safari was not a success. Serengeti was terribly dry, few animals were visible and even fewer plants. Then Mary went down with such a bad throat and cough that, with extreme reluctance, she was forced to return to Momela, leaving Vesey to his work in Serengeti.

She had recovered by mid-December and was out collecting with Samuel. She spent Christmas with Vesey and friends at Momela but all she wrote in her diary on New Year's Day, a date she had always celebrated with a party, was: 'Spent a quiet day.' So, very subdued, she began 1974, her last African year. But as usual she perked up and on 7 January she was off in the Land-Rover with Samuel and Mhilu to Bereku where she was again made very welcome by the foreman of the Public Works Department. Though the weather was 'very very hot' they collected every morning, resting in the shade after lunch. Then Mhilu went down with malaria and they had to go back to Arusha and the doctor. But a fortnight later, Mhilu having recovered, they went back to the woods and plains of Bereku and their familiar camping place and friends including an African named Hamish who attached himself to the party and made himself enormously useful. This time they were nearly the whole of February at Bereku, exploring woodlands, plains, dried-up lakes and the slopes of Hanang Mountain. And they only returned to Momela because Mary ran out of cash. She summed up the trip quite cheerfully:

> It's been a pleasant camp here. The Africans are very friendly and we've had visitors most evenings. Hamish has been invaluable as he knows the country and took us to places we would not have known about. He has never mentioned 'salary' but he will come to Arusha next week and I will pay him for the time he has been with me.

At Momela on 9 March, 1974, Mary and the flamingos (now increased to 12,000) were photographed by an American journalist but she seems not to have heard whether the photographs were ever published. On 14 March she botanised for the last time on the slopes of Meru: 'I collected a great many plants. The path was steep and slippery with loose earth, so we did not go as far as I should have liked and not really into the big forest.' Her final Meru plant was an *Indigofera*.

Two days later she was off on her very last safari. It was back to Bereku yet again and for nearly three weeks she collected with all her old enthusiasm, walking far through the forests. On the last day she wrote: 'We shall do no more collecting here, though a good deal more wants doing.' In the end they were defeated by the very difficult weather. There were many thunderstorms and nights of tremendous rain and on April 2 the last plants were gathered into the presses. On 3 April Mary wrote:

> Everything is soaking. This morning, after heavy rain last night, the camp is so wet and muddy we reluctantly decided to go back to Momela tomorrow. It is a fine sunny morning. We had thirteen presses to change and two presses from yesterday to label. Samuel has bad toothache.

The last plants she gathered were 'several tall grasses and a beautiful blue *Thunbergia*, a bush by the side of the road'.

*　　*　　*

So concluded Mary Richards' African experience. A month after her final Bereku trip she said goodbye to Momela. She gave Samuel her Land-Rover, and Mhilu a gift of cash. Samuel had served her well for six years; but the magnificent support she had always had from Mhilu went back eighteen years. At Ndundu and then at Momela he had been her cook, working in a well-equipped kitchen. But on countless safaris he had produced excellent meals amid tropical storms on primitive stoves or wood fires. Between meals, while Mary was out of camp collecting, he had baked many a loaf of bread, not in an oven but simply in a hole in the ground pre-heated by burning wood in it. He had also helped with erecting and taking down the tents and looking after all the camping equipment. When she was afflicted by an infection in her eyes it was Mhilu who had bathed them. As cook at Ndundu he had got meals not only for Mary ('Mama Richards' she always was to him) but also for her Abercorn friends who were almost daily visitors. ('Ndundu Hotel' he was heard to mutter under his breath one day.) And in travelling he had endured huge discomfort riding in the backs of Land-Rovers over some of Africa's roughest roads. Yet it was very rare for him to complain about anything. Though his English was poor it was much better than Mary's Swahili; and somehow they understood each other most of the time.

It can be reasonably argued that Mary Richards stayed a year or two too long in Africa. Maybe 88 is quite old to be roughing it in the African bush and keeping up the awesome discipline of plant-collecting, day after day. But as long as Vesey was willing for her to go on using a room in his house, the temptation to continue her life at Momela remained very strong. Before the end, however, she was beginning to irk even the tolerant Vesey by her insistence on pressing on with arduous safaris as if she were thirty years younger and was not now nearly blind. She longed to have him on all those trips, as so often in the past; but those days were over and most of the time he was busy elsewhere on his work in the national park service. And when he was at home at Momela he was much preoccupied with writing reports and scientific papers. So Mary complains in a letter home, written on safari:

> I don't know when we shall go back to Momela. Vesey has endless visitors which he leaves me to entertain as he shuts himself in his office and is always writing. I get a bit tired of them!! So we have come away for a bit.

Meanwhile Vesey, writing on safari in Serengeti to friends in the UK, complains:

> Mary is not here. I have had a most anxious time with her. She is not up to it these days. Her sight is no better and what's worse she has lost her wild enthusiasms. One must admire her indomitable spirit but it should be reserved for her garden not for safari in the wide open spaces of Africa. If only she would sit still a bit at Momela and enjoy the animals and birds . . . However she won't and thinks she can rush about as of old but is more and more disappointed and despondent. We set off on this safari together and dallied at Tarangire and Seronera for a while. When we stopped for lunch she said: 'Vesey, I am feeling so unwell.' So I at once suggested that we returned. But she wouldn't hear of it. Both Samuel and Mhilu said she had been collapsing in the Land-Rover on the bumpy road and were not prepared to go on. So I had to tell her I was not either . . . In the end I had to more or less order her to go back to Momela, which she has done and I hope she will be recovered when I get back in a few days' time.

Fortunately, these cracks in what had been such a long and productive friendship were not too severe and for most of the time all was well between them, especially when they could enjoy a leisurely hour or two watching wildlife round Momela's pools or at the Ngurdoto Crater.

On 30 April, 1974, she did the round of the Momela lakes for the last time. Flamingos, the last African birds in her diary, were still in their thousands. She finally left Momela on 2 May, Vesey driving her to Nairobi where she stayed with Peter Greenway while Vesey went to other friends. Next day she helped in Peter's garden and in the evening Vesey dropped in for drinks. He was his usual cheerful self and said he would come and see her off at the airport next evening. Instead, she was seen off by other friends who, as she had a long night journey before her, did not tell her that Vesey had died in his sleep the previous night. A cable was sent to Jack and Jonnet and it was left to them to break the news when she reached Doddington. It was, of course, totally crushing for her. Vesey had been such an influence in her life that it is inconceivable that she would have stayed in Africa collecting plants for 24 years if he had not been there to inspire her and be her companion in the field on so many days, weeks, even months. When she heard of his death she simply wrote in her diary: 'A terrible shock and a very great loss to Africa. He was a very fine scientist.' Very likely his death also shattered a secret hope. For though she had finished with collecting when she left Momela, it seems more than likely that she nurtured a thought of going back and staying with Vesey for a holiday sometime.

Certainly Vesey was a great loss to all who had so enjoyed his unfailing hospitality, his quick humour and his love of discussing every branch of natural history. He was a loss to the wider world because although he had produced learned papers in the scientific journals and had completed his book, *East African Grasslands* (which he did not live to see), he had much still to offer and had barely started on his philosophy of wildlife conservation to be called *The Kingdom of Pan*. Its contents were foreshadowed in his brief synopsis:

> Conflict has continued between the Kingdom of Pan and the Kingdom of Man until the present time. Only now are some of Pan's laws being understood. However the conceit of Man is unlimited and he usually only consults Pan after he has already devastated the natural resources of the earth. But Pan is extremely tolerant and resilient, even though Man has so much abused his favours . . . This balance between all living things and their living space is in our days known as the science of ecology. Man is only now beginning to comprehend its principles. But Pan has been administering and evolving them since the dawn of time. And the more we understand and appreciate them, the more we come to realise that there is very little conflict which cannot be resolved between the World of Man and the Kingdom of Pan.

*   *   *

As soon as she could Mary went to Wales and Tynllidiart, Jonnet driving her up from Kent. She was pleased to find her garden blossoming with rhododendrons and azaleas. 'It is nice to be home,' she wrote, 'but oh! I miss Africa.' Spring and summer she spent mostly in the garden. In July Sophie Blathwayt came to stay. On 3 August Mary had an 89th birthday dinner with Pam and Richard at Caerynwch. But there is very little else to report because at long last Mary had pretty well ceased to chronicle her life: 'It does not seem there is any point in keeping a diary now I am at Tynllidiart and my botanical work is over.' All the same she did manage a few sporadic entries until the following spring. She

226

reports going to the wedding of her grand-daughter, Sarah Heywood, in the choir of Gloucester Cathedral in October; she spent 25 December at Caerynwch ('a very quiet Xmas Day, so different from Momela'); in January, 1975, she received some plants for the garden 'which I put in but the ground is very waterlogged—we have had far too much rain'. A few days later she sent off her seed-list to Thomson and Morgan. That winter was a mild one and she saw no snow even on Cader Idris until 16 January. Next day she wrote: 'Garden coming on far too early. We have had no frost yet—*Rhodo praecox* is coming out and some of the bulbs are well up.' The final diary entries come at Easter, 1975. Kate and her family had come to Wales from Gloucestershire. 'Sunday was a lovely day,' reported Mary: 'Church at Brithdir. In the afternoon the young people went round the Precipice Walk. I sat above Maes-y-bryner in the car in the sun. I am too blind to do the walk.' Her last mention of the garden is that a hard frost that Easter weekend had 'caught the early rhodos'. And her last entry of all leaves us in Africa with thoughts of Vesey: 'Have a new list of plants collected on Mt Kilimanjaro and Mt Meru. I hear Vesey FitzGerald's house has been pulled down.'

Her last botanising day was 10 August, 1975, a week after her ninetieth birthday. She was taken to see the minute and inconspicuous bog orchid, a rarity which her friend, Dorothy Paish, had just found in the marshes of Tir Stent—a fitting place for Mary to enjoy her final encounter with a wildflower since, so close to Dolserau, her birthplace, it had been one of the haunts of her childhood.

She lived another two years, gradually declining. At first she was looked after at Tynllidiart, then at a nursing home on the north Wales coast and there she died on 12 August 1977. Her grave is next to that of Major Richards close to the door of Brithdir church. For 35 years she had been his wife; his widow for another 35. The churchyard at Brithdir is like a woodland glade and is at its loveliest in spring when what Mary used to call 'the Himalayan rhododendrons' are in bloom, big old trees that were planted under her direction. Early spring flowers on her grave are lesser celandine and Good Friday grass (*Luzula campestris*).

Many tributes were paid to Mary Richards by the botanical world. Dr Bernard Verdcourt, former Director of the East African Herbarium, Nairobi, summed up her life and achievements in his introduction to a delightful work, *The Mountain Flowers of Southern Tanzania*. Written in 1982 by Father Philip Leedal of Mbeya and Dr Phillip Cribb of Kew, it was based on Mary's travels in the Southern Highlands. Dr Verdcourt wrote:

> This book, an introduction to the plants of the higher parts of the Southern Highlands, is dedicated to Mary Richards . . . It is hoped it will enable many of the plants of the upland grassland and mountain rain forest, which she knew so well, to be identified . . . One word of warning—although the collecting of Mrs Richards and others has been praised here and in fact our knowledge of the flora would be non-existent without collections, everything is now under so much pressure from increased agricultural and industrial development, concomitant with the increasing population, that plants should not be picked with abandon. There is no need for everyone to have a private collection; only a few are needed in schools, colleges and museums. The Southern Highlands are already a shadow of their former forested glory. Let us conserve what is left for all future Tanzanians and visitors to Africa.

No one would have agreed more wholeheartedly with that than Mary Richards herself.

*   *   *

Looking back on the life of this courageous and adventurous woman who held the world of plants in such a warm embrace, we may well marvel at the single-mindedness she brought to her plant-collecting. Single-mindedness in some people can be tiresome but Mary Richards found the time and energy to be not only a great field naturalist but also to leave space for being fun-loving, laughing, cheerful and friendly towards a wide circle of friends. And there was more to her than that. There was the writer of the diaries which must contain not far short of a million words. After her plant-collecting these diaries must be rated her greatest achievement. It is one thing to collect plants all day in tropical heat in steamy forests, on burning plains or up formidable hillsides; and press those plants at the end of the day, in camp, perhaps in heavy rain, and label them and write notes about them. It is another thing then (or perhaps next morning) to write several lucid pages recounting the day's events. Yet, year after year, Mary Richards kept that chronicle going and clearly it meant almost as much to her as the collecting. The diaries are not merely botanical. They bring in the whole world of nature, landscape and people and they reflect the excitement that wild Africa inspired in her from the first.

Not that her diaries are perfect. She was a lark not an owl and at the end of a hard day she often flaked out and looked just like the young Linnaeus after a day's herborising, as famously portrayed by the French painter, Louis Prosper Roux. There is Linnaeus, collapsed in his armchair, his vasculum dropped at his feet, his dog as dead-beat as himself. So Mary's diaries were sometimes written when she was half asleep and could not remember the names of some of the day's plants. She left spaces, intending to fill them in next morning, but seldom got round to it because next day she was far too busy. And the notes she sent with her African plants were occasionally indecipherable by the botanists at Kew.

Though Mary never writes at length about people, they constantly flit in and out of her diaries because, whether she was in England, Wales or Africa, she was never a loner. The sociable side of her life at Abercorn might well be useful to anyone wishing to dig into the history of the Abercorn white community from 1951 to 1971—Mary Richards knew them all and often mentions them, even if only because they had given her a much needed cup of tea.

*   *   *

Many references to plants found by Mary Richards can be found in *Flora Zambesiaca*; *Flora of Tropical East Africa*; and in Diana Polhill's *Flora of Tropical East Africa: Index of Collecting Localities*. Mary Richards' African specimens are mainly at Kew but are also in herbaria in Africa, Germany, North America and elsewhere. Her British plants are mainly in the National Museum of Wales. The fullest obituary of her was by Edgar Milne-Redhead in the BSBI journal, *Watsonia*, in 1978. It contained one slight error: we learn from her diary that Mary Richards had already agreed to collect plants for Kew before she left on her first visit to Africa in 1951, not after she got there as that obituary states.

29 plants are named in her honour—one genus and 28 species. They are *Richardsiella eruciformis* (*Gramineae*); *Justicia richardsiae* (*Acanthaceae*); *Celosia richardsiae* (*Amaranthaceae*);

Pandiaka richardsiae (*Amaranthaceae*); *Polyscias richardsiae* (*Araliaceae*); *Impatiens richardsiae* (*Balsaminaceae*); *Cyphia richardsiae* (*Campanulaceae*); *Maytenus richardsiae* (*Celastraceae*); *Bidens richardsiae* (*Compositae*); *Bothriocline richardsiae* (*Compositae*); *Ipomoea richardsiae* (*Convolvulaceae*); *Scleria richardsiae* (*Cyperaceae*); *Euphorbia richardsiae* (*Euphorbiaceae*); *Faroa richardsiae* (*Gentianaceae*); *Gladiolus richardsiae* (*Iridaceae*); *Indigofera richardsiae* (*Leguminosae*); *Monopetalanthus richardsiae* (*Leguminosae*); *Tephrosia richardsiae* (*Leguminosae*); *Vigna richardsiae* (*Leguminosae*); *Aloe richardsiae* (*Aloaceae*); *Hibiscus richardsiae* (*Malvaceae*); *Ochna richardsiae* (*Ochnaceae*); *Chionanthus richardsiae* (*Oleaceae*); *Habenaria richardsiae* (*Orchidaceae*); *Pavetta richardsiae* (*Rubiaceae*); *Psydrax richardsiae* (*Rubiaceae*); *Allophylus richardsiae* (*Sapindaceae*); *Pimpinella richardsiae* (*Umbelliferae*); and *Cyphostemma richardsiae* (*Vitaceae*).

INDEX